Postmarked Moscow

Postmarked Moscow

By LYDIA KIRK

WILDSIDE PRESS

For Marian, Deborah and Roger

Author's Note

First written as letters to our two daughters and to our son when he was not with us, *Postmarked Moscow* is a record of our experiences in Russia from the time of our arrival in June 1949 to our final departure in October 1951. It seemed important to share these experiences with our children, to tell them of the friends we made, the sights we saw, the trips we took, the parties we held, the constant vexations and frustrations of Moscow life and the rare and rewarding glimpses through the chinks of the walls.

Lydia Kirk

Postmarked Moscow

IN MARCH 1949 THE
newspapers announced that Bedell Smith might retire from
the Moscow Embassy. I read the item, saw it repeated the next
day, and thought who my candidate for his replacement would
be. As a taxpayer I had just one, but as a wife and partner
in the venture I dreaded the idea. That candidate was my
husband, presently Ambassador to Belgium, Admiral Alan
Goodrich Kirk. I talked about it with him. He said it was an
impossible suggestion, that a general would never be replaced
by an admiral, even if that admiral had already spent three
years as a diplomatic head of mission. We had enjoyed those
three years in Belgium, we were still enjoying them.

Dad had gained the confidence of the Belgian people and
their affection, we had many friends and colleagues whom it
would be difficult to leave. We talked more about it and agreed
that if the call came there were two posts one could not refuse,
Russia and Germany, as both were fighting assignments. Germany was out of the question, but I still maintained that
Russia might be offered him. Dad refused to believe it. Weeks
wore on. The Atlantic Treaty was written and about to be
signed in Washington. Dad had worked on the Belgian end,
so was not much surprised when the telephone rang one
Saturday morning. It was Washington asking him to fly home
that very day, the Saturday before the final ceremony on
Monday. Although they specified nothing he assumed his visit
concerned some detail of the treaty.

I wasn't convinced, but I saw him off that afternoon, put
on evening clothes, and dined at one of the ministries where
they questioned me closely as to what my husband's trip home
might be about. The days passed. I heard nothing and was

beginning to be very uneasy. On Friday I called one of our people on the phone.

"Since you've asked, I may as well admit, Mrs. Kirk, the Associated Press has been on the wires for an hour asking confirmation of the Ambassador's appointment to Moscow."

So there it was. I'd known it all along, known it from the very first time I'd heard that Bedell was ill, known it because Dad was the very man I would have chosen myself. I knew, too, that he'd accepted. We'd agreed he must accept. Other posts one could refuse because one had served one's country long and well, in peace and war; one could refuse because one wasn't a rich man, because one deserved rest and material rewards, but this—no!

It would be interesting, of course, but our lives had been interesting enough and we hadn't so many more years ahead. Still, there it was. I'd gotten over the shock by the time Dad returned—at least I made a brave effort to make him think so. He'd been surprised when they asked him to go to Moscow, more surprised than I, but he knew what he must say, and he knew what I would say. He'd accepted.

Leaving Belgium was hard. There were problems there, problems that still seemed very important to us but which dwindled beside those we should face in Russia. Our friends were all very kind and we felt sad indeed when we sailed from Rotterdam, our cabin full of flowers and our hearts heavy with affectionate regret.

We spent a month at home. We visited relatives, doctors, dentists, signed powers of attorney, made new wills. It was like assisting at one's own funeral. Everyone was most solicitous, gathering around with tender, soothing words. Attentions were lavished on us, even the saleswoman at Saks leaned across the corset counter, as she read my name and address, to ask:

"Are you the lady whose husband is going to Russia? The blessing of God be with you."

I felt in need of just that, but our great consolation was the fact of Roger's deciding to interrupt his college course and spend a year in Moscow with us. As a sophomore of eighteen, he was young for his class. A year out would be desirable from many points of view. He'd already studied some Russian, had mastered the elementals of the grammar, and he hoped for a job in the Embassy where he could make himself useful and get on with the language. His professors at Princeton approved, even President Dodds agreed it would be a fine experience. For me, it meant all the difference, and for Dad, who had been separated from his son for nearly ten years of war and foreign service, it would be a wonderful thing.

Roger and I sailed June 8 on the Nieuw Amsterdam, Dad preceding us by a week, as he flew from New York to be present at the Foreign Minister's Conference in Paris. We joined him at the Crillon.

Our days in Paris were crowded with shopping of all kinds. We had long lists of supplies plus food and wines to be bought, and shipped in with us by plane. The Russians adhere strictly to the protocol of the Congress of Vienna, which specifies that Ambassadors may have free entry of goods *pour les besoins de leurs maisons,* anything not intended for personal use being subject to ordinary customs. There is an import quota set for an Ambassador; ours is the same as that of the Norwegian or the Greek, even though their chanceries may number six people and ours a hundred. Over and above that quota, free import of goods must be covered by a *laisser passer* and the goods must be accompanied by the Ambassador himself. It was obvious, therefore, that full advantage must be taken of any trip outside, not only because we knew everything in Russia would be prohibitively expensive, but because little would be available at any price.

During and just after the war a special plane was assigned to the Moscow Embassy. As the Russians no longer permit any foreign planes to remain in Moscow, our plane has been withdrawn and, instead, the American Air Force very kindly supplies a ship for official trips which the Ambassador may be required to make in and out of Russia. For increased fuel capacity, and to avoid any danger of forced landings in forbidden areas, it seemed wiser to use a four-engine transport instead of the usual DC-3. Dad, Roger and I took off from the Crillon promptly at two o'clock, June 26, a fine sunny day, with all the fashionable world streaming out to see the Grand Prix. We passed a line of coaches and fours, pretty ladies with sunshades riding on top, all bound for the races, a destination quite different from ours. But we embarked in style, as the Embassy had provided cars and a truck, along with a polite secretary with a flower in his buttonhole. The plane was waiting on the field at Orly, large, substantial and impressive, with the crew drawn up in a line by the ladder. The heavy luggage had already been packed in and we had to pick our way through boxes and bales, trunks and suitcases. "Operation Kirk," I called it and they actually sent a special loading officer to supervise the distribution of weight. Just across the aisle, along with the tennis racquets and my typewriter, I noticed Dad's shotgun. I thought of my good-bye call on Madame Pavlov, the wife of the Soviet Ambassador to Belgium.

"*Votre mari aime chasser?*" she asked me.

I replied yes, that he was very fond of shooting.

She shook her head disapprovingly.

"*En Russia, nous ne tuons pas les animaux!*"

As the lady herself was supposed to be a champion pistol shot, I wondered what she did kill, and how. Probably she shot more often in cellars than in open fields.

We were to spend two nights in Germany—one in Heidelberg, one in Berlin. Our first stop was Wiesbaden, where we put down at the American Air Force base. Generals Huebner and Cannon were there to meet us, the former commanding our ground troops, the latter our Air Force in the European theater. General Huebner had come from Heidelberg in his private train, a gleaming three-car affair that Frau Goering used for her shopping trips, back and forth, through Germany, to Vienna, Prague or Paris.

General Cannon and his wife rode up from Wiesbaden to Heidelberg with us. We were to stay with the Huebners in their fine, big house, formerly the residence of some member of the Bosch magneto family.

The Huebners had a party planned for seven-thirty, and

we found there were to be over a hundred guests for cocktails and buffet supper in the garden. It was good to see some old friends down from Berlin and a few of the French and British officers and officials; no Germans, of course, and no Russians. These last come to only very special functions—national holidays and anniversaries.

Next morning we drove about Heidelberg, a fascinating town, fortunately untouched by bombs and still looking like the decor from the *Student Prince*.

The Goering train took us back to Wiesbaden next day, and we flew from there to Berlin. Our trip was carefully scheduled between regular airlift flights, and it was interesting to hear the crew tell of that miracle of organization; of the control tower that sent our planes in at three-minute intervals, of the splendid safety record the pilots made, and the astonishing 'round-the-clock delivery of goods and personnel. The airlift had begun to slacken off when we arrived, but it was still impressive to feel a part of such a show. We flew low over Berlin on our allotted level—one could see the shells of ruined buildings—and came in at Tempelhof Airdrome. This is one of the finest in the world, with its great semicircle of open hangars under which dozens of planes can be lined up at one time.

A full honor guard of soldiers, with music, was waiting for us, two companies with a band drawn up at one side and a group of high-ranking American officers, including generals and admirals, together with Bob Murphy, the senior State Department official, and a big press contingent. The band played first the flag officers' march and then the Star Spangled Banner, at which point I bit my lip hard, for there we were, three Kirks on our way to Moscow with the airlift roaring overhead, the music playing, and the American flag streaming out in front of us. Dad reviewed the guard with the Commander of the Berlin garrison, and then we drove to the house of Admiral Wilkes, our ranking naval representative, where we spent the night.

Berlin, in this spring of '49, I found a horrid sight: no building or house left untouched in the heart of the city, trees cut

5

down, statues mutilated, the empty ruins of the government palaces blackened, destroyed, concrete and stone laid as low as the system they were built to glorify. Along the main streets there were numerous shops open, with what looked like handsome articles for sale, though with the thirty-cent mark and the added Berlin import tax anything new is very expensive. Antiques are still to be had and bits of silver, old Meissen, rugs, tapestries, anything and everything the "new poor," or the refugees, can sell in order to live. We were told that conditions were very much better than last year and that, with the airlift and the stiffened attitude toward the Russians on our part, the difference in the West Berlin Germans was noticeable. In all the Allied sectors food distribution had improved, black marketing was being stamped out, and earnest efforts to combat unemployment were being made.

The Wilkes lived on the edge of town in a comparatively intact area. It was hard to sleep, with the planes going overhead every four minutes, but the house with its large garden was pleasant enough.

We were awakened early next morning, the 28th of June. With an escort of military police before and behind, we drove back to Tempelhof where the big plane was waiting, loaded and ready for the take-off. With the officers we found Brewster Morris, one of the Moscow First Secretaries who had come down to meet us and travel back in the plane. There were also two Russians, a navigator and a radio operator, assigned to guide our flight. This is the usual procedure. Our planes are flown by our own pilots, but the flight plan is made by the Russians and they are responsible for everything but the plane's actual operation. They are civil aviation officers, never the same two, but they seem to know their business and they give no trouble to our people.

We settled ourselves amid our boxes and bales and took off at nine o'clock, flying along at a good height out over the Russian zone toward Poland and Moscow. We three and Brewster were the only passengers; there wouldn't have been room for anyone else, the plane was so loaded with supplies and baggage. There was little to see, the Russians having carefully routed us around any town or settlement that might have been of interest. The Polish farming country stretched out into what appeared to be marshes, scrub woods, and miles of land uncrossed by roads or railroads. What a hopeless country to invade! There's too much of it in every direction.

We roared on for five and a half hours. Now we were nearing Moscow. The plane went into a long glide and we put down at Vnukova, several miles outside of the city. As we taxied along the runway, I could see crowds waiting ahead. We were obviously a great curiosity, as there are no four-engine transport planes in Russia, our own only comes in two or three times a year, and this first trip with a new Ambassador was of special interest. The fences along the field were lined with people. The plane came to a stop. I straightened my hat and my lipstick and followed Dad down the ladder.

The whole Embassy staff had come out to meet us, also a Russian Protocol Officer and Dad's four officially assigned MVD guards, to whom our counselor, Foy Kohler, formally introduced us. On entering or leaving Russia theirs would be the first and last faces we would see. The Smiths had told us about them and there they were, four short, tough-looking fellows in dark suits, turned-down felt hats, and gun bulges on their hips. Their hands, when I shook them, felt hard and dry. We were never told their names. Only the American and the British Ambassadors are honored with this protection. The custom dates from the assassination of a German Ambassador just after World War I. From then on, the top three envoys, German, British and American, were assigned bodyguards, four of them on duty night and day.

We had met the top four but there is a squad of eight, probably twelve, as they have to keep watch-and-watch. Every time the Ambassador goes out from his house, they follow in a car immediately behind, and they surround him if he walks in the street; if he dines at a restaurant they sit at a table close by, the chief facing the Ambassador; if he travels by train, one stands guard outside his compartment. Only on Embassy property, his own or another, is he free from direct surveillance. This is furnished for his protection and, though it serves other purposes as well, I don't mind the idea. Certainly, if we said half the rude things about the Russians that they say about us every day, we'd have crowds throwing things at our Embassy windows. The Russians may be more apathetic, but I'm just as glad to have those armed men watching over us. Three sit in a car just outside the residence gates, while one stands on the sidewalk to give the signal and note who goes in and out.

Compared to the Belgian, the Moscow staff looked large; afterward Dad told me there were about a hundred and ten. The usual length of term is two years, in the case of military personnel somewhat less. This same rule holds true in many of the other missions, and it's the consensus that two years is about the limit; beyond that, one's nerves, health and general outlook grow a bit frayed. All told, our staff seem a very good lot. They should be, for Moscow can't be too easy; it's listed as a "hardship post," probably with reason.

The skies were gray and it began to rain. It almost seemed as though we had left the sunshine very far behind us as we motored into town. We were quite a cortege, Dad's guard car close to ours and the rest of the Embassy stringing out behind. No Americans have licenses to drive. In order to obtain one, they must pass an expert mechanic's test in Russian, practically an impossibility on any count. As a result, we must employ Russian chauffeurs who act as checkups for the MVD and send daily reports on all our movements.

The airport is about forty-five minutes from town. The road was wide, the country flat, with a few straggling houses of unpainted wood, many built of logs, much like those a child would put together in his playroom. Around the windows there were frames of fretwork. None of this seemed new, none of it looked well kept, no flower gardens round the houses, a row or two of potatoes or cabbages, but it all looked gray and wet and the roads leading off the highway were mud tracks down which walked children with goats and occasionally an old woman leading a cow. Entering the city, the main streets looked broad and fairly clean. There was evidence of new construction, but many of the buildings, even the large ones, looked shell-damaged. When I asked they said no, they were simply in need of paint and repair.

We swung off into a little square with an untidy green space in the middle and the ruins of an old church on one corner. Ahead of us was Spaso House, set back from the street behind high iron railings. It looked tidy and secure with the United States Embassy shield over the gate. Perhaps tidy is hardly the word to apply to so impressive a structure. It is an immense neoclassic palace, built in 1912 by a rich businessman who married into the nobility. He had two daughters and a good-for-nothing son. The latter fell into debt, quarreled with his father, and finally murdered the poor gentleman in the front vestibule. One of the daughters is still living in Paris, and I wish that I might learn more about the house from her, but hardly suppose she has happy memories of it or her family. After the Revolution, the Bolshevik Government took it over as an official guest house for the Foreign Office. Then, when we recognized the Bolshevik Government, in 1933, and Bill Bullitt was appointed Ambassador, he negotiated the lease of Spaso for his Embassy residence, as well as another lease of a large office building to serve as chancery and living quarters for the staff. We still rent both properties.

In architecture, as in much else, the Russians seem to lag a hundred years behind the rest of the world. Although we know the date of its construction, Spaso really corresponds to what we would call classic revival. Its proportions are gigantic, the ceilings some twenty-eight feet high, downstairs, and twenty on the second floor, not to speak of the main hall, which is eighty-two feet long and two stories high. From its ceiling hangs an immense crystal chandelier, almost the biggest I have ever seen. They assure me it is quite secure, that General Smith had it seen to immediately on arrival, but just one pendant dropping on a guest's head might cause international complications. The walls of the hall are faced with marble, there are great fat columns at each end and, where doors open onto a semicircular porch, there is a part set off as a salon, an agreeable corner with wide sofas in soft greens, two others in deep rose, low tables, lamps, all very attractive. Throughout the house the painting is fresh and light-colored and the furniture, though largely American reproductions of the pseudo-Williamsburg type and therefore out of scale for these huge rooms, is unobjectionable.

The whole house is far better than I feared; in fact, the effect is dignified and should not be difficult to live with. At one end of the Great Hall there is a small oval dining room, which the family use, keeping the big state dining room for official entertaining. Beyond this room there is a ballroom, a big one, opening onto a large enclosed rear garden. The ballroom is used for every kind of purpose. During World War II it was made into office space; now, between parties, it serves for movies and more often for indoor badminton, one of the few sports we can enjoy in Moscow.

Upstairs there are ten bedrooms, opening out from a wide corridor which runs around three sides of the Great Hall. I have a most comfortable suite of bedroom and sitting room, looking over the front garden to Spaso Square. When I have put a few of my own things around, the rooms won't be quite as much like de luxe apartments at Claridge's or the Waldorf. Actually, our government decorators did a fine job at long distance, and I am most grateful to find so pleasant a place in which to live. Everything, down to the last nail and pillow, had to be sent in, for nothing is available here at any price. The Soviet Government will rent furniture out of their storehouses, but most of it is utterly unsuitable to modern living and the complications that accompany such transactions are unending.

Dad is set up in style in a fine, big room just across the hall from mine. It is so large we intend using it as a kind of bed-sitting-room, for it has a fireplace that will be very pleasant on winter days and nights.

Living in the house with us are two Embassy Secretaries, both exceedingly nice. Dick Davis, a First Secretary and one of our Russian experts, is leaving this summer; John Keppel, a very attractive, intelligent young man, will stay on for another year. They share a corner apartment down the hall, and Roger has a room just beyond. At the moment John superintends the running of the house, so my worries on that score are over. I was frightened by the prospect of coping with Russian servants, marketing and accounts. Our counselor, Foy Kohler is also living here until his replacement arrives, so I sit down to table with five men, and I quite like it. Most families and the single girls live in Mokhovaya, the chancery building; a few have quarters outside; and there are two houses for bachelor service attachés and another for enlisted personnel and the men clerks.

We do not own any property in Moscow; actually, only two or three missions, among them the Finns and the Persians, have houses of their own. Even the British, who wanted to exchange their old Embassy in Leningrad for property here, have never been able to make a deal. We are all at the mercy of the organization called Burobin, a department of the Soviet Foreign Office, which deals with the needs of foreign diplomats—everything they may require—from Christmas cards to new roofs on their garages; from servants to tickets for football games. Like all other Russian departments, this one is a mass of red tape and bureaucracy. It manages to make our complicated lives that much more complicated.

I think the secret desire of every retiring Foreign-Service officer who has been posted in Moscow must be to head up a Get-Back-at-the-Russians bureau in Washington. There are so many things one could do to harass them, the kind of things that happen to us here every day: electricity failures, repair delays and consequent demands for damages from leaks and stoppages, lost luggage, cars inspected and found faulty for city driving, requests of all kinds mislaid or unanswered. There's no end to the game, and it would be such fun to play.

At the moment, there is fever-pitch excitement about the annual Fourth of July reception to be given here in Spaso. This turns out to be a soirée of four hundred people, all the American Embassy plus the entire diplomatic list and a selected number of Russian officials. It's to be at nine-thirty, with buffet supper and dancing afterward. All this was planned before we arrived, so I only have to stand in line and receive alongside Dad and Foy Kohler. By the Fourth, Dad should be officially accredited as Ambassador; meanwhile, Foy acts as Chargé d'Affaires until Dad presents his papers to the President of the Supreme Soviet, Mr. Svernik.

Our major crisis right now is the nonappearance of two trunks containing all my best clothes, which seem to have been left behind in Belgium. My secretary there will be so horrified she will tear the storage company apart. It's not only that the trunks have disappeared but that, when found, they will be difficult to forward here.

Postmarked Moscow   *July 4, 1949*

THE TRUNKS ARE found, but in an excess of zeal the Brussels people sent them to Berlin, hoping to catch us on our way in. There they sit until someone figures out a routing. Anyway, they are found and that is a comfort, although I am sorry not to make my début tonight in white brocade. It will have to be a red-and-white summer print I brought along in my suitcase, and I'll search the beds in the front garden for a small cluster of blue-and-white flowers to pin on the shoulder, giving the patriotic touch. Foy told me the gardener had done his best with the seeds on hand, but nasturtiums and marigolds and lupins seem the main crop. Flowers in Moscow are very scarce, even in summer. There are only two or three shops where any can be bought and, even then, it's mostly spindly green plants one sees for sale, along with a few wilted cut flowers—no roses or carnations, no hothouse blooms of any kind. I was wise to bring in a big sheaf of artificial products, which will stand me in good stead. Already, I've combined them with green leaves and filled big vases in the corners of the Great Hall.

In the city, most of the trees were cut down in the early days of the Revolution, but there has been some recent replanting and there are young maples staked along the streets. Except for the Kremlin buildings and the very few newly constructed

Government ministries in the heart of the city, the rest of the town is crumbling and even substantial structures look so poorly kept I should guess they would not last long. The State, I am told, has great plans for transforming the whole city but, as fast as they build anything up, what they've finished falls down. There seems to be no conception of maintenance or upkeep. Our people find that to be true whenever they install modern equipment or machinery in American-occupied premises. Here in this house we have two deep-freeze cabinets, bought only a year ago, which are already out of repair through neglect on the part of our Russian house electrician.

The Spaso house staff numbers about twenty, plus five women working in the basement who operate a steam laundry for all the Americans. There are two cooks; a kitchen maid and a scullery maid; three men servants: the two Chinese, Chin and Tang, and Stepan, the pantry boy; two cleaning women downstairs; three housemaids upstairs; two chauffeurs; two telephone operators; a gardener; a general handyman; and two yardmen. All this lot must be fed three times a day. None of them, except for the two Chinaboys, are experienced servants, but somehow the house seems to run and Chin, the Number One boy, keeps a sharp eye on all concerned. He and Tang came to Moscow with the newspaper correspondent, Demaree Bess, some fifteen years ago. They married Russian wives, had children, and stayed on here to work in the Embassy, as they could not get exit visas for their families. Chin acts as major domo. Tang, the Number Two boy, is his faithful adjutant, and between them they take care of us as only good Chinese servants can. Several times they have thought about going to America, to their former employers, but they are loyal to their families and reluctant to leave. Incidentally, today, Russians are not permitted to marry foreigners; such marriages, if performed have no legal status.

Yesterday was Sunday and we drove out to the *dacha,* or country house, rented by the Embassy. It's about twenty miles outside of town, on a wooded slope overlooking a small river. The site is quite pretty, set in grounds enclosed by a high board fence; the house, a plain stucco villa type, has somewhat the air of a deserted summer cottage. The grounds are overgrown and uncared for but the place serves a real purpose, for it is available to all the Embassy on Sundays and holidays. There's a shabby clay tennis court, as well as volley-ball court. Although the river water is too dirty for bathing, some of the boys keep a *kayak* for sailing, and the hardy few bring sleeping bags and provisions to camp out over weekends. One of the chief disadvantages is the road in from the main highway, which is full of ruts and deep holes, almost impassable for low-slung American cars. It's a refuge, however, and a precious one. Each year the Russians threaten to cancel the lease, for the area roundabout is filled with summer-vacation camps, which Eddie Gilmore, the Associated Press correspondent, tells me are unwelcome to the rather elegant *dacha* colony just over the hill behind barbed wire and high walls.

I was glad to see the sunshine for, so far, it's been cold and wet. They tell me Russian summers can be hot. I wonder. I look with longing at my sport clothes and bathing suits, for even when the sun comes out there won't be much chance to enjoy. We are permitted to motor out of Moscow on only four roads, and then only as far as the fifty-kilometer mark. Beyond that, there are three expeditions we may take by car, after informing the Foreign Office forty-eight hours in advance, giving the numbers of the cars and the names of the passengers. The longest trip is to Yasnay Polyana, the home of Tolstoi; then there are the monastery at Zagorsk, and Klin, the home of Tchaikovsy. On none of these expeditions are we supposed to stop en route, even to eat lunch by the road. As sure as we spread a blanket and take out the sandwich boxes, a militiaman will pop out from behind a haystack, telling us to move on, that we are in forbidden territory.

WE HELD THE PARTY.

The four hundred guests came and stayed, a good many of them until half-past three in the morning. Dad and I received at the entrance into the Great Hall. It was my first look at our diplomatic colleagues, and by ten the place was a sea of faces, American and foreign. The men came in white tie and decorations, or in uniform, the women in their best frocks—I still wished for my white brocade. Fifty Russians had been invited; about twelve turned up, Gromyko en tête. He wore a crumpled brown suit, and hadn't even bothered to shave for the affair. It was just in the midst of his office hours, of course—the Russians do most of their business late at night—but, having seen him looking very smart at New York functions, we hardly felt complimented at his appearance.

As per local custom, the heads of missions and high officials were led into the smaller dining room, while the rest streamed into the state dining room and ballroom beyond. Things went smoothly enough and there seemed to be masses of food, cold meats, salads of all kinds, ices and cakes, champagne, wines and whiskey. The rooms looked very handsome. They were designed for living in the grand manner, and the four hundred guests fitted easily into them. In the ballroom, the hired Russian orchestra obliged with American dance music and it was all very gay. I stood with Gromyko, and, asking about his wife, I was told she was taking a cure in Carlsbad. We spoke of our livers, of the strain put upon them by diplomatic life. Madame Gromyko's was responding to the cure. I congratulated him and her, and asked to be remembered, reminding him that we had met at a dinner given by Ambassador and Mrs. Warren Austin in New York, the year before. Forty-five minutes went by. As if by signal, the other Russians appeared from the big dining room. Gromyko shook hands, they formed in behind, and out they all went.

It's farcical, pretending to entertain these people, but it's a farce we must continue to play while we still maintain relations with them. As Dad has often said, he could understand clearing out altogether, but that would be a futile gesture while the Russians still keep a large delegation at the UN in New York. No use closing the Embassy here, having their Embassy closed in Washington, and some hundred or more of their trusted agents left on the spot in New York to circulate as they like.

None of the Russians brought their wives to the party. I'm told these ladies are practically never seen. Very occasionally Madame Vishinsky appears with her husband, sometimes Madame Gromyko with hers, otherwise the men come alone. I daresay they don't want their wives corrupted by Western sights and manners, but even in restaurants one often sees men dining together. With all their talk about the equality of women, there's a lot of the Oriental left in these people. It comes out in odd ways, in their prudishness of dress, in their public behavior, in their passion for evasion and concealment. The White Russians we knew in the West were not like this, but they were a different people, almost a different race, from these peasant folk now risen to a petty bourgeois level of taste and morality.

My own analysis is that the leaders in the Kremlin, the men who were young in 1912, have reverted to what seemed fine and elegant at that time. That taste they understood, that taste they therefore decree to be right and correct, and so you get a kind of aspidistra, turn-of-the-century atmosphere. It suits the elder statesmen who found some of the young moderns of the '30s shocking and incomprehensible. All these have been liquidated or disciplined into conformity. There is no writer today like Alexander Blok, the young revolutionary, no innovator in the theaters like Stanislavsky or Meyerhoff, no daring or imaginative architects; and musicians such as Prokofiev have been stifled, others are in exile. Shostakovich composes, but at the behest of the authorities. He's become a kind of musician laureate who grinds out musical odes to national events. It's too bad, for the Russians have been a gifted people and their folk art was colorful and vigorous. Now that, too, seems to be disappearing, and a dismal sameness, a gray monotony, creeps over everything the Soviets touch.

In spite of themselves, their national shrine is impressive. Red Square, which I saw yesterday for the first time, is an astonishing place, exceeding all one's expectations. For centuries it's been the center of Russian national life. Here history was made, czars were acclaimed or denounced, triumphs and executions held, over and over again the pavements have run blood, all within the shadow of the Kremlin walls. The Russian word *Krasny,* or red, also means beautiful, and the square has always borne this name. It's a vast place, empty now except for Lenin's tomb, the old round execution block, and the fantastic pile of St. Basil's cathedral at one end.

In the old pictures, the Square always looked crowded, for it was the main market place and the center of the city's life. Kremlin means citadel, and this settlement on a slight eminence looking over the Moscow River was the start of the city. It was first enclosed with walls of wooden logs and these were replaced only in 1571 with the present ones of brick. Czar Ivan III brought Italian architects to design them and to build the towers and gates, each one different, that are spaced at intervals. Inside the Kremlin there are churches, monasteries and convents, now converted to Government use; palaces, the largest now housing the meetings of the Supreme Soviet; and the great Kremlin Museum.

The place is closely guarded. Only three of the gates are used and foreigners enter only by one on the the side away from Red Square. The main gate facing the square was once topped by the most sacred of all ikons and flanked on either side by small chapels. These chapels have been torn down, and just along the wall to the left of the gate is Lenin's tomb, a red-and-black polished granite structure, faintly reminiscent of what we might call Masonic architecture. On each side of the tomb are tiers of stone benches to accommodate the spectators at the great state reviews. Behind stand rows of cedar trees, and at the rear are the graves of the Party great, the elect of the elect, the greatest of whom are buried under flat slabs set into the ground, while their lesser brothers' ashes have been set into the wall itself, behind tablets engraved with their names. The wall is of rose-red brick, some sixty feet high along the main part of the square, crenellated in strange swallowtail design on top.

The Kremlin is an impressive and never-to-be-forgotten sight. It has beauty and terror, not only because of its associations, but because the whole effect is striking with the gold domes of the churches and the massed blocks of buildings within. All day long, no matter what the weather, Russians stand and gape at this holy place. They come from all over the country, some being led in reverential groups, others just standing alone to look.

Yesterday, when we were looking, ourselves, we had an almost too realistic demonstration of what can happen in the Square. Ellen Morris, Brewster's very attractive young wife, a lively girl who has learned much about Russia and the Russians, undertook to show us around. We were riding in her car and suddenly, in the middle of the Square, it coughed and sputtered and stopped. Just then round the corner came fifteen or twenty trucks filled with security police soldiers in khaki and blue caps. They piled out, formed into lines and proceeded to clear the square of people.

Our chauffeur became very nervous, and we didn't like the look of it ourselves. We didn't know what was up, but the police certainly meant business. It was interesting to see how quickly they emptied the Square and cleared the adjacent streets. That wasn't too hard, as no one is ever allowed to cross the Square on foot except at one point; otherwise they must walk around the edges; but farther down, where the streets run into Mokhovaya Square in front of our chancery building, the men formed long lines and simply swept the people in front of them as a wave pushes seaweed toward the shore.

More trucks arrived and our chauffeur was really in a panic. Fortunately, just as a very big militiaman was strolling toward us with fire in his eye, the car started and we were hustled around the corner and into the Mokhovaya driveway. Afterward we found that the Bulgarian Communist, Dimitrov, had died and they were bringing him to lie in state at the Union Hall, once the old House of the Nobles. For hours after, the streets would be closed until, late at night, the Politburo members and other high officials would come to pay their respects.

Whenever the Politburo people move about, elaborate security measures are taken and, when it is a question of Stalin himself appearing, there are even more. Big shots always drive in long, black limousines with curtains drawn and one or more guard cars behind. The bigger the shot, the more guard cars he will have following him. These are touring cars with canvas tops so the guards can fire through them. Sometimes a car precedes, as well as follows. These cars are all equipped with special horns well known to the sensitive ear of both the militia and the public, who give way immediately. Two short blasts—every traffic light turns and for blocks ahead the cars drive down the middle of the road at high speed.

Dimitrov, they told us in the Embassy, was to be entrained for Bulgaria the next day. He died here in a Government clinic under somewhat suspicious circumstances, but they are doing the handsome thing by him now, everything short of burial in the Wall.

Until I've read more of Russian history, I've no desire to visit the Kremlin. When I go, I want to know just what I am looking at, for I've a suspicion that the guides are not too informative. The museum is not open to the public. It's a rare privilege to be allowed within the Kremlin gates, and it's one that is extended to us only at long intervals, perhaps four or five times a year when the Foreign Office permits us to submit lists of Embassy personnel who would like to make the tour. The party, which is met by guides, plus an English-speaking official of the Foreign Office, plus two or three secret-service men, is always given the identical tour, shown the identical things and nothing else.

I've two or three fat books by my bed, and am beginning to sort out the Czars and Czarinas and the dates of their reigns. Russian history is a dark and bloody record, from start to finish. Time and again, successive waves of invasion have thrown the people back into misery and confusion, with none of the so-called civilizing influences to lighten their despair, and uplift their spirits—no Crusades, no Renaissance, no Reformation, no French Revolution. All these influenced the Western world, but none of these reached into the wasteland of Russia; only faint echoes came through to further confuse a frightened people. Some of our news commentators might well take a course in Russian history, for it helps to know their background when we look at the Russians today. I often wonder how much the average Soviet citizen knows about his own background —probably not much, for it's certain that more emphasis is put on the Lenin-Stalin line than on ancient Slavic history. And yet Lenin and Stalin, as well as the man on the street, are the result of that history. All of them could have walked out of any page of it, and their motivations are closely akin to those of their ancestors.

There is an apartment house next door to Spaso; its windows look out over our front garden. Today, after lunch, as we were sitting on the terrace, we heard a frantic yowling, then screams of laughter. Looking up, we saw hands pushing a small black-and-white cat through the upper half of a window on the seventh floor. The cat scrabbled down the pane, hung on the window frame, then fell to the ledge where it remained yowling. More unhappy screams from inside, Russian screams. Afterward, Dad said the poor animal got down somehow, or just fell off—I didn't stay to look .The American mentality that calls out the fire department to rescue a cat from a tree would be incomprehensible to a Russian!

There are very few dogs to be seen in Moscow. Any foreigner bringing one in must be very careful to keep the animal indoors or it's liable to be stolen by the first passer-by. Now and again I've seen a German shepherd dog; the military use these for police work. But luxury breeds are rare, and there are caustic comments in the Soviet papers about the care lavished on dogs in the West as contrasted to that given poor humans. Cats roam the streets, stray alley cats and basement mousers. We've a shabby couple living in our coal cellar. One caught its head in a swinging door and the kitchen maid took him to the vet's down the street.

"Whose cat is this?"

"It belongs to the American Ambassador," the girl answered.

"Come, come, we've no time for jokes here."

"But truly, this cat lives at Spaso House and belongs to the American Ambassador."

"That shows," said the vet, "what filthy people these Americans are. Even their cats are dirty."

Postmarked Moscow   *July 12, 1949*

THE JULY 4TH PARTY

safely over, I've begun to settle into Spaso and into the Moscow diplomatic routine, so different from that of Brussels. There we saw our colleagues at official functions, those we knew best at other parties, but they were always mixed with Belgian friends. Here it will be like living on a large raft with every creed, nationality and color tossing about together. I take more interest, therefore, in the prescribed official calls which I am starting this week. It's the custom for newly appointed Ambassadors and their wives to call upon all heads of missions whose arrival precedes theirs, Dad calling separately upon the men and I on the women. Today I did two, the Mexican, Madame Joublanc Rivas, and the Polish, at hour intervals. All this usually involves drinking tea, never very good tea except at the British Embassy, and eating sweet pastries, although the Polish lady produced coffee topped with whipped cream. I found her very agreeable, a young square-faced woman with sad eyes. We spoke French, and said the usual diplomatic phrases to each other:

"You have been long in Moscow, Madame?"

"Do you have a family with you?"

Then the weather, quite a lot about the weather . . .

"Did you know Moscow before?"

"Yes," she said, "I was here during the war, I came here to enlist in the Partisan Army and to fight with my Russian comrades."

I'd heard the lady was a colonel and had gone with the Army from Moscow to Berlin. I asked her a few questions, but she said no more and we fell back again on the weather and the children, and ended with an enthusiastic discussion of the reconstruction of Warsaw, which I said I heard was phenomenal.

In satellite Embassies, in any Embassies, it's not really possible to have private conversations. Dad tells me to be wary. Talking with these women, I remind myself that everything I say is probably recorded, that my hostess herself must make a report of my behavior and conversation, that someone else makes a report of her behavior and conversation. It's too bad, the Polish lady was an interesting woman to whose experiences I would like to have listened. I had the feeling that she would have liked to be friends with me, but, even if cordial gestures are made toward us, we must be cautious. If the gestures are sincere, those who make them may come to harm; if they are insincere and we respond, we ourselves may fall into a trap. It's a horrid business.

The Mexican Ambassadress was quite different, a lively lady whose husband is a career diplomat, and who has been a long time behind the Curtain, here and in Poland. Her description of her flight from Warsaw during the war was superb. She took off with a group of frightened colleagues, just escaping as the bombs fell. She had on a tailored suit and, for some unknown reason, gold kid sandals. As she went out the door of the Embassy, she caught up a package from the hall table, the last mail delivery to get through from Paris. She opened it in a slit trench, into which they all tumbled on the outskirts of Warsaw, waiting for the planes to pass over. It was a set of false finger nails, the only luggage she had taken with her!

Madame Rivas is also the heroine of the Kremlin crow story. Moscow is full of crows, which we Americans call the Kremlin crows, great black birds who scavenge and swoop about in the most sinister fashion. One day Madame Rivas found one in her courtyard, trailing a broken wing. She is a warm-hearted creature, and she took the bird into the house and nursed it tenderly. Such a large bird, loose indoors, had practical disadvantages, so Madame Rivas made him a little pair of red-flannel pants, very effective she said, and very becoming with his black feathers. The wing healed and, still wearing the red-flannel pants, the crow flew off through an open window straight toward the Kremlin, probably to make his report to Uncle Joe himself.

The Rivas are about to be evicted from their Embassy by Burobin, though not on account of the crow. It's to be given to one of the satellite missions, and the Mexicans have been offered another much smaller house with only four bedrooms and no service quarters. When they objected, saying they had fourteen people to house, the Soviets said, "But you've plenty of space with four bedrooms. What more do you want?"

Chantal Goffin, the Belgian Ambassadress, has worse stories to tell of dealings with Burobin and the difficulties of arranging for repairs and service of all kinds. The Belgians have just moved into their Embassy after a year at the hotel, and Chantal has the house but no servants, except for a daily helper and an old nurse. We have enough trouble dealing with the Russians, but the smaller missions have hideous struggles, proving that, even in minor matters, it's power and prestige the Russians respect. One reason the Belgians have special problems is that Chantal has learned to speak excellent Russian, she is young and spirited, and accepts very little from any Russian officials, shopkeepers or servants.

Louis, her husband, also insists on his rights, so they've not had too easy a time. He told me of one maid whom they liked very much, a good, hard-working girl. She came to them in the mornings, and worked at a regular factory job in the afternoon. One day, the militiaman at the Embassy gate questioned her; the next day, he gave her a paper saying that she could no longer work at the Belgian Embassy or for any other foreigners. She asked why, said she needed the money, but was told that she was too young, that if she really wanted to work for foreigners she must go to a special school for two years. The girl was angry but had no choice in the matter but to come in, pick up her things, and tell the Goffins she was leaving.

Afterward, their other maid told Louis of the reports both

of them had had to make, even without special schooling! They were told to notice the habits of their employers; what they ate and drank; what medicines they used and how often; when they brushed their teeth and where they put their brushes on the shelf; whether their routine was regular and, if it varied, whether they seemed nervous or upset. Did they quarrel with each other? What was their manner toward their child? etc., etc.—all sorts of small details that, taken together, might make a pattern of their lives. These servant girls were not intelligent or highly educated enough to be real spies, but their reports filled in the picture of the subjects, and, if made faithfully, skilled people could deduce much therefrom.

I expect that's the kind of reporting which goes on from this Embassy, though we may have two or three expert operators on the job, Mike the doorman, for example, a former head-waiter who speaks several languages and creeps about the lower floor like a large cat.

You may ask why we have Russian servants in the Embassy, why we don't bring over Americans. In the first place, the cost would be prohibitive; and, in the second place, there's no housing for them. These old palaces, the only houses available for any of us in Moscow, were built in the days when servants slept below stairs with the black beetles—when heating and plumbing were luxuries only allowed the masters—and they are simply not equipped to accommodate a modern staff. We have a few people who "live in," but the majority go home at night; and even those who do live here put up with conditions we would not ask Americans to accept. The building is not ours, the Russians fight any repairs or improvements we suggest and substantial changes would never be allowed. If the place should be run with military personnel, we would have the morale problem, bad enough for the men who must be here on regular duty, but impossible for mess sergeants, cooks, etc., who would find no recreation or outlet in Moscow, and whose tours would have to be so short as to be useless. It's a difficult business, and for the moment we've no choice but to put up with the place as we find it. The two Chinese do the best they can, and, by and large, the staff try to please us and fit in with what must seem our extraordinary ways.

Last night we held our first dinner, a buffet supper rather, of thirty-eight, with small tables set around an open space in the Great Hall, so that it was a reasonable facsimile of a very swank night club. When we first saw that vast room, we decided it must be used for just such functions. With candles and champagne on the tables, and music from a good phonograph belonging to Dick Davis, the fourteen women in summer evening frocks, and the twenty-four men whirling them about in turn, it was all very gay. It was a young party, no heads of mission, but junior counselors and secretaries, Belgians, Greeks, Indians, British, Italians, Mexicans, French, and, almost the most attractive couple of all, the Israeli Chargé d'Affaires and his wife, a very accomplished beautifully dressed Viennese. English and French were spoken indiscriminately. Without any Russians or satellites present, there were no political problems to consider so it was simple enough to mix nationalities and have a jolly evening. Russians are never invited to such functions—if they were, they wouldn't come—and the satellites attend only formal National Day receptions.

Our menus for such parties have certain limitations, but Frieda, the Finnish cook, produced our old standby of Chicken Tetrazzini; there were salads and ice cream; and Dad and Roger mixed a marvelous whiskey punch that livened everyone from the start. The party was actually in honor of Foy Kohler, the counselor who is leaving—he's been our Far Eastern expert—and the Emmersons.

These last are very solid folk who have lived for two years in a kind of tumble-down shack outside of town, with wind whistling through the cracks in the walls and the drains overflowing in the cellar. They chose the place, one of two houses we've been able to rent, because it had a garden and their two children, nine and seven, have been able to go to the local grade school. These are the last foreign children to be accepted in Russian schools; I suppose satellites may be admitted, but ours are no longer allowed.

Mrs. Emmerson has been most uncomplaining, and the

family certainly deserves a great deal of credit for the remarkable way in which they upheld the flag in their small village. The children learned Russian immediately, and they got good marks in school. No Russian parents ever came to see Mr. and Mrs. Emmerson, but ice cream and chocolate bars induced some of the Soviet children to play with theirs and the young Emmersons, in turn, visited the Russian homes. It's what should be happening all over this city, and did happen once upon a time, but that family was the last to experience it. Now the Curtain has fallen, even for children at play.

It's hard to describe what the housing problems are in Moscow. We rent Spaso House and Mokhovaya, the Chancery building with its apartments for married officers and single girls. We have a few other apartments allotted us outside; the military have two houses for both bachelor officers; and one we share with them for enlisted personnel and male clerks. There's no chance of getting extra space anywhere, nor of renting anything privately; even hotel rooms are given to one man or one couple, and may not be passed on to another. With the exception of Spaso, none of these buildings is in good repair, one or two are in very poor repair, none is modern, none is very comfortable.

There is hot water in Spaso and Mokhovaya, but only geysers in the other buildings. These geysers must be lighted to supply bath water, and there are no facilities for hot water in the wash basins or in the kitchen. Efforts are being made to improve American House, where the enlisted personnel live. Conditions there have been appalling—leaks in the roof, broken windows through which dust from the cement works next door sifts through, rotted pipes, falling plaster. If there were any alternative, any other place to go, we would evacuate the premises, but there's nothing else to be had at any price. It's difficult to make anyone at home believe what these places are like, difficult for them to believe we must accept them, but the fact is that no amount of complaint to the authorities here, to Burobin, that bureaucratic horror, has much effect. We do the best we can with the American "know how" at our disposal, patching here, painting there. It's sometimes a battle to keep the rain out, the cockroaches down, and the men's spirits up, but our boys are a good lot and grumble far less than might be expected.

Spaso House I find almost handsome, and absurdly large, but I realize as I live in it that to a lot of people here it's become a symbol of the Free World, and our colleagues look on it with real affection and pride. No other mission has as fine a house. The British Embassy is magnificently situated on the Moscow river, just opposite the Kremlin, but it is a dreary building, pseudo-Gothic, very oldfashioned and very uncomfortable. The French Embassy is a hideously ornate affair, boasting one bathroom for its dozen bedrooms. Some of the smaller missions do better, with their smaller houses, but ours is certainly the most modern and the most impressive. Then, too, we have more facilities for upkeep, hampered though we are by Russian restrictions. For example, we have the only lawn mower in all of Moscow and the only deep-freeze equipment. It's true, the latter goes dead fairly often and we have to rush down to take the temperature of the food, in case of spoilage, blaming the houseman, or *dvornik,* who has forgotten to check or the city current, which is variable —but still we are far better off than our colleagues.

Roger, at present, is apprenticed to the building superintendent, a well-trained engineer, who came to this country to work before World War II and knows how to deal both with Russian officials and with his own employees. For Roger, at nineteen, this job is a fine one. He will be the leg man, bossing the workmen and working with them a good part of the time. It's even excellent propaganda, for, in this "land of equality," it seems difficult for the Russians to believe that the Ambassador's son is willing and able to work with his hands. They themselves are very rank-conscious.

Roger started promptly at nine, this morning, and I am very curious to see how he makes out. Certainly a knowledge of Russian plumbing and house repairs should make small adjustments at home child's play and qualify him later as an ideal husband. He goes on the records as an F.S.S. 14, the lowest-paid job in the civil service list, but the American taxpayers will get good returns for their money, as he is a conscientious and enthusiastic worker.

WE ARE JUST BACK
from the annual Red Air Force Show, an elaborate performance at which Marshal Stalin, the Politburo, high government officials, and the diplomatic corps assist each year. The special guests were given tickets for places in the aerodrome pavilion, but the thousands of other spectators were massed across the field, around which militiamen stood, shoulder to shoulder, making a living hedge. We three—Dad, Roger and I—plus the senior service attachés, were the only ones invited from our Embassy. With a placard on our car, we drove out of town, down specified avenues marked with stands of red banners. Once at the field, we had to show our papers before passing the cordons of police, after which we were ushered towards an open terrace at the right of the central building.

There we found the rest of our diplomatic colleagues, along with selected members of the Secret Service and uniformed police. The party folk and high Soviet brass occupied the roofs and balconies of the main structure, nearly two hundred yards removed from us, the very center balcony being reserved for Stalin and the Politburo. The general public never attends any of these ceremonies. They can watch from far off, from very far off, but the close view is the privilege of the elect, and even then only his immediate entourage can approach Stalin.

Fortunately some of us had brought field glasses, realizing that this might be our one sight of the Generalissimo. He usually appears in public twice a year, at the May Day parade in Red Square, and again at the Air Show in July. Even on

May Day, his own people never get very close and most of them only know he is there when they hear the salutes fired and the bands play. All this seems strange to us, but we should remember that Stalin considers himself God, and, as God, he shows himself very seldom to mortal men. He is constantly before them in pictures, in statues, his every saying is announced with reverence, but only a very few have seen him in the flesh.

We were therefore privileged. It was a few minutes before noon. Through the main gates came numbers of black cars, each followed by one or more guard cars. Important-looking men got out. Some we recognized, Molotov, Beria, a few of the marshals—then a small open automobile drove in, filled with armed militia, behind them the longest and blackest of the black cars, closely followed by another filled with militia. The cortege drew up before the steps of the central pavilion and Marshal Stalin, in a gray uniform, got out of the big car and walked rather heavily and deliberately up the steps, inside the doors, and a minute later appeared on the upper balcony, surrounded by the Politburo members. Down in front, a huge military band struck up the national anthem and the show was on. The Russians have discarded the *Internationale* for this new song, a very stirring tune which competes well with that other fine tune *A Life for the Czar*.

Although so far away, looking through Dad's field glasses we could identify the various figures in the box and note their respective positions around Stalin. That's always significant for, as a man drops out of favor, so he drops down the line. There were no seats on the diplomatic terrace, and I was grateful to one of the British attachés, who lent me his shooting stick. Sir David Kelly, the new British Ambassador, who arrived in Moscow just a week ahead of us, came over to talk with us.

We agreed it was absurd that Ambassadors and Ministers, accredited representatives of sovereign countries, should be quarantined off from the Government officials, sitting above and beyond us like the gods on Olympus. Not only that, but the Secret Service and the press photographers seemed to concentrate entirely on our people. Our naval attaché, Admiral Stevens, said that the Russian papers and news reels would undoubtedly carry pictures showing "American spies taking notes at the Soviet Air Show."

In all honesty, I must confess that it was a very good show, led off by General of the Air Force, Vassily Stalin, Stalin's aviator son, who flew past in a single-seater plane. There were exhibitions of fancy piloting by both men and women, there were sham fights, gliders and latest model jet planes—all very impressive. The last and most spectacular was the parachute drop, hundreds of parachutes colored like beach umbrellas, spilling out all over the field. The Russians have always been very keen for this sort of thing, though Admiral Stevens, who is himself a naval aviator, said they used very few parachutists during the war, and he supposed it may have been because of their well-known weakness in aerial navigation.

The show lasted two hours. At the end of that time, Stalin disappeared from the balcony, the cortege formed again, the other cars drove off, and we were then ushered to the rear of the pavilion and our own cars brought up from the parking lot behind. Driving back to the city, down the same carefully patrolled avenues, one of the long, black cars would now and again pass us, going full speed down the center of the road. This showed it was one of the big boys on his way home. On certain streets, they are the only ones entitled to use the middle lane; other cars, including those of the diplomats, must travel at single file close to the curb. Traffic regulations are very strict in Moscow, and there are any number of minor rules that make it confusing for foreigners.

We have no privately owned automobiles in the Embassy, but there are a certain number of duty cars available. Fortunately most of our people live in Mokhovaya, so getting to work is easy enough. Taxis in Moscow are quite plentiful, though the fares run high. There are good, modern trolley busses, although in the rush hours one must queue up for these and there's always the famous subway, of which more later—I've been promised a conducted tour by one of our young men. There are very few bicycles, and apparently also very few private

Russian automobiles. You almost never see women drivers—one or two driving taxis or trucks—but never a woman driving an ordinary car.

There's so much I'd like to ask about, to get straight in my own mind. I've been here now for two weeks, and I've talked with no Russians except the servants, the Foreign Office people who came to our Fourth of July reception, and the same men from the Protocol Division, whom I have met at other national day functions. There seems little chance of our ever meeting any others. Dad has inquired if I am expected to call on Madame Vishinsky or any other Government wives. So far, he's had no reply and even Madame Brosio, the wife of the Italian Ambassador and the senior lady of the diplomatic corps, tells me she has never been encouraged to pay visits to the wives of Russian officials. We cannot be friends with any one of them, and any Russians we may have known on former posts barely speak to us here and refuse any invitation offered.

There's no breaking through the wall—a discouraging business when one thinks of living two years in Moscow, one's social contacts confined to one's diplomatic colleagues. We knew all this before we came but it's hard to believe until one is on the spot. I don't ask to convert anyone, I don't expect to be converted, but, being a friendly soul, I would like to talk with these people.

As far as other restrictions go, there seems to be no reason one can't walk freely about town. I've promised always to take my identity card with me, and there I'm no different from any Russian, as to go out without documents is worse than going out without clothes. Taking careful bearings on one or two landmarks just around Spaso, I've ventured round the block several times and out along the Arbat, the famous old street which runs close by. The Arbat starts at Arbat Square, just up from the Kremlin, and runs far out into the country where the high Soviet officials have their *dachas,* or estates.

From the city limits on, the road is forbidden to us and we can only picture these estates. In town, the Arbat is closely patrolled by militia, and the white line painted down the middle of the street is a strict reminder for ordinary traffic to hug the curb. On the sidewalk, it's easy to spot the Secret Service men dotted along the route; the cut of their clothes, the very look on their faces is unmistakable. John Keppel says it's a game to count them as he walks to the office from Spaso, each day. As they see a foreigner go by, they will often stroll after him, walking down the block until they can pass him on to the next man.

Now that I've seen all this, I must reread that novel by the Australian correspondent, *The Room on the Route,* for that route was the Arbat. The shops along the street are poor enough, and the goods displayed look pitiful to Western eyes. The windows of food shops are always filled with cardboard models of whatever is for sale, cardboard hams, chickens, sausages, cheese, fruit; the bakeries even display varnished cardboard loaves of bread. I'm told this may be an old custom, perhaps dating from the time when ordinary folk couldn't read and the windows showed what was sold inside the shops.

All goods are free of rationing now in Russia; it's only scarcity that causes empty shelves, scarcity, and low living standards. At that, things have improved immeasureably since the war, and the people are better dressed and fed. That's hard to believe, when you come in from the Western world—this dingy, dusty mass of folk that throng the streets, what can they have looked like before? And the beggars, I've never seen as many or as pitiful ones. Curious, that in this enlightened land such creatures should be allowed on the sidewalks, in front of churches and shops, tugging at your sleeve in the markets. Surely there should be some way of caring for them, the crippled, the sick, the miserable.

Yesterday, Roger, John Keppel, and I went to look at a famous old walled monastery on the edge of town, the New Maidens, where two churches have been restored, one as a museum and one for worship. Here the beggars swarmed around the doors, pathetic creatures in rags, holding out their dirty hands and calling down blessings for every *kopek* you put into them. The New Maidens monastery was the favorite place of refuge of royal ladies of Czarist times, serving both as a retreat and as a prison. Peter shut his half-sister, Sophie, into a cell there and hanged two hundred of her supporters outside her window. Later on, it became a fortress against enemy attacks, and, when the French attempted to blow it up, as they left Moscow, the nuns put out the fuses and the fire. There's a dramatic picture of this episode in the museum church.

All around the monastery the crenellated walls were intact and the fine main gate still standing, but here, as everywhere else in Russia, nothing is cared for or kept up, and the restoration of the churches seems to have been badly done. The old tombs in the yard were cracked and broken open, grass grew rank everywhere, and there were big puddles of standing water in the pavements.

We went into the church, the first Russian orthodox church I've visited, except for one in Paris many years ago. Before the Revolution, there were four hundred churches in Moscow (I believe forty are open today) and at one time all these were shut, but since World War II a number have been restored. The present Patriarch made a bargain with the Soviets, promising his allegiance if they would give back the four great monasteries of Russia and allow certain churches to be made available for worship. This the authorities agreed to, even giving permission for a seminary to be created for the training of priests, although applicants must be acceptable to them and must refrain from political activity.

I was interested to see what kind of people came to church. We arrived just in time for vespers and the place was crowded, but the worshippers were largely women, most of them very old and very poor, shabbily dressed with their heads wrapped in shawls. They seemed very devout, crossing themselves and bowing, even kneeling and touching their heads to the floor. The two officiating priests appeared young, and went through their elaborate ritual with care and style. The church itself was plain inside, but there were numbers of ikons on the walls, with lighted lamps hanging near them, and queues of people forming up in front of their special favorites to kiss the holy images. There was singing; acolytes went back and forth swinging incense burners; the priests formed in procession and went from ikon to ikon. It was all very colorful, and must have been even more so in the old days when the church was ablaze with hundreds of candles, glittering jeweled covers over the ikons—now taken away to be melted down or placed in museums—and gilt embroidered banners and vessels of gold and silver.

With all this, I wonder if there was ever the gaiety one feels in the great Catholic churches of Western Europe, the transcendent glory, the triumphant joy of the service, for here the people seem to stand mute and the whole barbaric pageant goes on without their sharing in it except as dumb, almost bewildered, spectators. Then, too, for us Westerners much of the architecture and decoration of these churches seems ugly, both outside where the twisted onion-shaped towers still bear traces of gaudy paint, and inside where all the gold and violent colors offend our sense of purity and restraint. Perhaps it's what the Russian people need to brighten the age-old misery of their existence; it's perhaps why they have insisted that the churches be returned to them as an escape from drab reality.

The most astonishing example of Russian church architecture is St. Basil's, in Red Square, built by Ivan the Fourth, Ivan the Terrible, as a thank offering after his taking of Kazan from the Tartars. Unlike many of the churches inside the Kremlin, this was not the work of imported architects but was designed and built by Russians, and, it is said that, to make sure there would never be another like it, Ivan gave orders that the head architect's eyes be put out when the job was over. St. Basil's is in process of restoration today. Once an antireligious museum, it's been emptied of everything but historical relics, and the plan is to preserve and respect it as a national monument. Painters are at work splashing yellow and green and pink stripes around the domes, and the crosses have been regilded, those characteristic Russian crosses with the crescent impaled below, showing the triumph of Christ over Mohammed. This, too, dates from the time of Ivan's Tartar wars.

MY SIGHTSEEING
is interrupted by more calls. I am trying to get through the
list as quickly as possible, though, once I've finished, the business is only half over as these ladies must call back! I've been
to see the Czech Ambassadress, a tight-lipped young woman,
reputed to be very Red in her sentiments. Perhaps her coolness
toward me stems from an interchange of conversation she had
with Dad at the French Embassy on the 14th of July.

"How proud you must be of the fine showing of your tennis
team in the Davis cup matches," he said to her.

She answered rather shortly.

Next day we read that Drobny and his partner had asked
asylum in England and, of course, she must have thought
Dad was baiting her about it.

Ellen Morris went with me to call on the Hungarian. Ellen
is such a gay, cheerful young woman that even the most hard-
bitten of the satellites melt before her. She has worked hard
on the language here and speaks enough Russian to make
herself understood, also French and Italian when either of
those languages is appropriate. I must say I am grateful for
my own French. Mike, the old rascal at the door, is very much
impressed by it, but, like all headwaiters, Mike is a shocking
snob. In the old days, many Russians spoke French—before
the Revolution it was the court language—but it's heard only
occasionally today. In one or two bookshops, and in one of
the art stores, there are little old ladies who will say a few
words in French if there's no other customer standing by, and
in the Protocol Department of the Foreign Office a number
of the officers speak French more readily than English. They
used to tell the story in Belgium of a conversation between
Sergeiv, the Soviet Ambassador, and a rather foolish lady who
sat beside him at a dinner party:

"*Monsieur l'Ambassadeur,*" she asked, "*ou sout tous les Russes qui parlaient si bien le francais? J'eu ai connu tellement
dans le temps.*"

"Madame," he replied, *"ils sont tous morts."*

The French Ambassadress, Madame Chataigneau, comes to return my call tomorrow. She is a very shattered woman, still mourning the death of an only son killed during the World War II. The new British Ambassadress, Lady Kelly, has not yet arrived and the Italians are still away. A good many people are off on holiday. I expect during the winter we will all settle into each other's laps.

Postmarked Moscow   *July 22, 1949*

THE EMBASSY
mail pouches go out at intervals. We usually have two services a week, coming by air from the States to Helsinki, and coming on by rail from there in the care of two couriers; in between, there are "sea pouches." Sent by boat to Finland, these take well over a month to reach us, but all packages and periodicals and letters that are not stamped for air must come this way. Open mail back and forth to the States is discouraged. The letters are invariably opened, and often this fact isn't even disguised, for the envelopes are clumsily gummed back. Once we even had a letter with the Russian postmark stamped on the *inside*. The censor's hand had slipped.

I'm still missing my two trunks, but these will come in with Wally Barbour, our new Minister Counsellor who arrives next week. Everyone speaks very highly of him; Dad has met him in Washington and liked him immensely. His apartment in Mokhovaya is being put in order by the two maids who are staying on. Servants of any kind are becoming difficult to obtain and good ones are almost nonexistent. It's true there may not be many candidates to work for foreigners. Even if ordered to do so by Burobin, they become automatically suspect and must weigh better food and living conditions against a doubtful future, once they leave our employment. One of our young women told me of a maid who came to be interviewed, and who confided to her what the Burobin agent had said.

"Are you married?" he asked.

"I am a widow," she replied.

"Have you children?"

"Yes, two."

"Then," said the man, "you must realize that, if you continue working for foreigners, your children will be ineligible for superior state schools and later for government positions."

She answered him that she was very poor, that the children were young, and that she felt she must take a chance in order to make the extra money.

Yesterday, Roger reported a real crisis among his workmen, as one of the best of the younger men received a postcard in the morning mail saying he must report that day for his military service. Orders in the Soviet Union are arbitrary, no questions can be asked, but, as this man was one of our better workmen, it's quite possible he was picked out just to annoy us.

Roger is enjoying his job, and getting practice all day in the language as he orders his plumbers and bricklayers and carpenters about. He had a test in Russian given by a group of Embassy officers and came out very well. One of the board said Roger's showing gave him new respect for college teaching as his one year of Russian at Princeton had given him such an excellent start. It's really lucky he picked that subject. We had talked it over, and thought Russian a likely possibility for a young man with ambitions for the Foreign Service, little knowing how quickly it would be of use.

All our people make earnest efforts to get at least a smattering of the language as soon as possible. The women must know enough of it to direct their servants, for only one or two of the maids understand any English. We are lucky at Spaso, as Frieda, the head cook, is Finnish and she and her husband, Theodore, the gardener, spent some years in the United States and came back to Karelia, only to be declared Russian citizens when that province was annexed by the Soviets. Chin speaks English, so do the doormen, and we make out well enough.

In the house I expect my movements and habits to be reported on—that can't be helped while we have Russian servants, so it's fortunate I lead a fairly blameless life. So far as I know, I am not followed in the streets and I walk about quite freely. Perhaps it's just that I'm unconscious of being followed, for the Russians are devious about this, and, instead of men or women tagging behind, there's more apt to be someone across the way, or even in a car, watching you. I'm stared at in the street, of course, for, no matter how plainly foreigners are dressed, we are still quite different from the Russians and our shoes, especially, attract interest. Theirs are very poor, thin-soled, often made of artificial leather, many of canvas, and they are of all colors and shapes, the best of them like the cheap grade Czech shoes I used to see in Belgium. It's only the military that appear to have boots of real leather. Clothing for women is completely nondescript; now, in summer, the dresses are made of odd bits of printed cotton or rayon, the skirts short and narrow with no shape or cut to the garments, and no attempt is made to fit the wearer. Stockings are of thick cotton or rayon; there a few nylons for sale, but these cost twelve to fifteen dollars a pair in our money.

The ruble is artificially pegged at eight to the dollar (in the spring of 1950, this was cut to four to the dollar); the year before we came it was twelve; next year it may be two; it couldn't matter less to the Russians. Our Government compensates by giving extra living allowances to our people, but life is still very expensive in Moscow and it's fortunate we have so few temptations to spend money. So far, I've seen nothing to buy, aside from a few bits of old china and a very little Russian silver in the commission shops. These shops are state-run second-hand shops, and once held all manner of treasures, but everything now is pretty well picked over and "finds" are rare and usually overpriced.

Bookstores are everywhere, and they are crowded at all times. The Soviet Government is very proud of its campaign against illiteracy, and it's true they have made great progress on this score. It's true also that the written word is a weapon of propaganda, and their people must be able to read for it to be effective. Publishing houses work overtime, and enormous editions of politically important works appear constantly, and are as constantly exhausted. There are a few foreign books for sale in special shops. The English books I've noticed were novels by James Fenimore Cooper, Jack London, Mark Twain, English translations of Stalin on Leninism and of Lenin's works, some Shakespeare, and numbers of illustrated volumes on classic art and architecture. Some of our Embassy people have found some fine editions, remnants of old libraries, but anything politically suspect is not for sale.

Over and over again, the propaganda line is handed out; it appears in the newspapers, in the books, on the radio broadcasts. Reading and hearing nothing else, the people must believe it, or, if they don't believe it, they must accept it. It's maddening for us to turn on the Voice of America and to hear the whirring noise that means it's blocked all along the dial. Outside Moscow it comes through better—in some sections it's quite clear—but here in town the Russian language broadcasts from abroad are constantly "jammed." English language broadcasts they let by. The same thing holds true for the BBC; their Russian programs are also drowned out, and one wonders just what such a business of jamming must cost the Soviet Government.

We've no idea how many people in Russia have radios; we do know they listen to a lot of "canned" music and speeches that blare out all over the city, supplied by a cheap sort of plug-in public-address system. Some of the music, especially the men's choral singing, is quite good; the Russians have always excelled at that kind of thing. Perhaps one difficulty for a VOA listener, aside from the jamming is that no Russian is ever alone in a room. Housing conditions being what they are, he is bound to share accommodations with someone else, and might therefore be reluctant to be found listening to foreign broadcasts. This has also been offered as the reason why there are so few fires in these tumbledown houses. There's always someone on hand to put out a blaze!

Then, too, the militia are omnipresent. Militia are the ordinary police. Now, in summer, they wear white cotton jackets, with dark breeches, making them look a little like Good Humor men, with well-fitting high boots, and with business-like guns strapped to their waists. There must be thousands of them in the city; each large apartment house has one at the door, each street corner has one, there are often several to a block and, for any important occasion, they appear in droves. At football matches, Roger tells me, they make a human wall from the subway entrance to the stadium gates. MVD troops, such as we saw at the Air Show, are also used for this.

The men from Spaso—Dad, Roger and Dick Davis—are going to a big soccer match this afternoon, the Red Army team against Dynamo, the MVD team. It should be a good fight. I believe it was a terrific battle last year, and, quite naturally, the entire crowd cheered for the Red Army. The stadium is a fine one, said to seat sixty or seventy thousand people. Dad's bodyguards go in with him and sit directly behind, relaxing only to shout for their own MVD team.

After the men get back from the football games, we are to have some hot soup, and dress for the Polish National Day reception. These functions run to a pattern, starting at nine-thirty, when the entire diplomatic corps, plus appropriate Russians (there will be a lot at the Poles' reception), are sandwiched into drawing rooms and then led off to a buffet supper, the heads of missions and any high government officials being conducted to a special room or table. We Westerners are left strictly alone, no satellite doing more than nod to us, and no Russians whatever being introduced. It's fun looking at them, however, especially the marshals, with their stuffed uniform blouses and row after row of medals. It's true their blouses are stuffed. John Keppel examined one he saw hanging on a peg in a hotel barber shop one day. The chest was stuffed and heavily padded to give that fine curve they so admire.

Dad puts on white tie and decorations for these functions, and Roger wears his new tails and looks very nice indeed. I wish there were some lovely young ladies around to admire him. I've never seen any young Russian girls at these parties —even older ladies are rare—and the only two debutantes in the diplomatic corps are the Afghan and the Persian. They tell a funny story about the Afghan Ambassador, who is a devout Moslem. He is accredited to Sweden, as well as to the U.S.S.R., and chose to make his visit there at the time of the Mohammedan feast of Ramadan. This unfortunately coincided with the period of the white nights, when the sun never sets. As Moslems must fast during daylight hours, in Ramadan, the poor gentleman had just ten minutes of twilight in the twenty-four hours in which to eat.

Postmarked Moscow   *July 24, 1949*

GREAT EXCITEMENT.
I am to call on Madame Vishinsky next Wednesday, at five o'clock. I understand that I am the first Ambassadress she has received, so this must be a gesture of some significance. We did not put in a formal request, Dad simply asked Gromyko if Madame Vishinsky received and said that, if so, I would be very glad to call upon her and pay my respects. I wish that she would allow me to come to her home, but Dad thinks the call will undoubtedly be made at one of the state reception houses.

We don't know where any of the Russian officials actually live, as none of us, not just the Americans, but none of the diplomats have been invited inside their houses. We suppose they must have apartments in town, as well as their *dachas* in the country; some of them must live in the Kremlin itself; but we've no real information. Nor do we know what part, if any, the wives play in the lives of their husbands. Madame Molotov was head of the perfume trust at one time, but has not been heard of for several years. Madame Gromyko is sometimes seen with one of her children at matinee performances of the ballet. Madame Vishinsky is said to appear only rarely, and the others scarcely ever, in public.

My visit, such an ordinary occurrence in any other country,

is taking on added importance, for I begin to realize this must be a very special favor, not for me, but for the United States. I will go alone, dressed in my best clothes and my best manner. I daresay she will wear hers, to match.

Postmarked Moscow   *July* 28, 1949

MY APPOINTMENT
was for five o'clock, and the address given was the Foreign Office reception house, a kind of Blair Mansion, kept for state purposes. I dressed in a light brown-and-white summer print, put on my prettiest Suzy hat—Dad said I looked very smart—and went off, by myself, in the official car. As I left, I asked Mike, the doorman, who knows everything and everyone, if Mme. Vishinsky spoke French. "Surely, Madame," he answered. "She is not young, and she once belonged to the Old People."

The car drove through side streets to a big old-fashioned brick house set in the midst of well-kept grounds, protected by high walls. A sentry opened a gate for us, and we went up a drive to an imposing porte-cochere. The house was Victorian, and the grounds were ornamented with flower beds filled with cannas and red salvia. I was received by a footman in livery, at the bottom of the steps, and by a fresh-faced young woman wearing a summer frock and white cotton mesh gloves. These she kept on, throughout the afternoon. Speaking English, she ushered me into a large drawing room that opened onto a lawn and garden. The room was furnished in heavy pieces, all gilt and carvings, and there were huge vases of mixed floral arrangements, set on marble-topped tables.

Three ladies rose from chairs to greet me, Madame Vishinsky and the wives of two Vice Ministers, Madame Gusiev and Madame Zorin. Madame Vishinsky is a slight woman, about sixty. She looked very worn and sick, but was beautifully and very quietly dressed in a sheer gray silk frock, untrimmed, with fine old pearl earrings, no other jewels, and her hair was wound tight around her head in a bandeau, with curls on top. The hair was dyed that curious mahogany some European women, particularly elderly actresses, affect, but her coloring showed that she might once have had red hair, and certainly she must have been a very lovely looking young woman. I asked if she spoke French. She was greatly relieved to find that I did, but the three other women, the Ministers' wives and the girl interpreter, were apparently quite disturbed, especially the interpreter, who had thought to relay the conversation along a definite pattern from Russian to English and back. As it was, I became the interpreter. Neither Madame Gusiev nor Madame Zorin spoke any French, nor did the interpreter so, from time to time I turned with my most gracious manner,—

"Madame Vishinsky says . . ." "As I was just saying to Madame Vishinsky . . ." It was really very comical, and I enjoyed myself immensely.

Actually, our conversation was correct in the extreme. Madame Vishinsky at first seemed almost shy. Madame Gusiev was frankly curious, Madame Zorin more hostile and indifferent. We discussed the weather, that safe, never-failing diplomatic subject. We discussed Moscow and its new buildings.

"Our buildings," said Madame Gusiev, "must be quite different from the tall buildings in America. Yours seem so plain, like large boxes." I could have replied that theirs looked like wedding cakes, but thought better of it and decided she might have taken it as a compliment.

None of the ladies had been to America. Madame Vishinsky had been once to Paris with her husband. It was a beautiful city, she said, and she wished she might have stayed longer. Madame Gusiev had been to London and spent several months there when her husband was Ambassador. Madame Zorin did not look as though she had ever been outside Russia.

Madame Gusiev was dressed like a provincial lady attending her son's wedding. She wore steel-gray crepe, trimmed with touches of bright pink. Her hat was a monstrous affair crowned with masses of cabbage roses and ribbon bows, and her complexion was done to match the trimming of her dress. Madame Zorin was a large, plain-faced woman in carefully unfashionable clothes, shapeless and sand-colored, and without a hat.

We sat about a round mosaic-inlaid table. There was a lace cloth, five places laid for tea, dark blue Sevres plates, small gold forks and spoons. In the middle was a great dish of hothouse fruit, rare at any season in Moscow, and at each place were goblets and small liqueur glasses of Bohemian crystal. A perfectly liveried butler, speaking excellent English, appeared and offered us Russian wine and very dainty caviar and salad sandwiches, then either tea or coffee. We nibbled delicately, Madame Gusiev extending her little finger in the most refined possible way. The butler brought a tray of pastries, and again we nibbled.

"Have you seen the ballet?" asked Madame Vishinsky.

"No, I am looking forward to it very much. Will it open in September?"

"Yes, on the first, I believe."

"Do you have ballet in America?" asked Madame Gusiev.

"Indeed yes," I answered, "some classic and some modern. We wish we might have a chance to see your great artists there. Years ago, when I was a child, I remember the Diaghileff ballet coming to New York and the great success it had."

She made no comment.

We returned to the weather and agreed it was bad this summer. I admitted the Washington climate could be even worse. We expressed the hope that the winter would be mild.

"Will you leave the city for a vacation?" I asked Madame Vishinsky.

I was curious to know if she actually lived in town, and judged this to be so, as she said the weather had been too bad this year and her husband worked so hard and kept such irregular hours it was not possible to leave Moscow, then too, she had a daughter teaching at the Lenin Institute, a lawyer, like her father. I remarked that I had two daughters, a son, and also three grandchildren.

"I have none, my daughter is not married," she said.

"Does your husband speak French or English?" I asked.

"He used to, but he has very little practice," she replied.

This time, I made no comment and we returned to the weather. Subject matter is very limited, and one has the feeling that it's not quite fair to put any of these people on the spot, for they must be even more carefully watched and spied upon than we are. Altogether, if I had not realized where I sat and in whose company, I might have felt freer to talk and to ask questions. I could easily have imagined her to be one of the Russian emigrees one meets in Paris, very ravaged, a little bitter, and with many memories of her own. Her looks, her quality of voice and manner, were entirely different from those of the two other Ministers' wives, both of them straight Soviet products.

After the tea, there were more sweets offered, the fruit was passed and also ices in little gilt cups. I had already been there three-quarters of an hour and could not think there was anything more to come. I could have stayed, talking with Madame Vishinsky, if we had not been so carefully chaperoned by the other three, and even by the butler who must have been at least a General in the MVD. I really liked her and found her pitiful, as some royalties are pitiful—lonely and ill at ease. She seemed to enjoy my visit, but it must have been a long time since she had received in just this way; a long time, perhaps, since she had spoken French, and a very long time since she had been addressed as a woman of the world. Like royalties, who are timid and find conversation difficult, she made a stiff but very real effort to be cordial. Then, too, I think she was secretly pleased that we could talk privately together, even though our conversation was banal.

When I got up to leave, I said how much I had appreciated her receiving me, that I hoped we might meet again, and that she had given me real pleasure. She said she also hoped we might meet again, and very soon.

The young interpreter showed me out. I complimented her on her English.

"Did you learn it here?" I asked.

"Oh yes, at our special language school I hope one day to go abroad. That would be interesting and helpful."

45

"It would, indeed," I replied.

The footman opened the door. The Embassy car appeared and I drove out through the gates. I only wish I could have heard the three ladies' comments after I left. I feel sure Madame Gusiev and Madame Zorin finished off the cakes.

After a month of Moscow, I've tried to sort out my impressions of the city. It's not too easy. I've never known any central European country before, and I can't make comparisons between Moscow and Sofia, Moscow and Bucharest, Moscow and Budapest. But none of those other cities makes Moscow's extravagant claims to being the capital of the world's greatest empire; none of those cities claims the world's greatest building program or insists that its people are the healthiest and happiest in the world.

I was prepared to find Moscow a poor city, but a working city; I was prepared to find it alive and growing, a vital expression of the people's recovery from a long and terrible war, and of their hope and dream of a new world. Instead, it's a dingy architectural muddle, with nothing to offer of beauty but the stark, terrifying mass of the Kremlin itself. It seems to make little sense in either the Old World or the New. Rejecting the latter, its new aspect seems neither modern nor functional, and the much-talked-of city building program would seem to have been inspired by the Politburo's boyhood memories of bourgeois grandeur.

The new structures alternate between pillared brownstone and white-plaster wedding cakes. Only in the late twenties and early thirties did there seem to have been any imagination shown or any conception of modern design. The Lenin Library, with its tall, square-sided columns and straight, perpendicular lines, has style, and even the back of the Lubianka prison is impressive in mass, but architectural initiative seems to have been generally smothered by the same idealogical regulations applied to art and science.

One guesses the Soviet review boards, which pass on all phases of cultural activity, must be made up of middle-aged men and women conditioned by a fear that motivates their artistic, as well as their political, thinking. They cannot afford to be wrong.

They cannot afford experimentation or inspiration that may shock the rulers or the multitudes. "All art," says Stalin, "must be understood by the masses." The white plaster and knubbly brown stone, the loud blaring of the military bands, the cloying sweetness of their popular music, the mediocrity of their contemporary art, all this is easily understood. No criticism is invited or permitted. Stalin's dictum satisfies the people, without educating them or even interesting them. Only at the ballet and the theater is there escape from what seems to us monotonous and pedestrian; but here again, the ballet and the theater are part of a long tradition of Russian art, and some latitude is allowed.

There is even a dead level of taste in the clothing one sees. Men's suits are of shoddy material, and the lack of cleaning facilities prevents their looking neat; civilian shoes are often of ersatz leather or canvas; gloves are never worn except in winter; women's dresses are sacks, cut out of cheap printed cotton or rayon in summer, and coarse woolen in winter. The woolen dresses are dark-colored, brown or plum or blue. Skirts are very short, without gores or pleats. The dresses, even the more expensive ones, are loose-fitting through the body, and the occasional long frock one sees on an official's wife at the theater, or at a reception, is of much the same cut with modestly high neck, and elbow or long sleeves.

Jewelry consists of an odd string of amber or glass beads, the same ladies who might sport evening dresses sometimes wear what one's grandmother called "dinner rings," very fancy, of oval shape, often placed on the index finger. Wedding rings are not generally worn, although they are for sale in the shops, but their price may be a deterrent, the simplest costing sixty or seventy dollars in our money.

Underclothing is of the most rudimentary character, women's panties are not panties at all, but bloomers of bright blue or purple cotton knit. There are shirts to match, and astonishing brassières of heavy cotton cloth, also bright colored, fastening with three buttons in the back. These brassières, which are stacked on the shelves like cups in a china shop, all seem to be of the same shape and are so constructed as to give alarming figures to the women who wear them. Girdles of any sort are a rarity, and appear to belong more in the surgical-supply realm than in the esthetic. One splendid specimen I saw was of henna-red cotton, heavily boned, and fastening up the front with twelve pearl buttons.

Over the knit shirt and bloomer brassière combination the better dressed women appear to wear old-fashioned chemises of white cotton, edged with a little cheap lace. Nightdresses I have never seen for sale, and men's pajamas are used for travel and lounge purposes, apparently not for sleeping. The men's undershorts answer the latter need, they too are blue but dark, their undershirts are of the same lighter blue knit as the women's. There seem to be no wool underclothes for sale. It's summer now, although that makes very little difference in shop displays—the same flyspecked goods are shown in the windows at all seasons. A fair listing of prices of some of these items, translated into our money, would be:

Cotton knit bloomers	$7.00
Cotton cloth brassière	4.50
Man's shirt, cotton	15.00
Men's leather boots	75.00
Men's shoes	40.00 — 60.00
Woman's rayon silk dress of indifferent quality and style, the sort that might sell with us at $14.95	100.00
Men's suits, of second-quality worsted and poor workmanship	275.00 — 300.00

Of course, the ruble does not mean the same to the Soviet citizen as it does to us, because of the arbitrary nature of our exchange, but it does mean a great deal in terms of work hours and relative proportion of their "take home" pay. As the satellites feed their produce into Russia, things are growing better—better for the Russians, if not for the satellites. Czech shoes are beginning to appear in the shops, and the printed materials are probably Czech also. There is chinaware coming from Eastern Germany; the Dresden and Meissen factories are in the Soviet Zone. But the quality of all these things has been debased to fit the needs of the people, the quality and the taste. It's always the same story of dead, monotonous level.

CLIMATE MUST
have something to do with the way the Russians behave. There's simply too much of it. Never have I seen such a country. It's rained ever since our arrival. No wonder I read in the Memoirs of Caulaincourt that Napoleon, coming into Russia, was as hampered by the rains and mud as he was by the snows, going out. I can well believe it, and I expect it snows in the same violent way that it rains. Perhaps we are lucky not to have to travel far on Russian roads, for so few of them are well paved that the going would be impossible. The main streets in Moscow are all right, but the side streets look as though they'd not been touched since Peter the Great ordered the stones laid down, and there are great mudholes everywhere. Cars must drive at snail's pace. The Belgian pavés were bad enough, but these cobblestones are simply stones, most of them laid with pointed edge up; sidewalks are chipped and broken, some of them little more than dirt paths. It's true there is not much refuse about, because the Russians have no refuse—they eat so little and own so little. The last cabbage leaf is consumed in soup, and there are no fruit peelings to throw around, since there is no fruit. Apples are luxuries, selling at $4.00 a pound, and lemons anywhere from a dollar and a half to five dollars apiece, depending on the season. Oranges are nonexistent—now, later, they promise us some mandarins—and this year the wet weather has spoiled the summer berries.

I asked Chantal Goffin, the Belgian Ambassadress, to take me to market. She speaks excellent Russian, and, being Belgian, is a good housewife and a canny bargainer. I dressed in my oldest clothes, but Chantal went me one better in a mackintosh with a handkerchief over her head. She said I looked like a capitalist spy. We went to the big central market where the peasants and *kohlhoz*, or collective-farm workers, bring in their produce. Individuals are allowed to sell over and above what the State has set as their quota, not unnaturally they try

49

to keep the best for this purpose, as they can set their own prices in the free market.

The only vegetables—and this is early August, when gardens should be at their peak—were cucumbers, carrots, cabbages, a few shrunken onions, and now and again some small parsnips and handpicked mushrooms from the fields. These last looked very risky to me—horrid to die of eating Russian mushrooms —but they seemed much appreciated and I saw women buying one or two big ones, peering at them and weighing each one as carefully as we would cantaloupes at home. Some of the old peasant women had strings of dried mushrooms for sale, and Chantal told me they made fine soup. I saw women buy, not even a half or a quarter of a cabbage, but three or four leaves, two or three carrots, the same with onions.

All this goes into soup, for that's the main dish of the Russian people; even their meat, when they can afford it, is cooked in it. They have very few roasts, and broiling is unheard of. Meat for them is stew meat, usually beef in the north, mutton in the south, cut in chunks that you see housewives carrying home from market, sometimes unwrapped in their bare hands. If it's wrapped, it's in a bit of old newspaper crammed down into their string bags. The fat is cut away from the meat and sold separately, often used to spread on bread, for the people eat lard in this way instead of butter or margarine.

The average Russian diet, the diet of the worker and the small employee, consists of kasha, or porridge, in the morning for breakfast, with no milk or sugar on this but more often eaten plain or with oil; for midday dinner a bowl of soup, some sourkraut or pickled or fresh cucumbers, and a hunk of bread; for supper more bread and tea, brewed over and over again. The bread is excellent, and varies from the traditional dark loaf to white that is almost like cake. All this bread is made in Government bakeries and sold in Government-controlled shops. Black bread costs about 50 cents, white bread 75. There is no flour of any kind for sale, except twice a year on the November 7 holiday and on May Day. Then each person is allotted a certain ration (two to three kilos), and large posters announce that the Great and Beneficent Father Stalin will generously permit his people to buy flour in celebration of the holidays. Because of the way this distribution is handled and announced, the people are made to feel they are being given a present, rather than resenting the fact they've not had flour all along.

At the moment, there is a great lack of the particular grain that makes black bread, a real hardship, as the people prefer it to the white; besides, it is quite a lot cheaper. They are compelled to buy the white, therefore, and must spend a good proportion of their food budget to do this. We don't know whether the bad weather is general throughout the country, but if so it will mean considerable suffering later on. As in India and China, these people ask and expect very little, but they must be fed to work, and bad harvests can mean famine for large sections of the country.

I asked Chantal about dairy products. Here in the Embassy we use only imported powdered milk, and I think we are wise. Milk is handled through a chain of shops, well kept and clean, but what happens to the milk before and after it reaches the shops one can't know. We see it brought in from the farms in huge cans, and the saleswomen ladle it directly from the cans into any containers the customer brings along —open pans, pitchers, soup kettles. I've seen no milk-delivery wagons; in fact I've seen no delivery wagons of any sort. Even beds and carpets are carried by their purchasers through the streets, the women shouldering as big loads as the men.

Furniture stores are another revelation. The stuff is wretched and very expensive. Beds are invariably metal, usually nickelized; mattresses are thin, stuffed with cotton or straw. Carpets are nondescript. Lampshades are all of a pattern, orange with fringe. I think there must be a State lampshade factory, over-fulfilling its norm each month, for I've never seen any other variety for sale. There are two sorts of chairs, hard armchairs covered in mottled tapestry, or bentwood sidechairs with cane or wooden seats. There's no chintz for sale, and I've never seen any figured curtains at the windows. I've become a great window peerer, looking unashamedly into basements and ground floors as I pass along the street.

Windows are curtained with bits of white cloth, and occasionally a panel of cheap lace, the sills often filled with straggling plants. Russian plants seem to grow in a special way, all stem and stalk with a rare, very timid bloom at the top. Sometimes there are bouquets of weeds or nasturtiums, set in bottles. Hothouse flowers do not exist.

Furniture is sometimes covered with white cloths, tables sometimes have handknitted doilies on them—that's about the sum total of decoration. Many of the rooms look very clean, the walls whitewashed or distempered in light blue; others are very shabby and dirty. Invariably, the entrance halls and stairs are filthy; this is true even in the better buildings. I see this because I look through the doors, not because I go inside, for none of us gets a chance to visit Russians in their homes. The courtyards are also very dreary—muddy or dusty, depending on the weather, and filled with rubbish; no attempt is made to plant or pave them. Sometimes you see a broken bench or two, and the old women sit there to watch the children. That seems to be the mission of the old in Russia.

The Soviets boast that construction is going on everywhere. This is true in Moscow, and we hear it is the same throughout the Union. Near Spaso Square, on what is called B Circle there are several large buildings going up. I watched the workers yesterday, and contrasted their way of doing things with what I had seen last year in Italy. There, also, there is a lack of structural steel, but the Italians are master masons, whereas these people build as children pile up castles on the seashore, setting one brick on another with little or no mortar between, throwing plaster on, and making a few passes with a trowel.

Most of the plastering and painting is done by women, who approach the job as though they were whitewashing a barn. They seem to get more whitewash on the window panes and on themselves than on the house. These women are mainly peasants recruited out of the fields and paid by some curious system of so much a square foot, not the square feet they have covered but the square feet they are expected to cover, divided amongst the number of workers. This unskilled labor earns about a hundred dollars a month, although the rate in rubles is far less than that. Whether the job is done fast or slow seems to matter not at all, and, if the supervisor is away, the workers often sit on the sidewalk or squat on a pile of lumber and go to sleep. They seem a sexless lot, looking cheerful enough but I should think more possessed of patience than of enthusiasm. Many of these girls are housed in dormitories, and all they own is the right to a bed for so many hours a night.

The one real gesture toward civic cleanliness is seen twice a day where there are paved streets and sidewalks. The law requires that these be washed. Householders are responsible for the streets, and must clean off the snow in winter and hose them down in summer. In addition, the streets must be swept, and this is done by women with twig brooms, often very old women. The Government takes care of large squares and the very wide avenues. At any time of day, you can see "twenty maids with twenty mops" sweeping heaps of dirt into small pans, hardly bigger than dustpans. It takes them hours, but man and woman power is cheap in the Soviet Union.

Large construction jobs are done mostly by forced labor. Some German prisoners are still being used (these were no longer seen after 1949), but mostly they are Russian, both men and women. One always knows where forced labor is at work, as there are high board fences around such places, with guard towers at each corner, and armed sentries. The British White Paper reports that one in ten of the entire population is employed in so-called corrective labor. The Russians insist this is a proper and humane way of dealing with criminals, and far better than shutting them up behind bars. Perhaps so, but their definition of a criminal differs so much from ours that no argument is possible. Here people are arrested and sentenced to long terms on the slightest provocation; every kind of petty misdemeanor entails severe punishment, and there is no redress or appeal from final judgment.

We have lost many servants out of the Embassy; one boy, the son of one of the maids, has already done six out of ten years in a northern labor camp. He was a chauffeur for one of our officers, and, without rhyme or reason, was spirited away and accused of being too friendly to the Americans. He was given a choice of confessing and doing ten years in Siberia —or else. He figured that he was young and strong and could take a chance. The mother hears from him two or three times a year, and is allowed to send him occasional packages of clothing. When he has completed his term, he will be sent to a specified area, on probation, but can never return to work in Moscow. That is the Promised Land which will forever be denied him. The British Counselor's wife tells me that she has lost four maids this year, the Luxembourg Minister's wife two, and so it goes. Any imagined deviation, any small jealousy of one servant for another, with consequent taletelling, is enough to place an individual under suspicion. It's a terrifying business. One day the person is at work, another day he is gone. Sometimes an excuse is given of illness or trouble in the family, more often he simply doesn't appear any more. This happened to one of the employees in the British Embassy. When an Embassy officer went to complain to the Russian Foreign Office about it, saying the servant had been in the Embassy employ for several years and was a faithful worker, the Russian looked at him astonished:

"How is it possible," he said, "that you should take such an interest in the affairs of a minor Soviet citizen?"

Russian history tells us that there has always been some kind of system of police terror, but this one is more embrasive, yet it would be wrong to imagine any general revolt building up. The people are too patient, and the vision of rewards, the symbolic cardboard roasts in the shop windows, the bicycles no one can buy, the glitter of the Army Day pageants, and the once-in-a-lifetime trip to the Ballet, all this is substituted for the religion which used to sustain them through other dark times. They hope life will be better for their children. They are told it will be, told over and over again with the same fervor with which the priests once promised their fathers and mothers paradise in heaven.

YESTERDAY, WE
made our first expedition outside of Moscow, visiting the
Zagorsk Monastery, forty-five miles away. When I told the de-
parting British Counselor, Geoffrey Harrison, that we were
going, he said I'd be sorry—that, once I'd been there, I'd have
nothing left to see, and that he was saving it for his last week
in this country. Now that I'm back, I'm quite ready to go again
without waiting for my last week in Russia, for it's the traditional picture one has dreamed of: bright-colored onion-domed
churches behind a walled enclosure; bearded, long-robed priests
conducting services for the faithful thronging in pilgrimage
to the tomb of St. Sergei; huge black crows wheeling around the
domes, in and out of the tall trees in the monastery yard and
below; and, in front of the church doors, knots of miserable,
ragged beggars, their hands out for *kopeks*.

Zagorsk, the shrine of St. Sergius, and once known as the
Trinity Monastery, is the headquarters of the Patriarchate. As
it is beyond the fifty-kilometer limit prescribed for foreigners,
we must ask, forty-eight hours in advance, permission to go
there, giving the names of the party and how many cars there
will be. Word is then passed to the local police, who check the
car at the fifty-kilometer post and look to see that the proper
number of people are inside.

I'd been told this, but didn't believe it until I saw the security policemen standing in the road. It seemed a foolish gesture in our case, as our car was followed by not one, but two,
guard cars with four MVD agents in each. Actually, the Russians are quite wise to send two cars on these expeditions, as
one car invariably breaks down. Two men, two cars, two
horses, two everything, are needed to do the work of one in
this country.

We took our lunch with us, but it was the usual in-and-out
weather we have come to expect in this part of the world, so
we could not spread our blankets and picnic in the woods. We
compromised by eating alongside the cars, running for shelter

when a shower passed. Two men from each MVD car got out to stand guard around us. We offered them some of our sandwiches, but they declined. Dad doesn't seem to mind, but it gives me an odd feeling to be munching away under the eyes of the police.

Zagorsk was a pretty sight as its walls and towers loomed up against the skyline. First founded in the fourteenth century, it is built like many of the monasteries of the period, set on an eminence and surrounded by a heavily fortified wall. For years the richest in Russia, the monastery once owned numerous villages and a hundred and twenty thousand serfs, and had an army of twenty thousand men available for its defense. The oldest of its churches contains the miracle-working tomb of St. Sergei, and before 1917 over a hundred thousand pilgrims flocked each year to pray at the sepulcher. There are still pilgrims today. I saw several come to kneel before the elaborate silver canopied tomb and lean over to kiss the coffin lid as they left. One bent old woman was polishing the steps below with a small rag, and seemed to be doing it as a kind of penance.

Behind the main church there is a very good Government museum, and on beyond are a number of other churches and small chapels, a holy well, the Patriarch's palace, the convent itself, a divinity school, a library, and scores of attached outbuildings. We were lucky in finding a pleasant young woman to guide us about, and she seemed gratified that we were so much interested in all she had to show. She was a tiny person with a quite lovely face, very earnest about her work as a student of art and archeology. I am always impressed with how small most Russians are, short and heavy-set, square-faced with broad cheekbones, flat noses, small eyes, straight hair, and strong legs and arms. It's rarely that you see a pretty girl and almost never a pretty woman; neglect of person and hard work age them too fast. The men are better looking, but they too are short and thick, typical somehow of the pictures one sees of the barbarian invaders, of the hordes that swept down from the north to blot out the civilization of Roman Europe. Even the Russian athletes have no grace about them; they move like machines, with the emphasis of a punch drill.

Our little guide took great pains to show us the best of the monuments and all the treasures in the museum, especially the ikons, pointing out what was characteristic of each period and artist. The early ikons were left uncovered, but later there arose a fashion of fixing sheets of silver and gold over the pictures so that only the hands and face of the subject were left visible. The Virgin's image, in particular, was adorned with richly jeweled ornaments, crowns and collars set with pearls and precious stones, or worked in fine enamel. In adddition to the ikons on display, there were marvelous vestments sewn with jewels, embroideries of all kinds, and panels to be used as covers for the coffins of royalties or church dignitaries, golden missals, and communion vessels, most of them the original property of the monastery.

Many of the ikons in the churches were in process of restoration and our guide told us there was a school of ikon painters in the monastery. Judging by the work already completed, I would think the old ikons might better have been left alone, for the new colors are too gaudy and the spirit of the old pictures is lost. I'm told by one of the British who has seen the restored frescoes in the Kremlin churches that those are better done, but these in Zagorsk bid fair to be ruined.

The Orthodox Church in Russia has apparently made a hard and fast bargain with the Kremlin and is subservient to its edicts. When the Patriarch of Constantinople followed the lead of the Pope in excommunicating Communists, the Patriarch here came out immediately against him, and he never misses an opportunity to affirm his loyalty to the Soviet regime. He must do so if he wishes to maintain his position. It would seem that the Soviets allow religion to be administered today as they do certain drugs, the "opium of the people" being permitted them in small amounts, intended to ease the pain of the old and the forlorn. But the official attitude of the government has not changed. A recent article in *Komsomol Pravda,* the young Communists' newspaper, reads as follows:

Religion cannot help hindering the building of Communism, for it represents antiscientific reactionary ideology which prevents man from understanding the laws of the development of nature and society, educates him in a spirit of humility and submissiveness, and instills in him the idea of the impossibility of changing an order of life allegedly established by God.

The editors go on to point out that the Party and the Soviet State do not close churches or forbid church ceremonies, because such measures are not considered effective in combating religion. However, they state categorically:

> Religion is in no way a personal affair for either Komsomol or Communists, and belief in God and participation in church ceremonies, even weddings or christenings, is incompatible with Komsomol membership.

Small wonder that one sees so few young people in the churches. To attend regularly, they would have to be courageous indeed!

As we left Zagorsk, the sun came out and our ride home was a pleasant one. After so long in the city, it was good to get into the real country, away from the dingy drabness of Moscow. It's true there's not much variation in the landscape —mile after mile of uncultivated fields with small copses of white birch and pine trees, now and again a stretch of farm land centered around a village or a group of shacks, the houses of unpainted, unplastered wood logs with window frames of gingerbread fretwork. Electric light seems to have been installed along the main roads, but water supplies are completely primitive, householders walking long distances to the common pump. These small houses must be dreadfully hot in summer, for the windows are carefully battened down and only one narrow upper pane is made to be opened. All along the edges of the sash there is a packing of cotton or rags, and sometimes the walls are overlaid with layers of grass or straw. The houses look highly inflammable but, as we said before, every house is lived in by so many inhabitants there is always at least one person awake in each room, no matter what the hour.

We passed a few small herds of cattle in the open fields; single cows being led by old women along the road; many goats—the children seem to be trusted to watch these; but very few chickens or geese. The road was narrow and bad in spots, widening only as we approached the city again. Here we had to make a wide detour to avoid construction work but, as we turned off, I could see the gangs of men and women digging away, under the guard of armed MVD troops, and further on we came upon a large party of Red Army soldiers, also working on the road, under guard, probably a disciplinary battalion. Both men and women looked strong and healthy, but it's a strange sight to Western eyes.

Postmarked Moscow   *August 15, 1949*

DICK DAVIS, ONE of our star boarders, has left. There's always a big turnover in this Embassy, as the two year rule is generally enforced and, in the case of military personnel, it's reduced to eighteen months. Most of the other missions have the same policy, especially for junior officers. I'm sure it's a wise one, for two years of this fairly abnormal life should be enough; after that, the officer's usefulness diminishes, the objectivity of his viewpoint declines, and he's apt to become either indifferent or over-prejudiced.

To replace Dick, who goes back to head the Russian desk in the Department, we have George Morgan, an attractive, highly intelligent ex-professor of philosophy, who joined the Foreign Service after serving some time in the Army. George is the author of the article signed Historicus that made such an impression when it appeared in *Foreign Affairs* last year. He has a scholarly, profound mind and, with that, a sense of style and humor that makes him a good companion. We are very much pleased that he has come to live in Spaso.

Saturday afternoon was fine and hot, and George took me for a walk in Gorki Park, the largest of the so-called Parks of Culture and Rest. This pompous name is characteristic of modern Soviet language, and means nothing more nor less than a public park set aside for the enjoyment of the people. There are three or four of these in Moscow, all very much alike, the one we chose being laid out along the Moscow River in grounds that once belonged to large estates. One or two of the old houses are still standing on the river bank, but seem to have been turned into factory clubs or employees rest homes.

We paid a ruble apiece to enter, and walked down a long esplanade by the river. There were not many people in the park, Saturday being a working day in the Soviet Union, but there were children playing ball; there were some boys playing the Stick Game, a cross between duck-on-the-rock and ninepins, consisting of hurling a long stick at a pile of wooden blocks to knock them out of a square; and further along there was a cleared place where bigger boys were playing soccer. We turned away from the river, past an outdoor movie theater where the program advertised a picture of life on a collective farm. Opposite, there were a reading room, full of Party publications and propaganda magazines, and an open-air pavilion for chess players. The tables here were full of old men, very intent on their game.

There was also a small lake, with two or three couples rowing about in boats, and, beside the shore, an outdoor café. We stopped to have some tea served in glasses, and paid a ruble extra for a slice of lemon. People around us seemed to be eating snack meals—bread, cold cuts, and pickled fish—and drinking vodka, beer, or colored soda lemonade. Russians seem to eat at all hours, almost as though they had no set time for meals; and they dawdle along over their food, which is set before them all together, without regard for sequence of courses, the ice cream coming with the smoked herring.

There were a few young couples, but Russians are prim in their public behavior and the lovers sat well apart, saying little to each other. One can't help being impressed with how silent everyone is, certainly silent as contrasted with our own noisy exuberance. Even in Russian crowds this is true; no one speaks or shouts loudly, their faces show little expression, and they look no different walking in the park on a fine afternoon than streaming home from work in the subway, nor are they dressed any differently. It's only on very special occasions that better clothes are worn—after all, they have so little to change into.

From the entrance gate, every few feet of the way, there were placards posted saying that the park and all its facilities are provided for his people by Comrade Stalin. He therefore asks them not to pick the flowers, not to walk on the grass, not to scatter any rubbish, but to enjoy the beauty he offers them. In addition to the placards, we were never out of hearing of loud speakers placed among the trees and in the various buildings, blaring forth speeches of all kinds, with occasional musical interludes.

The wind came up, and it was quite dusty. Even though not walked upon, the grass was none too well kept and the trees were straggly, but it was pleasant to be out in the sunshine, especially in the late afternoon, when there is a kind of golden glow in the sky and everything is apt to look better than it really is, even in Moscow. And yet one can't help wondering about these Parks of Culture and Rest. I was reminded of the books of the early Socialist Utopians. This whole place was obviously planned for simple people with simple needs. Is it done by cynical, very sophisticated minds who know what the masses like or decide what they must like—or is it a more honest expression of popular taste?

Yesterday we made up a picnic party and went farther down the Moscow River where the grounds and woods surrounding Lenin's former country house have been opened to the public. While Sunday is not a legal holiday, it has been found more convenient for many professions and trades to allot that day for recreation. Stores remain open, but construction and industrial work is shut down, and many factories reward their employees by sending them into the country in trucks—no ordinary workers have private cars or even bicycles. Thus the fields and woods around Moscow are filled with holiday makers and bands of small children and Pioneers, or older boys and girls, in Komsomol groups.

We had with us Wally Barbour, our new Minister Counselor, such a nice man. We are delighted with him, and feel he will be a great addition to the Embassy and the diplomatic colony. Six feet, three, and weighing well over two hundred and fifty, he is a big man in every sense of the word, and Dad says his judgment and approach are as broad as he is himself. He is a bachelor, but so understanding of human problems, as well as of political events, we are fortunate to have had him chosen for this post.

He and George Morgan will go with Dad, if he is able to arrange his interview with Stalin. George will act as Dad's interpreter, and Stalin will probably have one or two for himself. The interview is more in the nature of a courtesy call than anything else, and was represented as such to the Russian Foreign Office. Sir David Kelly, the British Ambassador, was received by Stalin ten days ago; otherwise, none of our colleagues has been so honored.

Dad seems quite calm about the whole affair though I should be very nervous in his place. Somehow, to me it would be like facing the Divinity, or Saint Peter, or any aged gentleman whom absolute power and years have made impervious to human appeal. This man in the Kremlin has been so built up before the world he seems a kind of force rather than a human being. Even Lenin, enshrined and "stuffed," appears more approachable; but Lenin alive may also have been terrifying.

Roger and I went to visit the Tomb, the other day. It's open to the public four afternoons a week, and, rain or shine, there are always long queues of people waiting to go in. Sometimes the line reaches for blocks, although, once started, it moves fairly fast, as militia men posted every few feet prevent anyone from pausing and keep the crowd orderly and quiet.

The mausoleum is built against the outside of the Kremlin wall, midway between the two main gates on Red Square. Set in the wall, at the left of the Tomb, are the graves of high Party dignitaries, and tablets to prominent Communists, including three Americans: John Reed, Bill Haywood, and Paxton Hibben.

To avoid the necessity of standing in line, we presented our diplomatic cards to a militiaman at the door of the mausoleum, and were immediately admitted. We walked in, side by side, under the eyes of more militiamen, picked Security Police guards fully armed with rifles and drawn bayonets. At the door two stood at attention, their feet on small red-velvet cushions. The entrance is on the ground level. Inside, we turned left and walked down a winding flight of slippery black stone steps. More guards stood on the stairs and motioned us into single file. The air grew colder as we neared the death chamber, which is kept at icebox temperature.

In the middle, on a bier under a large canopy of glass, Lenin lay, with a black-velvet pall drawn to his chest, his hands at his side, his head on a dark-satin pillow. By some trick of lighting, his face seems illuminated from within so it gleams with a kind of faint, translucent yellow. He wore a dark suit, collar and necktie, and his hair and beard were neatly trimmed. Geoffrey Harrison, the British Counselor, said that, when he last saw him, there were gloves on his hands, but there were none the other day. We walked respectfully around him and out. The people in front and behind us showed no expression of emotion—one would hardly say of interest—and yet they come each day by the thousands, many from the other end of Russia.

I had thought this experience might be a trying one, but Lenin on his couch looks more like a wax image than anything else, and, except for the elaborate staging and the atmosphere of dramatic ritual, he's no more actual than any figure in Madame Tussaud's. One of our young men asked me, afterward: "Did you notice his feet under the pall?" He insisted there was some question about them; indeed, he wondered whether they were there at all!

It's a macabre business, of course, this embalming of Lenin and exhibiting him to the gaze of the people; but here, again, it's possible that there is historic precedent for such an idea. Throughout the sixteenth and seventeenth centuries of Russian history there was a succession of royal pretenders, false czars and princes who appeared, to claim thrones and inheritances, and who represented themselves as persons said to have died or been killed years before. The most famous of these was the false Dimitri, the young monk who declared himself the Czarevitch whom Boris Godunouv was supposed to have ordered murdered. Dimitri was actually crowned, and reigned in Moscow for a short while before he, in turn, was killed. But the pattern persisted and numerous other cases occurred.

People were ignorant and gullible; ambitious men played upon their piety and superstition so that they could be enlisted under any pretext, provided enough promises were made them and enough holy banners shaken out. It's conceivable that Lenin's successors, consciously or unconsciously, may have had all this in mind and that they thought it wise to present Lenin, embalmed, to the people, an actual ever-present proof that, dead, he lay enshrined for them, a symbol of a mysterious all-giving power that is delegated now to his disciple who rules in the Kremlin, over the wall.

Postmarked Moscow   *August 20, 1947*

I WENT TO CALL Dad just before dinner last night, and found him emerging from the bathroom. He smiled.

"It's an old Navy regulation," he said, "to take a bath and put on clean underclothes before going into action."

His call at the Kremlin was scheduled for ten o'clock in the evening. Wally Barbour joined us for dinner, as he, with George Morgan, made up the rest of the party. At a carefully calculated ten minutes to ten, the three men set off. Roger, Brewster Morris, and I gathered downstairs in the Blue Room to await their return. Brewster had arrived with two Embassy stenographers, in case notes had to be transcribed when they got back. When he figured the party was safely inside the Kremlin gate, he called the press correspondents, Eddy Gilmore and Tom Whitney, of the Associated Press, Henry Shapiro of the United Press, Harrison Salisbury of the *New York Times,* and Andy Steiger of McGraw-Hill, so that they could file their stories before the news came out over the Soviet radio.

It was nearly eleven when our men returned, looking very pleased with themselves. We adjourned upstairs and heard all they could tell us about the visit. They had stayed thirty-seven minutes, twelve more than the British!

Once inside the Kremlin, they were directed to the main office building, where they were received by a succession of aides, guided through corridors with guards posted all along the way, and finally introduced into a plainly furnished room, with a table and chairs set for the visitors. Marshal Stalin rose to greet them and walked toward Dad, shook hands, and seated himself at the table. With him were Vishinsky and his interpreter, young Troyanovsky, son of the former Soviet Ambassador to the United States. Dad said the conversation was a bit stiff at first, but cordial enough. The Marshal even went so far as to reach for his pipe and light it. The Press afterward told Dad that that was a mark of high favor. General subjects were discussed, brief reference was made by Dad to the Lend Lease question and to the jamming of the Voice of America. When the last was mentioned, Stalin turned to Vishinsky to ask, smiling:

"Do they say very wicked things about us?"

Dad said that Vishinsky seemed very nervous and hopped around Stalin like any overzealous young aide, whenever the Marshal so much as blinked. At the conclusion of the interview, Stalin shook Dad's hand most warmly, saying he would be delighted to see him again at any time. Altogether, our three men seemed to feel that both the Marshal and the Foreign Minister had been more than agreeable, according to Soviet standards. Knowing Dad, I'm sure that the interview was conducted in great style on his part, for he is good at that sort of thing, and no doubt the Russians responded.

Dad reported Stalin to be stalwart and strong in appearance, with graying moustache and hair, and neatly dressed in a well-fitting military uniform without decorations. His voice was strong, his eyes were clear; certainly he appeared in good health, and his whole manner had the simple confidence enjoyed by great and powerful men. Apart from his age and natural accidents dependent upon it, there seems no reason to believe he cannot still live for years and hold supreme power all the while.

Next day, the Soviet papers all headlined Dad's visit, and I suppose there will be long articles and much speculation at home about it. Any interview with Stalin is important—he gives so few—but this was more in the nature of a formal call than anything else. Although he is not the official head of state, it seems only fitting that a new American Ambassador should be received in person by the Marshal.

Postmarked Moscow   *August 24, 1949*

LAST NIGHT, WE held our first formal dinner of twenty-two in the State dining room. The table is a vast mahogany affair, yards across, so broad that Chin, the butler, has to climb on it to arrange the centerpiece, and one of the Russian maids has been seen to polish the top by lying across it and wriggling her rear back and forth! Anyway, it looked very elegant last night with three great bowls of marigolds—the only flowers that seem to have survived our wet summer—and the best silver and glass all out. I've never felt quite the same about marigolds since our old English nurse told me they were made into garlands and cast on the corpses floating down the Ganges—but they were all the garden offered.

We had the Italian Ambassador and Madame Brosio; the Australian Ambassador and Mrs. Watt; the Siamese and Canadian chargés; a British and a Belgian secretary; and some of our people. These parties are all like a UN committee meeting, but that can't be helped. The Italians are just back from a vacation trip to the States. I found them charming. He is from Turin, a strong anti-Fascist and a very fine man, tall, handsome, and extremely intelligent. She is a sweet-faced woman, beautifully dressed. Both of them were very enthu-

66

siastic about their journey, part of which they had made by bus through the Middle West.

The cook gave us a good dinner, even though her heart was not quite in her work, as her husband, the gardener, was hit on the head by the dumb-waiter and is languishing in the hospital. Still she pulled herself together and produced a very creditable meal. None of it was quite up to Belgian standard, but menus have to be contrived from our deep-freeze, plus what can be bought in the local market. This house is surprisingly handsome when dressed for a party, and I'm only sorry we can no longer put on the kind of prewar shows they held here, with ballerinas dancing in the Great Hall, pirouetting under the chandelier, gypsy orchestras, and Russian scientists muttering in corners. It must have been very picturesque, and certainly much more fun.

One wonders what the Russian servants think of dinners such as last evening's, especially the women, who must contrast the scene with what they see among their own people. Mrs. Watt, the Australian Ambassadress, told me she felt certain that Burobin sent some of the girls to us to be trained in housekeeping, table-setting, menu-planning, and general deportment. She had had two or three who left to go to Soviet families, probably to coach Generals' and Ministers' wives in the ways of the world! We know there is a school of etiquette for foreign officials themselves, we've heard they are taught there how to behave in effete Western circles, what to wear and when to wear it, how to enter and leave a room, for no Soviet diplomat should ever feel any sense of social inferiority *vis à vis* his foreign colleagues. There must even be a wardrobe reserve their ladies can call upon.

Elizabeth Cabot, the wife of our Minister to Finland, tells of their tour in Yugoslavia just after World War II. As the country was living under an austerity program, our ladies had been told to keep their clothes and entertainments as simple as possible. Not so the Russians, who gave extravagant parties, and whose wives wore expensive furs and elaborate gowns and jewels.

"Along came the first of the year and, with it, a general

shift in the Russian Embassy personnel," said Elizabeth. "And what should we see but the new lot of wives all wearing the same gowns, the same furs and jewels, as the last!"

This evening, Roger and I are going with two of the younger military attachés to see a puppet performances in the Summer Theater. Dad is staying home, because it's really very cold, and he says it's permissible to catch a chill at a football game but not at a puppet show. He and Roger are making plans for their trip to Stalingrad next week, forty hours there by train with return journey by air. This week end, John and Roger intend flying to Odessa, hoping it will be warm enough to bathe in the Black Sea. Once there, I trust they are politely received, for just lately our Embassy travellers have had bad luck with their sightseeing expeditions.

Our Navy dental officer is just back from Astrakhan, where he was never allowed inside the hotel, nor would the police permit him even to sleep on a park bench, so he ended up by settling down on the sidewalk until he could get back into the railway station and take the first train home! Although a dental officer he carries the naval title of Commander, so I suppose the Russians decided he must be a spy and treated him as such. All our military are watched even more closely than the State Department personnel, down to the assistant Attachés who have two and three followers with them at all times. Unlike Dad's, these are not official; but they are the same, day after day, and use such amateur disguises as eyeglasses, a patch of face plaster, or a change of hat.

Postmarked Moscow   *August 26, 1949*

HIS FOLLOWERS

even came into the puppet theater, the other night, so Stuart Warwick, our nice assistant Air Attaché, told us. We were unconscious of them, and I hope they enjoyed the play as much as we did. It was an artless little comedy, but the marionettes were beautifully made and manipulated, and there seemed more lightheartedness about the production than one expects of the Soviet theater—even the puppet theater. The producer, Abrasov, is very well known and has been awarded one of the coveted Stalin prizes for his work. There is a long tradition of puppet theaters in Russia, and certainly this was better than any I have ever seen.

In front of us sat a row of high-collared Generals and their families, both children and their General fathers sitting rapt in delight. These rare aspects of the Russian people are the good ones; we would like to think they are truer than some others. If so, it seems cruel that so much talent, imagination and creative urge should be channelled into the dull business of Sovietizing society. Some of our experts tell us that the people are intolerably bored by the streams of propaganda shouted at them from all sides, and that they heartily enjoy sly digs at authority and the occasional hidden criticism that creeps into the plays and the press. But they are a patient people and so long-suffering they do not complain, especially as it's a question of conform or starve. Rebellion of any kind in Russia, even of a minor sort, is a hungry and dangerous pastime.

Patient they certainly are, these people. I've been watching the women at work on Mokhavaya Square, in front of the Embassy Chancery building. They are repaving the street, pouring and smoothing asphalt, and operating the steam-roller machines. These girls are dressed in cotton skirts and shirts, or jackets, kerchiefs over their heads, their legs in thick cotton stockings, with thin shoes to which the hot asphalt sticks in lumps. Only along the railroads have I ever seen any women wearing trousers in Russia, and our own girls tell me that even in winter no woman wears ski pants in the street. Working in asphalt is a dirty job and a hard one; but there seems no job that is too rough and hard for these women to do. You see them everywhere, heaving stone and bricks, unloading trucks, shoveling sand and gravel, plastering, painting, all with the same plodding submissiveness, more animal-like than human.

Much of the labor is unskilled, and reports say that girls anxious to come to Moscow are recruited in the country and told they can get here only by signing manual-labor contracts. As most of them have had no superior schooling, they would hardly be able to do any other work, but the sight of them out there shuffling about in the asphalt is shocking to our eyes. After work, trucks come by to pick them up and off they go, loaded on top of whatever load the truck may be carrying, indistinguishable from the sacks of cement or flour or rags. In theory, this may be a "land of equal opportunity," but I should say the women bear the greater burden.

One cannot help wondering about their health, for surely it must be affected by such hard work. I asked one of the correspondents who has lived here for years.

"Yes," he said, "there are special hospitals for those girls. They look strong, but a couple of years of hard labor can tear them to pieces. They are sent in by the hundreds to be patched up and, if unfit, shipped back to the country."

I've asked for permission to see a Russian hospital, any Russian hospital, but, so far, have heard nothing from my request. I've also put in to see a school, a day nursery, all manner of things, but doubt whether I hear anything from any one of them.

The hospital would particularly interest me, after the visit I had from the wife of one of the British Secretaries. This woman, a frail, pretty little thing, very refined and timid, had a baby last year in the Moscow maternity hospital, supposedly the most modern of its kind. Monthly periodic visits were made, previous to the baby's birth, but no real examination was suggested and she felt very nervous when her husband brought her to the hospital door. There she was told that she could not be admitted until hard labor had actually started, and that until that time she must wait at home or outside the building.

As this was her fourth-child, she insisted they let her in and they finally did so and allotted her a cubicle such as one sees in hairdressing parlors, where she was prepared for delivery.

She was then led down a hall to the labor room, where four-teen women were going through birth pangs, all within sight of each other! The doctors—all women—went from bed to bed, or table to table, and justified the arrangement by explaining that obstetricians were in short supply!

I asked if she were given any anesthetics.

"No," she replied, "their methods were much more crude. Things were going along too slowly to suit the doctor so she finally became exasperated with me and said: 'If you can't manage yourself, I'll have to help you. Take a deep breath and count ten.'"

The poor woman obeyed, not knowing what was in store, and, with that the doctor, a huge female weighing a good hundred and sixty pounds, threw herself bodily on top of her to force the birth.

Once the baby arrived, mother and child were taken out and placed in a smaller ward, but even the after-care was less than rudimentary, and the obligatory diet (no outside food was allowed to be brought in) was appalling. This, mind you, was in the chief Moscow maternity hospital! It's possible that the wives of high Soviet officials are given different treatment. We know that the officials themselves get quite different treatment from anyone else, and that doctors and rare medicines are reserved for their special use. But here was the wife of one of the British diplomatic secretaries, a woman who would certainly tell at home of her experiences—and this was the kind of treatment given her!

Our own doctor, the American naval physician stationed in our Embassy, has no license or permission to practice in Russian hospitals. He can treat us on his own and our responsibility, but any case involving hospitalization must be sent to the Polyclinic, the one Russian hospital to which diplomats are admitted. There the patient is assigned a doctor, and he has no choice about anything from that time on. Hospitalization is supposedly free for the Russians themselves, but we are charged an all-inclusive price covering room, board, and medical care, usually amounting to about forty-five dollars a day.

Contrary to the poor Englishwoman's experience, the doctors' technique is often quite good, but the hospital equipment is poor and the methods are very rough-and-ready.

The Dutch counselor had a ruptured appendix last spring, and was hurried off to the hospital in the night. Two women doctors performed an hour-an-a-half operation on him, during only forty-five minutes of which he was under anesthetic, and that a local one. When he screamed that he was in pain, the doctors told him to lie still and relax, and one said:

"Recite Pushkin to yourself!"

Meanwhile, they ordered the nurses to strap his arms and legs to the table and proceeded with the operation.

The Dutchman also told how, when he was convalescent, he used to ask his friends to bring him American fashion magazines, and soon he had the nurses from all the wards swarming round him, begging him to let them look at the pictures. On his table was a most precious gift of a roll of soft toilet paper that another of his friends had brought him. One of the nurses picked it up and asked curiously:

"What is this?"

It's true that Russian toilet paper, when they have any at all, comes in small flat packets so I suppose she had never seen anything like our American variety.

I can only hope that I remain healthy. I will say the people in the streets look hardy enough, but perhaps we don't see many of the sick ones. I've noticed a lot of poor creatures, however, walking about all bandaged up, with bits of gauze and rags tied around their heads, but I daresay many are too frightened or ignorant to apply for help or treatment, and therefore doctor themselves. We know also that, even though a Soviet doctor gives a prescription to a patient, this doesn't necessarily mean that the patient can get the drug prescribed. The pharmacy will tell him it's out of stock, or simply say it's not to be procured anywhere. And even the penicillin issued on Russian prescription is far inferior to the kind we have at home.

JUST AS WE THOUGHT
summer had left us for good, it's back again. I'm glad, for I
hated to think we must seal ourselves in so soon. They tell
me that for the cold season, our windows are shut, and stuffed
with bits of cotton batting which grows grubbier and grubbier
as the months go by, the only ventilation coming from one
small hinged pane, oddly known as a "Fortescue," probably
in memory of some visiting Englishman who insisted on fresh
air! The Embassy engineer tells us that, in spite of its immense
size, Spaso is well heated. Mokhovaya, the Chancery, relies
on city steam, but, once that is turned on, it's supposed to be
quite adequate. Now we are all thinking about our winter
clothes, trying to decide just how cold we will be outdoors.
Last winter was so mild that no one bothered with arctic
equipment, but one can never tell.

A large part of the Russian population, men and women,
go about in coats of padded and quilted cotton, very much
as the Chinese do, and, like them, they are practically sewed
into their clothes until spring. Even now, you see many of these
coats being worn, undoubtedly because they are the only garments their owners have. I have been poring over the Sears
Roebuck catalog and am about to order for Roger some items
suitable for lumberjacks in the Yukon—long underwear, heavy
trousers, and pile-lined coat.

The State Department Information Service has mailed copies
of the catalog to all Missions in Behind the Curtain capitals.
I hope the Czechs, Bulgars, Hungarians, etc., are impressed.
I remember reading last year that there was a queue a block
long to examine the catalog on view in the window of our
information library in Prague. No wonder the Czechs insisted
that it be closed down, for that sort of propaganda could be
more effective than any number of eloquent speeches. It's a
pity we can't circulate the catalog here.

Speaking of libraries, the Lenin Library here in Moscow
is one of the largest reference libraries in Europe, but foreigners

cannot enter the door without a card from the Government authorities. Even to apply for such a card, however, you must prove that you are a serious student, and you must also submit a note showing the subject in which you are interested and the books you want to consult. Even by conforming to the rules, none of our officers has been able to get a card, for some years, and applications are not encouraged.

It's true, of course, that books are pecious in Russia. The people have so lately learned to read that it's as if a whole new world were just opened to them. They flock to bookstores and seem willing to buy anything from, tracts on contour farming to propaganda leaflets and children's folk tales. American favorites are still Jack London, James Fenimore Cooper, Sinclair, etc., but one rarely sees foreign books for sale. In their own literature, Dostoevsky has been banned, Chekov is allowed, and Gogol and Gorki, but Pushkin, the poet, is their real literary idol. I have been reading a most entertaining life of that gentleman by Henri Troyat, published in France last year. I should imagine the author to be a Russian, for his knowledge of Russian history, character, and background is most convincing. Pushkin was the grandson of a Negro slave of Peter the Great's, a slave he later liberated and showered with property and honors.

In spite of their ancestry, or because of it, both grandfather and grandson seem to have been irresistible to women, and the younger Pushkin's love life was very spirited indeed. The book catalogs them all: Annas and Olgas, Lydias, Anastasias, Sophies and Eugenies—he needed two or three for each poem he wrote; and he left notes behind, both on the poems and on the ladies.

Reading the accounts of life in Petersburg, as well as in Moscow, I'm anxious to visit Leningrad, for I feel I'm better informed now about dates and personalities. In spite of the Soviet preference for Moscow, it must be more of a city, well laid out, with buildings that have style and beauty. They say we should plan to go twice, once to see Leningrad in the winter, when the river is frozen, and again in the summer. But right now I've my heart set on a trip out to Paris and London, the end of September. It won't be a long one, but I'd love to just walk about among gay and friendly people.

Postmarked Moscow   September 3, 1949

THE CITY IS QUIET
again. Yesterday, it was like Grand Central Station when the summer camp groups are returning. There were children everywhere, alone and in packs, with mothers, fathers, grandparents. The shops were crowded—clothing stores, stationers, barbers. Every schoolboy must have his head shaved, either as a sanitary or an economic measure; and every schoolgirl must have new ribbon bows on her braids. Until late last evening, children sang and played in our square, but early this morning a procession of them took off with a bugler. Now they are all shut in the schools, or half of them at least, for the overcrowded conditions make it necessary to hold morning and afternoon sessions, just as we do in some of our own cities. The Pioneers, the junior Komsomol group, have a song "Thank you Stalin, for our happy childhood." And they're right, theirs does look like a happy childhood. Russians are exceedingly fond of young children and very indulgent with them. Children are natural tyrants, so they seem to fit into the Soviet pattern quite well, perhaps because it is an instinctive one for them and they take kindly to wolf-pack discipline, a logical introduction to what must come later on. All groups, even the youngest, must submit to daily doses of propaganda, but they accept the Soviet line as their fathers did the catechism, made more palatable with banners and drums and puppet shows and dances. Then, too, I think children really enjoy having something or someone both to love and to hate —on the one hand, Stalin and the Motherland; on the other hand, the wicked capitalists, and the monsters of the Marshall Plan.

As I can't visit a school myself—I've still heard nothing from my request—I asked one of the servants in the house to tell me about the two grammar schools, the girls' and the boys', that her children attend. In city schools, children enter after their seventh birthday, and usually go for seven years after that. In the villages, this period is cut to five years' compulsory attendance, sometimes less. This is another reason for parents' wishing to come to the large cities to live, as they feel their children have a better opportunity for schooling than in the country. Candidates for secondary schools are chosen in various ways, some for merit, some because of party influence.

Most children whose grades are average or lower are recommended for trade schools, rather than for more formal education. The few who show special talents in the arts are allowed to pursue those interests. At the moment, cadets for the new Naval School have all been taken from groups of war orphans. Orphans, by the way, get very preferential treatment as being foolproof Party material without ideological or family ties. In most schools, there are parent-teacher groups, and every so often a number of parents are invited to school assemblies, it being obviously to the interest of the teachers that the parents be as well oriented politically as the pupils. There are no organized game periods, but ten minutes out of each hour are spent in the corridors, exercising or walking about—this in the primary grades; the recitation periods in the secondary schools are much longer.

The children's health seems fairly good. There are the usual contagious diseases, but polio, from all we can learn, seems rare in the Soviet Union. We have no figures on tuberculosis or rheumatic fever, that former curse of European childhood; in fact, we have no figures at all and must rely on what we can see and observe with our own eyes. The children do not look fat, and their color is often sallow, but, like their parents, they are a hardy stock, and again it may be that, by school age, it's a question of survival of the fittest. We've no way of checking infant mortality.

As for the babies, we find it horrifying to see the way they are wrapped and swaddled, up to the age of six months and even later. The streets are always full of women carrying these bundles, the size of which shows how many covers there must be around the child. Even on the hottest days, the whole will be topped off with a wadded quilt and the pocket tied, top and bottom, with ribbon bows. As there are so few baby carriages to be seen, infants must go out in their mother's, more often their grandmother's, arms. There is a report written by the English anthropologist, Geoffrey Gorer, in his book, *The Great Russians*, in which he claims that this practice of early swaddling makes for later subservience and docility. Young Russian children don't appear inhibited, however. It's only when they are 'teen-agers that they begin to lose expression from their faces, which finally become set in the patient, joyless mask of their elders.

Postmarked Moscow   *September 5, 1949*

IT'S TRUE THAT I
was once shipwrecked in the Potomac River when the boat, going downstream, went aground in a fog and all the passengers had to climb over the side to be taken off by a friendly tug. But I never dreamed that such a thing might happen to me, years later, in Russia, on the Volga Canal. For a moment, yesterday, it looked very likely.

We had rented a small river steamer for a Labor Day Embassy picnic and were cheerfully returning from same, when the boat began weaving to and fro. Mothers clutched their children and people rushed out of the enclosed cabin, grabbing passports and identity cards. You can't even afford to be shipwrecked in Russia without your papers! The boat gave a few more dreadful lurches, and Wally Barbour, the Minister Counselor, and senior officer present, rushed to the bridge where he found the Russian captain out cold, and the helmsman with one languid finger on the wheel, the other hand on a vodka bottle.

Wally spoke a few stern words, someone went below to order a jug of strong coffee to be handed around the crew, and we came back more or less on course. Then, because of either the coffee or the words of authority, we put on steam and reached port, docking without accident, but it was quite an experience. Fortunately for all concerned, Dad, the old sailor, was not aboard, he having refused in order to attend a championship football match with the French Ambassador.

The picnic had been great fun. We were about eighty people, including a number of other foreigners and all the enlisted men and clerks from American House. We sailed down the canal for a couple of hours to a pretty wooded island, big enough to accommodate lunch groups, a baseball game, volley ball, even swimming for a few hardy souls. Ellen Morris and I took a walk toward the end of the island and were, of course, stopped by a breathless militiaman, who appeared from nowhere, saying, "Not allowed. Turn back. You can go no farther." This invariably happens if you stray off the beaten track, even on an uninhabited island. What they thought two women could find there, I can't imagine.

It's true that entire area is out of bounds for foreigners and we had to get express permission to voyage down by boat, all motor traffic in that direction being forbidden. If there are bridges or factories or dams or gas works, these installations constitute military targets, in Soviet eyes, and as such are something we might wish to spy upon.

Reading the headlines in the papers that came in this morning, I realize that the situation in Jugoslavia must look very menacing, the Finnish strikes are very serious, and the whole of this part of the world is in an inflammable state. Actually, while the Jugoslav controversy is of greatest importance, most people do not think the Russians will act at once. What the Soviets hope for, of course, is that Tito will meet up with a well-placed bullet, and I feel sure there must be sharpshooting agents scattered about with just that mission in mind. As for the Finns, they seem to have gotten the best of their strikes, though the papers here are playing up the idea that the workers are being terrorized by the Army.

As you may have read, one of the many Peace Conferences was held in Moscow last week. The chief of the American delegation was a Negro, while the British included the Red Dean of Canterbury. This cleric was seen at the ballet, wearing the Red Star on his coat, along with his crucifix, a Russian blonde on either arm. I believe the British can do nothing unless he commits some criminal action, and the Church is also powerless, but he certainly makes a spectacle of himself with his Red Star and knee gaiters.

None of the members of any delegations, the American or the British, come to call or even put their names down at their Embassies. We never see them except in the lobbies of the theaters, walking about the big squares, or waiting in front of the hotels, to be taken off in special busses. When delegations from abroad arrive in Moscow, they are immediately taken charge of, and their every moment is planned for. They are allowed no time of their own, no time to see anything that is not on their prearranged schedule. It's even rare that they have any Russian money. One Italian trade unionist wrote of trying to buy post cards at his hotel newsstand. As he had no money, his guide stepped up and said he would supply much better cards, the Italian mustn't think of buying any. Result: the cards given him showed all the finest views of the finest buildings taken from the finest angles—no others were available, said the guide.

The visiting delegates, whether they be American, British, Canadian, French, or Italian, are all motley groups. Most of them look bewildered—all look quite tired, and well they might, for they are kept busy day and night. They come with ready-made opinions and prejudices, which they are reluctant to change, and it's the rare and courageous man who dares write a minority report, once he arrives home. The simpler-minded might like to, but, after accepting the generosity of their Party or their trade union, it seems plain ungrateful to voice or publish unkind comments—far easier and safer to follow the Party line and praise everything they saw and heard.

There may soon be rumors about us at home, for Dad and I were surely conspicuous sitting in the very midst of the Soviet dignitaries last evening. It was the Bulgarian National Holiday and the Ambassadress, a grim old party with straight gray hair, a determined moustache, and a hard revolutionary eye, invited the entire corps to a h_ge party at the Métropole Hotel. We had some young people dining here with Roger, so we were a little late in getting to the reception.

When we arrived, the guests had already gone into the supper room, and I stopped by the door to chat with the Italians and British while Dad went up to the head table to speak to the Ambassadress. In a minute he came back, motioned to me to join him, and explained that she had asked us to sit down at one end of her table. Down we sat under the amazed eyes of our colleagues, who goggled at us from across the room. Beside me I found Gromyko; beyond him a gentleman whom he presented and told me was the Secretary of the Supreme Soviet; then came the Ambassadress; and on her right Vishinsky; then Marshal Budenny, the fierce old cavalry General, with his sweeping moustaches.

Opposite us were some nameless satellite dignitaries, and just opposite the Ambassadress was the famous ballerina, Lepechinskaya. One of the two top dancers, she shares honors with Ulanova, but, in addition to being an artist, she is also a Party member and a member of the Supreme Soviet. She is about forty-three, thin, quick-moving, as intelligent-looking as a bright and lively bird, speaks both French and English, and has a hard animation that keeps her dancing from being really great. The technique and brilliance are there, but little tenderness or feeling. Fortunately Ellen Morris, who is an ardent ballet fan, had spoken of her that very morning, so I asked if she were not dancing Don Quixote next week, explaining that I had been told if I saw her in that ballet I would see one of the finest performance of all time. She beamed, and we drank a toast together.

There were more toasts. The Ambassadress rose and made a speech, none of which we could understand. Dad leaned across me and said to Gromyko, "You must warn me, Mr. Minister, if I am drinking confusion to the United States."

Gromyko smiled and answered: "That would have to be in

vodka, something very strong. This is only white wine!"

Down the room, I noticed two of our newspaper correspondents looking at us aghast, and I could see our colleagues whispering among themselves. It was very comical, especially as there were no other Ambassadors at the table, not even any of the satellites. As we rose, Marshall Budenny came over to drink a toast with Dad, saying, "A soldier greets a great sailor."

It was all what one expected of Moscow parties: caviar; immense cold salmon; fancy illuminated ices; Soviet ministers in gaudy uniforms; others in crumpled brown suits without ties: the Bulgarian Ambassadress in nondescript black, with a red ribbon and star pinned on her bosom; the Marshals in light-blue tunics, their chests covered with medals in rows, like cabbages in a garden; the ballerina, badly dressed in wispy chiffon, but with fine diamonds swinging from her ears. It was, as I said, what we expected such a party would be, but our share in this one was pure luck. Ordinarily, we would have been carefully shunted off at a far table with our alkaline friends, within sight of the Russians, but no more. Dad was delighted and I must say I enjoyed myself immensely. (Since this was written, our relations with Bulgaria have been broken off, and we and our former hostess no longer speak to each other.)

We got back to find the ground floor of the house in darkness, as Roger and John Keppel and their young friends were staging a murder game and playing sardines all over the upstairs. I believe there's been more animation in Spaso since our arrival than for many years. Roger is enjoying himself, no end, both his work and his out-of-hours activities. What a pity that he can't meet or see any young Russians. At one time he had considered entering the Moscow University, but we were told this was not possible, that the only foreign student is the daughter of the French naval attaché, who is completing her fourth year; since she entered no others have been accepted. But what a silly business it is, the son of the American Ambassador here for a year, especially to study Russian, and finding no opportunity or even possibility of meeting up with even one young man or girl of his own age, the only Russians he can talk to being the workmen he directs in the Chancery courtyard.

The same conditions exist for all foreign diplomats and their children, the satellites excepted, although I often think those wretched people must be even worse off than we are. They are constantly under suspicion by their own compatriots and by the Soviets. Any slight hint of deviation is fatal, and they must follow the ebb and flow of events at home, as well as here. At any time, they may be caught up and called to account.

Our trip out into the free world has been put off, now, until early October. We must be back here the second of November, in time for the celebration on the seventh and the traditional show in Red Square. Along with the parade on May first, this is the big event of the year, with a procession hours long and the Politburo lined up on top of Lenin's tomb, wearing fur-lined overcoats and hats, and blowing snow off their moustaches.

Right now, the weather is good, with wood smoke in the air and a kind of Indian summer haze over everything. The autumn is short here, so we are told we must enjoy these days as they come. Already, leaves have fallen and the gardener is sweeping the drive. Such a lot of sweeping as goes on in Russia—the dust, the gutters, the snow, the leaves—all with twig brooms, the kind we associate with Hallowe'en witches.

The town is full of people. They've come back from their holidays, and the parks are so full of children one realizes how empty they seemed during the summer. Yesterday I went shopping with Ellen Morris and the wife of one of the British secretaries. No matter what time of day, the shops are as crowded as ours during the Christmas rush. Compared to the population, there are few shops, of course, and many of the people are sightseers, not buyers, simply coming in to wander about and push alongside the counters to see what others are buying. The system is to pick out an article, then go to the cashier, tell her the price, pay, return with a slip showing a cash transaction, and then stand in queue again to claim the article chosen. You can imagine that, with this lengthy process, traffic becomes snarled and the scene is one of utter confusion.

Even though there is often a cash register in her booth, the cashier does all her sums on an abacus, and wooden beads rattle back and forth until you would think you were in San Francisco's Chinatown. There is very little to buy—that is, very little any of *us* would want to buy—and, with our exchange rate, prices come high.

The largest store in Moscow is the Mostorg, once a fine department store. I suppose you could still call it a department store, but I found nothing to buy except a few toys; wooden dolls that fit one into another; small stuffed animals with a Russian look about their faces; and a bright-colored picture book. In the silver and china stores, commission shops where goods are brought in for sale, there were a few bits of interesting silver and some highly priced porcelain, but the rest trash for the most part, the kind of thing one finds in the back corners of any grandparent's attic. Gone are the days when there were real treasures to be picked up; the last of these appeared at the Foreign Minister's Conference, in 1946, when the Soviets filled the shops with every kind of article from their storehouses to impress and tempt the foreign visitors. As for ordinary purchases—thread, buttons, soap, cosmetics, yard goods —what's offered is so bad and so expensive that none of us would think of buying so much as a pin. We are all quite self-sufficient, having come equipped with every conceivable necessity, and I hope our supplies won't run out before they can be replenished from home.

Postmarked Moscow   September 15-17, 1949

MR. VISHINSKY
should be happily ensconced on the Queen Mary today, with cordial memories of our cook's lemon pie. He lunched here on Tuesday, the first time any Soviet citizen, much less the Foreign Minister, has taken a meal in the Embassy for two years.

Dad had spoken to him some time ago, saying he hoped that he would come to lunch before leaving for the United States and the General Assembly. Then, about ten days ago, he wrote him a personal note asking if Monday or Tuesday would be convenient, and explaining that it would be a very small men's lunch with only our own Embassy staff members present besides the two gentlemen he hoped the Minister would bring with him.

After five days—the Russians seldom allow less time to respond to anything—an answer came that either day would be convenient, and that Mr. Vishinsky would be most happy to come to lunch. The men here in our Embassy were astonished, but Dad says it may well be that the man was never before invited in just that way. Too often he would have been asked to large dinners, where he would be trotted out like a tame bear, in front of other members of the diplomatic corps, and, by accepting one such invitation, find himself compelled to accept them all.

In any event, he came on Tuesday and apparently enjoyed himself immensely. He brought with him the head of the American desk and an interpreter, Mr. Pastoev. For our side, there were Wally Barbour, our Minister; Admiral Stevens, the naval Attaché; George Morgan, our Russian expert; and Brewster Morris, our Counselor. Both Stevens and George Morgan speak excellent Russian, so they could do interpreting themselves and check on what was being said. Mr. Vishinsky understands both English and French, but he always speaks Russian to our people and has their English interpreted for him.

I gave the gentlemen roast ham, the last string beans out of our garden, and lemon pie which Chin and Tong served with Oriental deftness, so all went well. Dad was greatly pleased, and everyone applauds the gesture. No other Chief of Mission has done anything like it, but coming just before Mr. Vishinsky sets out for New York, it was a natural gesture and, we hope, will be accepted as such by the press.

Absurd, isn't it, that a quiet lunch, the Foreign Minister coming to lunch with an Ambassador accredited to his country, should make such news? I laughed, contrasting it with the many times Mr. Spaak had come to our house in Belgium, and the easy friendly footing we felt ourselves on with him.

During the course of the conversation, Dad told Vishinsky that he intended going away, himself, for three weeks next month, and that we had an old saying in English, he hoped the Minister would not misunderstand:

"When the cat's away, the mice will play."

The interpreter translated, Vishinsky thought a moment, then said:

"Ah, but you made a mistake in translating the gender of the cat. In this case it would be a tomcat!"

All laughed heartily, for this seems to be the kind of give-and-take humor they enjoy. Of course, Vishinsky knew that in coming here he was not creating precedent—the visit could so well be excused on official grounds—and, as he was leaving next day to be gone some time, there would be no question of having to trot over to the British or French Embassies the following week.

I would not like the impression to get about that we have become intimates on the strength of my one formal call on Madame, and the one lemon pie Mr. Vishinsky ate here. I doubt whether our acquaintanceship goes any further, but after all, the Italian Counselor in Brussels said their Embassy in Moscow wrote that the two most important men in Russia were Stalin and the American Ambassador and that, in spite of the fear and suspicion they feel for us, the Russians have admiration, as well as hatred, for the United States.

So far, our personal triumphs have been four: Madame Vishinsky received me; Stalin not only took out his pipe when he received Dad, but lighted it—which he did not do for the British Ambassador; we fell into the seats of honor at the Bulgarian's the other night; and yesterday Mr. Vishinsky came to lunch. It may not seem much, but it's apparently more than has happened to other Chiefs of Mission; and yet it all came about quite naturally. As one friend said to us in New York, "Perhaps you'll be all right—you don't look scared." So far, anyway, we're not.

We drove to Yasnaya Polyana last Sunday, a very pleasant

excursion. It's the longest motor drive we are allowed, even with permission from the Foreign Office, and, as Dad and his little men stayed home, we were forbidden to stop anywhere en route. We thought this only applied to towns along the way—to Tula, for instance, where there is a big iron foundry. Not so, for just as we finished our picnic lunch by the wayside, a militiaman popped out from behind a bush, saying, "You cannot stop here, you must pack up and go away. This is a forbidden area."

There was nothing anywhere around us but birch trees and a few cows, and where he'd come from we'd no idea, but Soviet policemen spring from the grass like dandelions. He walked away and we started to pick up our things. He came back to make sure we were leaving and when he was satisfied hailed a peasant's cart, wished us good day and rode down the road astride a large mattress. We thought some of settling down again, but decided he might have a mate near-by; militiamen often travel in pairs, like cobras.

The Tolstoi house, the old family estate, now a Government-owned museum, is a simple place, white-plastered, with clean white painted rooms. It reminded me very much of Black Hall, in Connecticut, where my great aunts used to live. In fact, it had a distinctly New England atmosphere about it, even to the smell. The family living room was very like the one I remembered as a child, a student lamp in the middle of a big table set for tea, piles of books and papers about, a hard couch with a plaid blanket thrown over the foot, the afternoon sun coming in through paned windows, old prints tacked a little crookedly on the walls.

Perhaps what used to be called plain living and high thinking produces the same effect everywhere. The Soviets have made a great cult of Tolstoi, though one has only to read his books to realize how abhorrent the new tyranny and oppression would be to him and his gentle disciples. One guesses that, like many men who live on noble but impractical theories, he may have been somewhat trying as a husband and a father. One sympathizes with the wife, a tiresome, nagging female, but she had ample excuse for her bad temper—she had thirteen children, and, as if that were not enough, copied all his literary works in longhand, redoing *War and Peace* seven times!

Around the house there are still remnants of the farm, and some fine woods in the heart of which is the author's grave, a simple mound set around with ferns. It was pleasant in the woods and very quiet, with the first yellow leaves drifting down onto the path. Autumn comes early in Russia, and there's already a feeling of frost.

Next weekend will be uneventful; we've made no plans, as just lately the social schedule has been a heavy one.

Wednesday night, we had dinner with the Finnish Minister, a fussy little man, who begged me to come one day to try his Finnish bath set up in the basement of the legation. I was not too enthusiastic about accepting, remembering the shattering experience of a pretty young Swiss Secretary's wife who told me of attending last year.

"I thought it was a ladies' party, Madame. As you see I am very, very nearsighted, and without my glasses I am quite blind. I came to meet my girl friend, the Minister's Secretary; she had not come down yet, but the maid told me I could undress and wait for her in the *sona* room. I did so. I left my glasses with my clothes and walked into the steam room. I could see nothing, until suddenly toward me came two figures. Imagine, Madame, they were gentlemen and there I was, quite naked, nothing on at all and, Madame, one of the gentlemen was the Minister, the other his counselor. And worst of all, Madame, though I knew I had nothing on, you see, I am so blind I couldn't tell whether it was just the same with them!"

Thursday, we had a formal dinner here of twenty-four, then sixty more guests came for dancing, a very gay evening, the music supplied by an amateur orchestra, made up of some of our young men, led by Eddy Gilmore, the Associated Press correspondent, who played the drum.

Then, last night, we dined, fifty strong, at the British Embassy. Their ballroom looks out over the Moscow River toward the Kremlin, a most dramatic décor. Roger distinguished himself by asking the daughters of both the Afghan and Persian Ambassadors to dance. These young ladies, plus the daughter of the French naval attaché, are the only diplomats' daughters who go out to parties. Fortunately, we have a number of very attractive girls working in our own Embassy, and there are others from the Dutch, Norwegian, Swedish and British Embassies, who go about and manage to keep our young gentlemen quite happy. These girls really have a very good time, and, as they are generally very carefully selected, we've a very fine group with a high percentage of good looks and intelligence.

I like Lady Kelly, the British Ambassadress, who has just arrived to join her husband. She is half French, half Belgian, by birth, very vivacious, with a quick wit and real curiosity about this place and the people who live in it. What a pity that neither she nor I can get about to talk with the Russian wives, to meet them in the ordinary way and to learn something of their lives.

Eddy Gilmore told me Dad's lunch for Vishinsky made real news and brought comment from all papers at home. That shows the absurdity of our situation.

Postmarked Moscow   *September 22, 1949*

THE SMELL OF camphor in the house even penetrates my first autumn cold. Dad and Roger are unpacking heavy suits, preparatory to starting for Stalingrad tonight. I am just as glad that I decided not to go with them, for forty-eight hours in a Russian train might find me with pneumonia at the other end, and pneumonia in Stalingrad could be an uncomfortable business.

The trip is duly heralded in the press and they will have Harrison Salisbury, the *New York Times* correspondent, along to give a first hand report. Roger has an elaborate set of travel orders, "to accompany the Ambassador as Secretary and Interpreter, and to make observations and reports on matters of interest." We have prepared a large store of food and liquor, so they should not want on the voyage—bread, butter, canned meats, fruit juices, and jam. They go in a "soft car," as differentiated from an "international" car. This means there are four berths in each compartment, and no washrooms between; pillows and linen are obtainable, but must be paid for, extra.

They should be very tired men by the time they reach Stalingrad, for the softness of the car doesn't refer to springs or wheels. The hardest aspect of Soviet travel, however, is the sanitation problem. Madame Litvinov, the English-born wife of the former Soviet diplomat, was once quoted as saying, "Think of an entire nation that has never learned to pull the chain." And certainly the public lavatories are filthy spots. Lady Kelly recommends carrying an enamel pot in a box, a very practical idea I suggested to Dad and Roger. I wonder why the Russians aren't all afflicted with dysentery, typhoid, all kinds of diseases. Probably they've gained a fine immunity to these things and it's only effete Westerners who succumb. Like Polynesians who die of measles and chicken pox, we've no resistance.

We are curious to know how many of the bodyguard will go along with Dad, and whether any special effort will be made to lay on a tour at the other end. Our military Attaché, General O'Daniel, went last year and reported the local authorities had been most polite, detailing an officer to explain all the battle, and, incidentally, to prevent the General's seeing anything on his own account. One bright feature, he said, was that caviar was only half the price there that it is in Moscow. Here, at twenty dollars a pound, it's nearly as expensive as it is in New York. As all our friends are persuaded we live on it day after day, and will be disappointed if we don't bring any out with us next month, Dad will try to lay in a store.

I had thought to go to hear the opera tonight, but the theater is drafty, and, as no one is allowed to wear a coat inside, I think I will sit by my own fire. This rule about coats applies to all public buildings. "It's not cultured," the Russians say: *Nie culturnie!* Every museum has an immense cloakroom, where coats and hats and galoshes must be checked. Many require rag slippers to be put over visitors' shoes. It's quite a trick keeping these slippers on, and it's a funny sight to see parties shuffling along over not too well polished floors.

We've not put on heat in the house as yet, and it's chilly. The thermometer was 44 this morning, but I've wrapped myself in wool. With the lowered English pound, I hope to make some judicious purchases of woollen garments in London next month, for I fear they will be more useful here than my Suzy hats.

The Western press and radio have been filled with the story of a Russian atomic explosion. Here, there has been no announcement. We knew, of course, that sooner or later the Russians would manufacture the bomb, and we shouldn't be surprised if there has been a test. We could never hope to keep such a secret to ourselves. If World War II had not interrupted their experiments, perhaps the Russians would have succeeded before this. It's not too nice to think about.

I suppose the Soviet public will be duly apprised of the explosion in a few days. No event is immediately headlined here. When anything serious occurs, there's a definite wait until the propaganda machine goes into action and the Party line can be ground out to the entire country's press and radio.

Postmarked Moscow   *September 30, 1949*

AT LAST, WE'VE been to the Kremlin. I was very glad that the visit was not arranged earlier, for I wanted to wait until I had more knowledge of Russian art and history. Now I've the chronology fairly straight, so I knew better what I was looking at. These Kremlin visits must be applied for well in advance and the names of the party submitted to the Foreign Office. The museums are not open to the Russian public, and the Kremlin precincts are closed and heavily guarded at all times.

Including Dad, Roger, and myself, we were a party of about ten, all from our own Embassy, with George Morgan acting as interpreter. Our tour was scheduled for eleven o'clock, and we were told it would take about three hours, so we bolstered ourselves with hot coffee and ordered a late and hearty lunch to be ready on our return.

As Dad led the party in his own car, we were allowed to drive through the Kremlin gate—ordinarily all nonofficial visitors must enter on foot—and we were admitted after two stops, when our diplomatic cards were examined and checked by the militia on duty. Just driving through the gate excited me, for I've looked at those sixty-five-foot walls so often from the outside.

The Kremlin is situated on the highest part of the city and, once one is on top, the view over Moscow and the river winding below is very fine. As a fortress, it still appears impregnable. It was even able to resist the Great Fire of 1812, when Napoleon exclaimed: "They've set the city on fire themselves. What a people! What barbarians! They are Scyths!" Now, I believe, the Soviets claim it was the French who put the torch to the first house, but that's hardly possible, as history relates that Rostopchine, the Governor, ordered all the fire-fighting apparatus removed and, after that, opened the prison gates and sent gangs of common-law criminals around to set fires in various parts of the city.

Our cars drove up in front of the Great Palace, a huge building facing the river, and constructed in 1838 on the site of two former palaces. We got out and were met by a woman guide, a Foreign Office representative in gray uniform, and three additional Secret Service men who joined Dad's four and stayed with us the entire time. The various buildings and grounds inside the Kremlin are as neat and polished as tiled bathroom fixtures, the only really well-kept spot I've seen in the Soviet Union. Even the blades of grass looked as though they had been straightened that morning.

We were led into a central square surrounded by churches, three large ones and the high bell tower of Ivan Veliki. These churches are in process of restoration, so we were not allowed inside. Most are Italianate in feeling, with superimposed bulbous domes, more odd than beautiful. It's true that the czars, from Ivan III down—that is—from the mid-fifteenth century —all employed Italian architects, and their influence is predominant throughout Russian public architecture, churches, palaces, and administration buildings. This continued to be so until the end of the nineteenth century, and it's curious to see Renaissance and classic detail combined with bright yellow and white plaster, all shut behind high Russian walls.

With pride the guide showed us the Czar cannon, the largest cannon ever cast in the world, although she admitted it had never been fired. With equal pride, she showed us the largest bell ever cast in the world, and again she admitted it had never been rung. She marshalled us carefully around the Square and back toward the palace. Beyond, we saw long lines of buildings which were once monasteries and barracks, but which are now offices or residences for Kremlin officials. Over the largest there flew a red flag, so we supposed this must be Stalin's headquarters. We would like to have asked questions about this, but were hardly encouraged.

The Great Palace is a kind of period piece. Disrespectfully I was reminded of the United States Hotel in Saratoga; its furniture was of that era, only very grand indeed with heavily upholstered sofas and chairs in satin and bright brocade, little marqueterie tables, big marqueterie tables, inlaid rosewood pianos, fretwork music stands, round seats with palms sprouting from the middle, the whole illuminated by lights from hundreds of crystal chandeliers, every one of them turned on for our benefit. After its completion, the Czars rarely used the Palace, coming to Moscow only for their coronation and other state visits. The rooms, one after another, looked unlived in and untouched, the furniture as carefully arranged and as new as if the decorators of the day had just left.

One feature impressed us all—there were clocks in every room, and every clock was working. Remarkable clocks they were, the kind that had revolving moons and stars, that showed you the minute, the hour, the month, the year, that had nymphs and dryads dancing around the face, and little drummer boys striking the hours. When nowhere in the world today a watch or clock repair man is to be found, it's obvious they must all be shut up in the Kremlin dungeons!

I suppose there must still be dungeons under the Old Palace, bits of which they showed us. Most of the old buildings were torn down when the New Palace was built, but what remains in the rear has been connected to the New by staircases and corridors, including the rooms where Ivan the Terrible and Czar Boris lived. These last were pure theater, painted red, blue, yellow, with low, vaulted ceilings and tiny windows, below one of which Ivan hanged a row of his enemies on hooks!

Another window was famous as the one through which each day a box was drawn on a string. In the box were petitions from the Czar's subjects—petitions that had been placed there by poor people huddled below, hoping for answers to their requests. Today there is an office near Mokhovaya Square, supposedly open to any Soviet citizen, where individual complaints may be lodged, and forwarded to President Shvernik. I once looked in the door and saw rows of chairs, all filled with patient, pathetic creatures waiting, as their ancestors did before them, each one with his written complaint, ready to be put in the modern equivalent of Boris' box.

From the Palace we went to the Museum, where the imperial treasure is shut into display cases. The crown jewels are not on show, but there is a wealth of silver and gold plate, church vestments stiff with precious stones, marvelous services of porcelain and enamelware, and a final and touching exhibit, a cabinet filled with the Easter eggs given by the last Czar to various members of the imperial family. The first of these eggs was a surprise for the Empress, designed to please and amuse her, for she was always a sad and melancholy lady.

The gift was so successful the Czar ordered it to be repeated each year, and the eggs became more and more elaborate. One opened, to show a perfect model of the imperial yacht, in gold and jewels; from another there came a tiny gold train, a replica of the Czar's own, that could be wound up with a little gold key; another unfolded like a flower, and each petal showed a jeweled portrait of one of the royal children. All these eggs were made by Fabergé, the court jeweler, the latest and perhaps the most interesting being dated 1917, fashioned in gun metal and gold, the egg sitting on top of four artillery shells.

Beyond the silver plate and jewel collections were other rooms housing state carriages, coaches, and sleighs, and then a costume exhibit of imperial regalia and coronation robes. At the end, when we had seen everything possible, the guide made us a little speech, which George Morgan interpreted.

"All this, once the property of the Czars, now belongs to the people of Russia. The treasure is theirs to guard and enjoy." It is certainly guarded, but hardly enjoyed by the people. We were the only visitors in the Museum that day. One could scarcely say the public has the right of entry—probably no more than fifty people a month ever see these things, and then they are selected groups, admitted as a privilege rather than as a right.

I'd like to go again, but not for a while. I want to read more of my history and look for certain things when I go back. The guide was perfunctory, skipping over what was most interesting to us. Another time I hope to get into some of the churches and see less of the cannon and the bell.

Postmarked Moscow   *October 3, 1949*

SATURDAY NIGHT,
just as we were dressing to go out for dinner, John Keppel, the young Third Secretary who lives in Spaso, came into Dad's room to say that the Foreign Ministry had rung up, asking that Dad come to see Mr. Gromyko at once. Very well, said Dad, he would be there in twenty minutes. John and I both remarked at the military reaction to any emergency. All be-

comes calm, almost aggressively calm, movements are slow but precise, the voice becomes almost gentle.

Actually, the matter turned out to be very tame—the Russians simply wished to present a formal note of protest against the founding of the German Republic, and the note had to be given in person to the three Ambassadors, British, French and American.

When Heads of Mission go to the Russian Foreign Office, they are received in a bare room furnished with a desk, unused, and three or four chairs. On no account are they ever admitted to the Minister's private offices. Time schedules for the Russian Government Departments are quite different from ours. Work begins late in the morning, around eleven; lunch may be at four; and dinner may be anywhere from ten to twelve at night. Appointments are often given for nine-thirty or ten or eleven in the evening, as if these were normal working hours.

Shop people and industrial workers keep still different hours. Shops shut between one and four, whereas industrial workers are assigned to shifts, some starting at six A.M. Theaters and concerts begin promptly at eight P.M.; the plays are very long; even the ballets are not over until nearly midnight. Matinees start at twelve, and go on until mid-afternoon. I've not been able to discover when the majority of people eat; it seems to vary with the profession and the trade. Not only that, but, with the actute housing shortage, housewife must have to wait in line to shove her pot on the common stove. In most of the older houses there's only one kitchen and, with some fifteen or twenty families using it, there must be a lot of queuing up.

The servant problem grows increasingly difficult throughout the diplomatic colony. Every applicant must be passed by Burobin—the Government organization that handles all requests from foreigners—whether it be for rat extermination, a new roof, or a new housemaid. If an individual is rash enough to work without proper registration, he or she is liable to heavy penalties, nor can one Mission transfer a servant to another. A maid who has been authorized to work for the Mexican

Embassy cannot go to the Belgians. I daresay each one must receive special training and instructions before being sent out, but, by and large, they are such a simple lot that one can't take them too seriously as spies. It's true one always has the sensation of being watched; as yet, it's not bothered me too much but it may before our time is up.

OUR POOR MILITARY
Attaché, General O'Daniel, and his wife were returning last week from leave in Germany, with their provision of clothes and stocks for the winter. They were told that the train from Helsinki to Leningrad did not carry a baggage car and their goods would have to follow. When the bearer of a diplomatic passport accompanies his belongings in person, especially if he is a Senior Officer, these goods are not usually subject to duty; but let him be separated from those goods, and the privilege is forfeited!

Even though the officer in question may have a *laisser passer* in proper order, this applies only to whatever luggage he may have with him—result, when the O'Daniels' trunks came through, a few days after their arrival in Moscow, the Russians refused to consider them as accompanied baggage and the unfortunate pair were charged thirteen hundred dollars' worth of duty. Such is courtesy in the Soviet Union.

Admiral Stevens, our naval Attaché, who is shortly to be relieved, sent his heavy luggage off the other day, as he and his wife are flying out with us this month. When anyone, diplomat or civilian, leaves Russia he must declare everything he sends out, and must prove, to the satisfaction of the authorities, that any articles purchased here do not fall into a prohibited category. The Russians will not permit silver, art objects, rugs, books or anything of special value or interest to be taken out of the country without heavy duty, and in many instances permission is not granted at all.

In the case of an Ambassador the rules are more lenient, but the Stevens boxes were all opened and a lot of things returned to them to be accounted for and repacked. Among them were three old rugs which they had bought in the United States when they were first married; some naval prints the Admiral had had since he was a Lieutenant; Mrs. Stevens' court train of white and silver brocade, which she had worn in London before the war and was saving for her grandchildren—this was declared art material; a dozen ten-cent-store plated teaspoons bought at Kresge's, classed as *valuable silverware;* and some English books, which were questioned. Altogether an absurd lot of oddments were returned to the Stevens and had to be shown to the Soviets a second time, with convincing proof of previous ownership.

You might think the Soviets were going out of their way to be disagreeable to our military personnel, but it's the same with everyone. Very often it's not the official who is to blame, it's the system which does not allow any one person to take initiative or to make decisions. A Government employee is handed a set of regulations which he must follow to the letter, any authority for deviation must come from higher up, and the fellow just above him must ask the fellow above him, and so it goes all the way from the smallest and most humble militiaman to the Kremlin itself.

Postmarked Moscow   *October 6, 1949*

MY THREE MEN
arrived back safely by plane from Stalingrad, very enthusiastic about their trip. They went very thoroughly over the battlefield, studied it along with the published accounts of the siege —some have just appeared, written by the German generals

97

concerned. Dad says it's still a marvel to him that the Russians were able to resist successfully. The Germans would only have had to make one last thrust and the Russians must have capitulated.

The visas for our American plane crew have been granted. We expect to leave early next week for Germany and Belgium. I'm counting the hours—only sorry that we must leave Roger behind, but he's determined to stay on the job, holding down Spaso House with the two other men, John Keppel and George Morgan.

Postmarked Moscow　　　*November 6, 1949*

IT'S CURIOUS TO be back. Our holiday was a good one, Moscow and Russia seemed a dream while we were away, now it's the world outside that's a dream. It might have been harder to return if I hadn't known I'd see Roger's smiling face at the airport, unfamiliar almost, for he'd topped it with his new astrakhan fur cap. I must get one for myself, for it's already quite cold and we've snow flurries every other day.

We came back to find the city engaged in feverish activity, all in preparation for tomorrow's holiday. Everywhere red bunting is being tacked up, portraits of Lenin and Stalin have blossomed in every shop window, and, blown up to gigantic size, they adorn the fronts of public buildings. Embassy chanceries are busy writing cables to say that Molotov's picture appears on the right of Stalin's whenever the Politburo's is shown as the order of precedence is important. The streets are crowded with soldiers brought in to take part in the great parades, and late in the evening there are big civilian groups in front of our Mokhovaya building, marching back and forth across the Square, training for the "spontaneous demonstration," with cheer leaders coaching them who would put our college men to shame.

Red Square is splashed with color, the buildings opposite Lenin's tomb being entirely covered with red banners. The tomb itself is being handpolished by a squad of reverent women, while Security Police in blue caps stand by watching every swab of their rags. Stair carpets have been laid for the Party great to walk up to the top of the tomb, where they will stand around Stalin to view the parade.

Rumor has it, however, that Stalin will not be there tomorrow and that Molotov has been brought back from the conquest of China to head the show. Elderly gentlemen are safer basking in the Crimean sunshine than reviewing troops in Red Square on a November day, and we will probably be told that Marshal Stalin has prolonged his vacation on the advice of his doctors. At seventy, the doctors and the Party are taking no chances.

Postmarked Moscow   *November 7, 1949*

WE BREAKFASTED

at eight this morning, and left the house at nine, in order to get to Mokhovaya in good time. All streets leading into Red Square were closed at nine-thirty and cleared except for troops forming up for the parades. Dad inquired whether his party would be permitted to cross our square on foot without going around the edge as we must do ordinarily, and was assured there would be no trouble.

We assembled in the entrance of the Chancery and started forth in a group—Wally Barbour; General O'Daniel, the military Attaché; Captain Draim, the new naval Attaché; the Morrises, plus the Norwegian and Swedish Ambassadors and their families, whose cars had been left in our chancery courtyard. Dad and Wally wore heavy overcoats and silk hats which occasioned considerable merriment and interest from the crowds outside; the military were in uniform, Roger looked smart in his new astrakhan hat; while I was as muffled as a Chinese grandmother, under my heaviest fur coat, giving a stylish stout appearance. We proceeded majestically across Mokhovaya Square and up the street leading into Red Square, the sides of which were thickly lined with soldiers and spectators. We were stopped three times to show our cards and passes; even Dad's Little Men had to show theirs. This may be a public event, but the public cannot attend except as participants in the so-called spontaneous demonstration, the civilians march past at the end of the military parade.

Shoulder to shoulder, Security Police soldiers in khaki-colored wool with blue caps stood around the edge of the great empty space. We walked past them to take our places to the left of Lenin's tomb, in the front rows of the permanent stone benches which flank it on either side. Our section was already crowded with our various diplomatic colleagues and with officials from the Russian Foreign Office, other sections being set aside for Soviet dignitaries. The sun was at our backs, behind the Kremlin wall, still very low on the horizon, though it was nearly ten o'clock, but the day was clear and fine and, bundled up as we were, it was not uncomfortable.

Just across the square were blocks of Red Army troops standing at attention, with bands massed in the middle. At a few minutes before ten, there was a clatter of hoofs and two impressive generals rode by, followed by their orderlies, the Minister of War, and the commander of the Moscow garrison. The Minister was a heavy man whose horse rocked back and forth with him, so that he looked like an animated statue from off a pedestal in a public square. Before each company of troops they reined in, said something to the leader, and the men answered with three hurrahs.

When all had been inspected, the Kremlin clock pealed ten. The members of the Politburo, a string of men in dark overcoats and hats, walked out the side gate and mounted the stairs to the top of the tomb, where they stood in a row. The Minister of War rode up, dismounted, and joined them, guns boomed the salute, and the massed bands crashed into the national anthem. Everyone took off his hat, except the Politburo—perhaps the same idea as not drinking your own toast, although Russian orators invariably answer applause by clapping their own hands.

The march past began, the Moscow general on horseback at the head of the column. All their Generals seem to be large men, and most of them are stouter than the average. The clothes of both officers and men are good. The officers' gray overcoats remind one of prerevolutionary pictures; the cut is much the same, double-breasted, tight-belted, and long-skirted. The boots worn by all ranks are the only good-looking shoes to be seen in Russia. But the sound of these boots striking the stone pavement is chilling. The Russian marching step, or parade step, is much like the German goose step; the feet are stamped so hard that the men's cheeks shake.

There were detachments of infantry, long lines fed into the square from each side, moving as regularly and precisely as streams flowing into a river; there was the Navy, headed by an Admiral as portly as any of the Generals; there were four cavalry detachments, very smart indeed, and horse-drawn artillery that reminded me of the old Saturday drill-shows at Fort Myer. The Security Police marched by, solid blocks of them, visible symbols of this police state, and just then the sun came up over the top of the Kremlin wall to shine on their blue caps.

More bands—the music throughout was excellent—and then the motorized divisions, the Red Army on wheels. These made up the greater part of the parade as they do of any army today, and the clatter of the trucks and tanks on the cobbled stones seemed to go on for hours. Overhead the Air Force had its own show, bombers and fighters in formation and streaks of jets.

The military display lasted an hour and a quarter, and then it was the turn of the civilian organizations, factory unions, sport clubs, school delegations. There was an impressive sight when their massed flags came by, silk banners of all colors streaming out over the heads of the moving people. At the close of the military parade, Security Police moved in, separating the marchers by every five men, one line of Police facing in, the next out, so the loyal Soviet paraders' every step could be watched. We stayed to see half an hour of this, and then, surrounded by Dad's bodyguards, started back toward Mokhovaya Square. Here we had to cut the lines of marchers, which the Little Men did neatly but firmly, and our party came through with only a few good-natured jeers at Dad's and Wally's hats.

As our Chancery fronts on Mokhovaya Square, with a view up the street into Red Square, beyond, it's a good vantage point from which to watch any of these celebrations. Only Chiefs of Mission, Counselors and the Senior Service Attachés are invited into Red Square itself on these occasions, so everyone else crowds into the front apartments of Mokhovaya, where all our Embassy personnel keep open house for the rest of their diplomatic colleagues.

We joined the party at Wally Barbour's, where we had hot rum punch and looked down onto the marching columns. The people's demonstration lasted from eleven-thirty until mid-afternoon, a steady flow, as organized and controlled as the military parade that preceded it. Later this evening there will be dancing in the street, and searchlight and fireworks displays. Here at Spaso our own servants, plus their families, have had a huge holiday meal, with fresh meat stew, sweet sugared bread, coffee, and drinks. The atmosphere when we came home was decidedly cordial!

That was hardly the word for the gala Party Meeting which we attended, by invitation, last night with the rest of the diplomatic chiefs. This is the special Party Meeting graced by members of the Politburo, one member of which is chosen to make the keynote address, the speeches being followed by an elaborate concert featuring turns from opera and ballet, and lasting on into the night. We were not too anxious to go, as the main address was sure to be directed against the United States, but Dad said we must show ourselves this once. The Bolshoi Theater, the great opera house where the affair was held, is a magnificent old place, still looking as it must have looked in Czarist days, decorated in crimson and gilt, with six rows of balconies, and great glittering crystal chandeliers. The eagles over the imperial box have been replaced with the Soviet seal, otherwise it's the same. Dad and I sat in a side loge, as stuffed with Ambassadors as raisins in a cake. I was in a front corner seat, and tried to appear as haughty as possible, especially when Malenkov, a Politburo member and the speaker of the evening, thundered against the Amerikanski Capitalisti. Behind us Sir David Kelly, the British Ambassador, was counting the times Amerikanski were mentioned. He got to twenty-five and was rather miffed at hearing England named only once. We left before the concert began. What a curious idea, to invite people to come to hear themselves insulted. Dad says if he must go next year, he will simply appear in time for the singing.

Postmarked Moscow   *November 9, 1949*

YESTERDAY, ALONG with the rest of Moscow, we were recovering from the day before, and the whole Embassy appeared a trifle languid. Dad, Roger, and I went to the Foreign Office reception given by the Minister and Madame Gromyko on Monday evening, a formal affair held in the big State reception house where I called on Madame Vishinsky. All the rooms were thrown open and filled with the elite who are eligible for such functions: the Diplomatic Corps and the Foreign Office personnel; high-ranking Russian military men; the Marshals and Admirals; Soviet writers and artists; and distinguished foreign Communist visitors, such as Professor Joliot Curie and Marcel Cachin from France; a Chinese delegation, to whom special attention was paid; and the new East German representatives. These last two groups were seated at tables in the main room, with Russians told off to entertain them and make a fuss over each one. The rest of us stood about in the inner room, a kind of VIP corral where the diplomats were all herded together.

Dad asked Gromyko to introduce him to one of the Marshals, who turned out to be Vosolovsky, late Commander in Berlin. The Marshals' dress uniforms are terrific—dark trousers, and light-blue tunics with wide gold shoulder boards and stupendous rows of medals. When a man is cited for the same medal a second time, he wears a second medal; and this particular Marshal had eight identical ones in a line across his breast.

The Marshal asked where Dad had served in the war.

"As Commander of American invasion forces in Sicily and Normandy," answered Dad.

"Normandy," remarked the Marshal, "that was the Second Front."

"No," answered Dad—all this interpreted by Gromyko—"that was the second Second Front."

"How so?" questioned the Marshal.

"The first was in 1939 and 1940—Western Europe," replied Dad.

The conversation stopped there. All three men—Gromyko, the Marshal, and Dad—bowed politely to each other.

Both at the theater the night before, and on Monday at the reception, I thought the Russians we saw were well dressed, not perhaps according to our standards, for there is no attempt at or understanding of style, as we know it, but there certainly is nothing of the proletarian collarless "dirty shirt" effect. These are the Party folk, but they have risen to a point where they can afford what they term culture and taste. The men do not wear evening clothes, but the Foreign Office officials and the military were in resplendent uniforms.

Most of the women at the reception wore long dresses of dark colors. Décolleté styles are frowned upon as bourgeois decadency of taste. Madame Gromyko was muffled in black velvet, with high neck and long sleeves, and most of the other women's frocks were made in similar fashion. Fortunately, I brought out my white brocade, which, though cut square in front, is high in back and, with jewels and gloves, produces quite an impression and still remained in the note.

Aside from Dad's encounter with the Marshal—and he asked

for that introduction—we talked with no Russians but our hosts, nor were we presented to any. Some of our older colleagues could point out prominent figures, at whom we looked—that was all—and they looked back at us.

Now the holidays are over, we can settle in for the winter. It looms long ahead, but the prospect of a real vacation in February will help to get us through the Great Cold. We have a very congenial household, with John and George Morgan, and I am sorry to think that both will be leaving Moscow before the spring. Ellen Morris is a tower of strength for me, a very energetic, stimulating young woman. She speaks considerable Russian and its great fun going with her to the plays and ballets. The theater is a great resource for all of us; it's only a pity that most of the modern plays are strictly propaganda and many so violently anti-American that we feel conspicuous in attending them.

It's fun to wonder what Moscow must have been like before the Revolution. The streets, I feel sure, were always ill paved and badly lighted, but the number of once elegant dwellings makes one believe there was considerable wealth in the city. Stalin remarked to Dad that the war had interfered with the city's rebuilding, some projects had had to be abandoned and others delayed, for want of material and labor. The plans he said were all made, and would go ahead as soon as opportunity presented.

After the 1917 Revolution, many of the brightest young men and women in the country were sent to study abroad to bring back knowledge and ideas. During the war, many of these same young men and women were lost, others were liquidated as tainted by Western corruption. Their younger brothers and sisters are now locked behind the Iron Curtain, none go abroad today, nor do foreign engineers and technicians come to be employed in the Soviet Union or teach in its schools, factories and universities. Whether it will be possible for Russians to develop ways of life, on their own, that will be able to compete with Western civilization, is problematical. Sooner or later, it would seem, the gates must open either inward or outward. Right now, the tangible rewards for the Russian workers—an extra few meters of housing space, an extra few tickets for the Bolshoi, an extra few rubles to buy food, an extra few days of vacation in a crowded rest camp—seem meager enough. Heretofore, they were sustained by the drama of revolution and the war. Now, it remains to be seen whether the promised paradise offered their children's children will be sufficient to compensate for their own life of hard labor and grinding monotony.

Just above the steeple of the old church in the Square, in front of Spaso, I can see the skeleton of the newest Moscow skyscraper. It's to go much higher, twenty-six stories, and it's to be quite rigid, no swaying in the wind like the top stories of the Empire Street. The newspaper *Pravda* assures its readers that no one can live comfortably at much greater heights than twenty-six floors above the ground, many New Yorkers being known to suffer from nausea and dizziness brought on by the constant movement of the buildings. One of our chauffeurs said there was talk of tearing down the church in the Square next year. That would be a pity, for it's very sweet, even in its decayed condition. The whole of Spaso Square must have been pretty at one time. There are still a number of the old houses left—that is, there are bits of them left, for each day they crumble more and more.

These houses of the old bourgeoisie were all of much the same pattern, with pseudo-Greek temple façades, the front often of one story and a half, with a more substantial structure behind. Entrances are at the side, carriage entrances that once had wrought-iron grilles; a few still hang on rusty hinges. There are small gatehouses and outbuildings, and stables and sheds in the court. Larger houses belonging to the nobility or rich merchants were similar in design, often with added wings in the classical manner, and deep gardens. Now the gardens have been built over, and the courtyards are dirty patches of rubble and mud.

No pictures taken in our worst slum areas could be more dreary than the surroundings of Russian dwelling places. Even when new apartments have been put up, no provision has been made for landscaping around them, and yet every man, woman, and child seems to have a craving for living green things. They carry sad little bouquets of weeds and grass as they walk about the streets, and every window I pass is filled with tortured little plants growing out of milk bottles or tin cans. Some are so choked with these straggling plants, I wonder how any air at all gets through to the people inside.

Even now, when it's quite cold, the eagerness of the Moscow citizens who flock into the public parks shows they crave space and sunlight. But even the parks are badly kept, especially the lawns. I don't remember having seen a lawn mower all summer, not even in a shop window. Except for the lawns inside the Kremlin, the only ones that look moderately neat are those alongside the outer walls, laid out in what was once the old moat. Here are tidy beds of flowers—cannas, snapdragons, petunias—and well swept paths with wooden benches, where the young mothers and grandmother *baboushkas* sit with their babies wrapped tight in layers of blankets.

There are almost no baby carriages in Russia, just as there are almost no bicycles. The reason for the latter's absence may be the roads, as well as the high prices, for rattling over the broken cobbles of the side streets would be destruction to any machine. Only the main streets are well paved, and even those have a thin layer of asphalt that has to be constantly renewed. Sidewalks are very bad, far too narrow for the most part, and, except in the center of town, along the boulevards and around the Kremlin itself, are very broken and badly patched.

The long winters are somewhat responsible, for the snow and ice lie for months on the ground. But householders are required to keep their walks as free as possible and it's a constant battle, waged with twig brooms and primitive shovels, even to keep the surface properly swept. The brooms are like those we use for hearths, and, day after day, hour after hour, old women sweep the streets and squares of the city, brushing dust in the summer and snow in the winter.

I've seen mechanical watering carts but never street cleaners. Garbage wagons are fairly neat, the lids shutting tight like large hoppers. The Moscow garbage problem, however, cannot be very great for everything possible is consumed. I have counted the cans waiting for collection in front of large apartment houses. In no case have I seen more than three or four, and I've watched women come down with a handful or two to dump inside, hardly the amount we would dispose of after each meal.

Postmarked Moscow   *November 13, 1949*

WE HAD PLANNED
to have a picnic at a monastery just out of town, but this morning the light froth of snow that fell last evening has evaporated into mist and murk, and it seems wiser to lunch at home and play badminton in the ballroom. The latter sport is a lifesaver, as I can see that exercise will grow more difficult out of doors.

I've provided myself with all manner of footgear for walking in wet, and snow, and cold, but it's not too comfortable even so. The footgear I bought at home, but waited to buy my winter headgear, and yesterday I purchased a most convincing Russian hat, a round fur turban of mouton to match my brown coat. I look a little like Anna Karenina's mother in it, but it is warm and tight on the head and should protect me against wind and cold. Suzy might not approve, but I am quite pleased with it.

Ellen Morris took me to the Mostorg, the B. Altman's or Marshall Field's of Moscow. There was a great crowd at the millinery counter, but we pushed our way in. After I made my choice, a disappointment to the saleswoman, who had hoped I would buy something finer than the hundred-and-thirty-ruble model I selected—that's $32.50 in our money and quite expensive enough, I thought—I looked back to see all the other women asking for the same hat. The fashionable foreign lady had given the lead! The business of head covering for women is all important here. In the summer young girls go bareheaded, but a kerchief is still the mark of decency and no older woman would be seen in public uncovered. Perhaps it's a leftover from early Oriental influences. I always held it against Saint Paul that he insisted women cover their heads in church; but then, he had a real bias against our sex.

In spite of loud insistence on equal rights in the Soviet Union, so far as hard work is concerned women get the short end, and there does seem to be a kind of Oriental taboo about taking wives to social functions. In restaurants, too, there's a preponderance of men, and, when women do appear, they are usually young, so it seems the older generation are left home to mind the house and the children. When I say "older," I mean women from fifty on, for Russian women age fast, their life not being easy at any time.

What a pity that none come to our parties here. As late as 1947 and 1948, while Bedell Smith was Ambassador, certain ones used to come—artists, writers, musicians, scientists. Now all that has changed; the word has gone out and invitations are neither given nor suggested. But we do have pleasant times among ourselves.

Our dinner, Friday evening, another formal dinner of twenty-four, was a real success, although there was a very mixed bag of guests. We had the Luxembourg, Finnish, and Israeli Ministers, along with the French Chargé d'Affaires, the new British Counselor and wife, the Swedish Air Attaché, and several couples of our own. It was all very animated, and the Israeli gentleman, who speaks only Hebrew, German, and Russian, made me a low bow and said, through George Morgan's interpretation, that it was a well-recognized fact in Moscow that the American Ambassadress, Mrs. Kirk, belonged by right and spirit to the younger set! Next Wednesday, we have another party, which will include the Norwegian Ambassador, lately up from a sick bed, and the Indian Ambassador, a distinguished philosopher, who will eat only a little rice and boiled vegetables, so the dinner may not be as gay.

Roger is in the midst of a terrific round of social activity, as three very popular members of the Embassy staff are leaving and there are young people's parties every night, to which, in spite of the Minister's remarks, we are not always invited! Our own parties, combined with the theater and the ballet, leave us very few evenings free, and the time passes more quickly than I would have supposed.

Last night, we went to the opera to see *Prince Igor,* a very colorful production with marvelous Tartar dances in the last act. Dad's little men were delighted; one muttered so to John Keppel as we went in. I'm sure they must welcome a night's entertainment, for otherwise they sit, three of them, in their small car outside our gates, while one keeps watch on the pavement. They seem a fairly cheerful lot, however, and I almost missed them when we were on vacation.

I wished I had had them to push the crowds aside when I went shopping yesterday. I returned to the Mostorg, for Ellen told me it was a sight to see the people thronging in to buy the newly arrived Czech-made shoes. Sure enough they were lined up in the aisles in long queues, and the stairs were as jammed as those leading from a suburban train platform at rush hour. The shelves seemed full of goods, but everything displayed was of such uniformly bad quality and taste that they looked like the prizes offered in a honky-tonk shooting gallery.

I passed the kitchen utensil counter and was thankful I had laid in a supply of pots and pans in Belgium, for these poor tin jobs looked as if the bottoms might burn out with the first using. Goods from the satellite countries are just beginning to appear all over Moscow; generally speaking these are of much better grade than anything made here, but even so, they're not top grade. I've never seen anything that is better than bargain-basement level.

The same is true in the food shops. Essentially, much of this food must be good but it's so badly prepared and presented for sale as to be unappetizing. We use a great deal of canned goods at Spaso, and our cooks are delighted with what we brought in. Last night, we had an excellent lemon pie made of synthetic lemon powder. Even that abomination of all time, canned spinach, is not too bad when successfully seasoned.

Our meats in the deep freeze keep well, although we must always be on the alert for failure of current or breakdowns in the mechanism. Then there is scurrying in the basement, and chickens and chunks of roasts are hurriedly shifted to iceboxes and back, as carefully guarded as money being transferred from one bank vault to another.

It's easier to come back here than I thought. Before I left for France, I dreaded the return—so different from the first time when there was the excitement of the adventure and a kind of spirit of dedication. Now both are still there, but tempered with the certainty of a comfortable, fairly secure daily life. We have no personal anxieties, provided our health remains within the bounds our Embassy doctor can handle. Our servants are good enough, the food is sufficient, and our living quarters are adequate and well heated. Our Embassy staff we know and like. Roger is with us, and the two men who live here in the house are congenial companions. Even so I thought it might be hard to come back and leave behind the familiar aspect of the civilized world, but I find myself more reconciled to the months ahead than I had thought possible.

I find I am interested in being back, because the country itself is interesting, and because I want to know more about it and about its people. Even though we have so few contacts with Russians, just being here allows us to absorb the feel and look of the place, and one reads in the faces of the people much that cannot be put into books or even in accounts one hears outside. Gradually patterns emerge, patterns of thought and of behavior, and it is especially useful to sort these all out and compare them with those of the worlds beyond the Curtain.

Postmarked Moscow   *December 3, 1949*

OUTSIDE DAD'S
window, the thermometer sticks steadily at eight or ten above zero, and the snow has settled down over the city. Snow is becoming to Moscow; even Custine said in his letters from

Russia, *"Je comprends qu'on visite la ville l'hiver. Elle parait mieux sous six pieds de neige."* Six feet of snow does improve it, no end, wiping out a lot of the dingy ugliness and giving light to the landscape. It must have been a great sight when the churches were gaily painted and the domes gilded. Today, only about forty have been restored and, even so, the gilt is a little thin.

We went, last Saturday, to a vesper service in the big cathedral. There are no seats in Russian churches, and the people were crammed in so tightly it was all one could do to stand —mostly old people and mostly old women, but there were more men than I should have imagined, and all appeared devout. They looked very poor, and the line of wretched beggars at the door seemed a part of the whole scene.

The entire ceremony appeared unreal; the masses of shuffling worshippers were like crowds brought onto a stage in some great play. All the service takes place behind a screen, so that the congregation has no direct part in it. There is almost constant singing, first from one side of the church, high up from a balcony, then from the other, curious minor—almost dissonant—chants, sometimes sounding like wails. There is a tremendous show of gold and glitter, ikons placed over ikons (most of them very bad paintings), immense chandeliers and huge candlesticks, lights everywhere. Perhaps it's the warmth and the light and the glory that attract the people, especially those who cannot pay for other glimpses of beauty, but the churches are never empty. Services are held several times a week, and each is as crowded as the one we attended.

I am persuaded of the essential religiousness of the Russian people, and think it obvious that the Government has taken advantage of this deeply rooted characteristic to channel it toward the cult of Lenin, Stalin, and the Party.

One of our colleagues, supposedly very leftist-minded, told me of attending a concert the other night—the closing concert of the Soviet Academy of Composers. "It was a great disillusionment," he said. "There were symphonies led by the foremost Russian orchestra leaders, Prokofieff was there, and Shostakovich played his new composition, the one intended to reinstate him in the good graces of the Politburo. It was a musical ode to Stalin's Reforestation Program! All these men, and the men and women who listened to them, knew what good music means, they had made it themselves, and all of them were there to witness the public prostitution of their art. The look on their faces was tragic, and the sounds were such that I never want to go to a modern Russian concert again!"

This complete levelling of art in all forms—painting, architecture, music, household decoration, clothing—cannot be emphasized too much or too often. It's all done by political dictum, which insists that every thing be within the comprehension of the masses, but which imposes on those masses vulgarity of taste and mediocrity of expression—not even honest vulgarity, but a tawdry, cracker-box prettiness that smells as bad as their synthetic perfumes. These perfumes are frightful; they have a touch of patchouli, nutmeg, and mace, but mostly dead mouse, about them. The hotels reek with the stuff, so do the more elegant shops, not to speak of the Generals' wives you pass on the streets.

Two or three unfortunate families belonging to our Embassy and many of our colleagues must live in hotels, and these are dreadful places. There is only one modern one, the Moscow Hotel, now reserved for party big shots and distinguished Communist visitors like Paul Robeson or the Dean of Canterbury. They make great claims about this hotel and say, of course, it is far better than the Waldorf, in New York. Actually, it's more like a second-class commercial hotel at home, the kind where the Kiwanis Club meets on one side of the main lobby and the Lions Club on the other. Ours, I am sure, are better lighted, better furnished, and certainly cleaner.

The three other hotels, the National, the Metropole and the Savoy, are dismal spots, dusty and musty, with remnants of pre-Revolutionary trappings that haven't been aired or even shaken out since 1917. Our young people who are assigned rooms in these places are good sports and make do with what is given them, but it can't be too pleasant especially as, added to everything else, there's the certain knowledge that there are listening devices in every room and the hotel personnel is watching and reporting on all that happens. We've no choice but to put our extra officers into hotels, for the Soviets never give us enough housing space for our needs; so, if our Government decides the Embassy staff requires so many people, into the hotels they must go, cooking in their bathrooms and piling their belongings in packing cases along the walls.

It's hard to convince the Russians, the Burobin officials, that we need more apartments, for they themselves are used to community living. The new blocks of flats going up all over town are divided into four- and five-room apartments, that's true, but each one is designed to accommodate several persons or families for which there will be one bath and one kitchen, these placed at the end of the flat to be accessible to all. No one speaks of "his" house or apartment—one says that he has so many square meters of home space.

The daughter of the French naval Attaché—the one foreign student from our group at the Moscow university—told me that her comrades asked her, when she said her sister was getting married, in France, "Which family will she live with, his or hers?"

There is no question of a young couple's setting up housekeeping for themselves; or, at least, that would be the exception. There is simply not enough housing space, nor money to pay for it. Even when the babies come, the grandmother, the *baboushka,* takes care of them, and the parents carry on with their work.

This French girl is finishing her fourth year at the University. She is a clever girl and seems to have managed to hold her own with her classmates. I asked how many students there were in the Moscow University. Ten or twelve thousand, she told me, most of whom receive pay from the State. This pay varies with their marks, and, if their marks are too low, stops altogether. Students are chosen from medal-winners in the lower schools, with a very small number of others who must pass a very stiff entrance examination.

The course is a five year course with a great number of subjects required. Classes are two hours long, with discussion periods instead of recreation breaks. On graduation, the student is assigned to three years of practical work, in any part of the Soviet Union to which the Government decides he or she must go. Naturally there is fierce competition for good posts, and Party influence often enters the picture, the politically undesirable getting the worst of all.

The hardest workers of all among the students are the Komsomols, for they must give extra time to Party meetings and do propaganda work in factories and farm cooperatives, all the while keeping up with their studies. Lodging is provided for those students who cannot live at home, and their meals are taken at special cheap restaurants. Helene Pelletier, my French friend, elected work with the Russian Language Group as her major course. To complete this, she must study seven languages in her five years: Russian and Russian philology, old Slovan, Ukrainian, Polish, Czech, German and English and pass satisfactory examinations in each one. She says that as there are so many subjects to be covered, much of the work is cramming and learning by heart and there is little time for individual thought or research, especially as all courses must be accompanied by a lengthy and exhaustive study of Leninism and Marxism, which must be perfectly mastered.

The chief recreation of the students is the theater and the ballet, far more than drinking or dancing parties, and the poorest of them find money to buy cheap seats for entertainment a night or so each week. Some of the students are married, but I gathered that romance did not figure large in their lives. Russian approach to sex is more casual than sentimental, or so our Embassy young men tell me.

Postmarked Moscow   *December 7, 1949*

OUTSIDE IN THE
Square there's almost a Breughel scene—scores of children playing, dark spots moving against the snow. The children are the

best part of Russian life, and it's strange to see them so swaddled and wrapped as infants, so free as children, and so mentally swaddled and wrapped as adults. Usually its an old *baboushka* who goes out with the baby in her arms. Quite often the child has a pacifier in its mouth. I've rarely heard one cry. Tiny children who can walk are stuffed into fur coats that reach to their heels. They look like little animals, with bright eyes shining out below hooded caps. I saw one yesterday in a red-fox outfit that made him resemble an angora kitten, and another in a blue fur-bordered mantle that came straight out of *Boris Godunov.*

Actually, these winter costumes are becoming to the Russian type, grown-ups as well as children. Some of the men wear magnificent fur caps, Army officers especially sport high ones of gray astrakhan. Many women wear fur coats, but they are badly cut and the fur itself looks of poor quality. The general effect, however, is an improvement on the usual drab clothing one has seen all summer and fall.

No slacks are worn. Even the women working in the streets wear skirts, and long hair is also the rule. Many of the bobby-sox age go in for the most complicated system of braids, laced and interlaced, and the ballerinas wear tightly pleated coronets. At the opera and the theater, one occasionally sees women, expensively dressed according to Russian standards. They seldom wear long frocks, but their skirts are longer than the average. and the materials are satin or velvet, black or plum or wine color, and invariably they trail a silver-fox fur over one shoulder. Between the acts they walk around and around the lobby with their escorts, usually high-ranking Army officers, with now and again a pause in front of the buffet selling ices and bright-colored drinks.

Sunday night we went to hear the Red Army Chorus. The audience was less refined than at the Bolshoi and more unrestrained in their enthusiasm, stamping and shouting approval of their favorite songs and dances. It's an immense men's chorus, accompanied by wind instruments, a dozen or more accordion players and guitars and balalaikas. The noise is impressive. We sat in the tenth row and were nearly blown out of our seats. I was sorry that there were not more soldier songs. The ones they did sing were great fun, but the rest was straight Party stuff, hymn after hymn to Stalin, to the International Students' Union, to the Democratic Youth, etc. The dancing was fantastic, grand leaps into the air and more knee jerks than you could imagine. I came home quite breathless, dry in the throat, and sore in the legs, just from watching it. No one enjoyed the performance more than Dad's bodyguard, who roared with delight throughout.

Postmarked Moscow   *December 13, 1949*

THE WORLD LOOKS
sodden gray outside. Most of the snow has melted, and the remnants have frozen over into a dirty smear of ice. I hope that we will have a fresh fall for Christmas, for Moscow looks dreary indeed without its winter coat. The shops are quite bright with trees and tinsel ornaments, all presided over by Grandfather Frost, a white-bearded fellow in a long sparkling overcoat and cap, the Soviet counterpart of our own Santa Claus. There seems no thought of presents for grown-ups; the preparations are all for the children, but toys are expensive and of poor quality. It's not Christmas that will be celebrated, but New Year's, for naturally the Soviets have abolished the official celebration of Christian holidays, and the trees are New Year's trees, not Christmas trees.

I am going shopping tomorrow for ornaments for our own tree, which will be set up at one end of the big central hall in Spaso. Like everything else in this house, it must be large to be effective; and Morris, our expediter and commissionaire, has promised to bring me a huge one, along with masses of fir and pine to put about the rooms. Morris is a curious little man who looks like the vendors of naughty post cards at Pompeii, and who is quite as capable as they in finding you anything or anybody you want. His rakeoff, like theirs, must be well over fifty per cent but he is a useful adjunct of the Embassy.

Among the less shady episodes of his past was a period of stewardship on an ocean liner, during which time he rose to the dizzy rank of Captain's private table steward. Now he darts about Moscow, selling and buying anything that comes to hand—including us no doubt! But he is an ardent admirer of Roger's, and assures me that the Embassy workmen are astonished to see the boss's son holding down a job, and a hard one, "I tell them that's the way you learn to be a boss in America," said Morris.

It was Morris who provided us with our new assistant cook. The old one was a dreadful creature, left over, like the black beetles, from some other regime. He was dirty, impolite and a sly sort of spy, his spying taking the form of spreading lies about the other servants, rather than about the masters, and there was endless trouble. He was also dishonest and made away with untold amounts of good American food, which he either ate, or sold on the black market. Finally, even Morris complained, so we decided that something must be done about him and off he went with Morris's assurance to us that another cook would be found to replace him.

A stout lady of cheerful aspect is now installed in our kitchen. This makes two very stout ladies there, and I hardly see how there is room for them both in front of the stove, but all seems peaceful for the moment below stairs, and food supplies have ceased to dwindle. That is, they dwindle a little but the little is the traditional amount.

It's a job to keep everyone happy, for these Russians are intensely jealous, one of another. No kind word, no present, must be given to one without giving to all, everyone must share and share alike, not because it's the new Soviet philosophy, but because they are really children, much like our own Negro servants of two generations ago.

WE HOPED FOR A
Christmas snow and here it is, deep, deep, snow. Late last
night and early this morning, the *dvorniks,* the house men
and women, were out with shovels and spades, shoveling,
scraping, shoveling, for the law says that sidewalks and streets
must be cleared within a few hours after the snow has fallen.
As I have said before, the implements they have to work with
are fairly primitive. In some cases, the twig brooms, already
worn out in struggles with the summer dust, must be used,
and, as the snow keeps falling, it's a losing fight. But Russian
patience does not question the elements or the task in hand.

Happily, no one has suggested that parades be held for
Stalin's seventieth birthday tomorrow, December 21, although
there are bound to be celebrations of some kind. Standing
for an hour or two in Red Square would be difficult in this
weather, though there's been no falling off of the queues waiting to visit Lenin's tomb. I read they have found a new embalming method, and that Soviet technicians are already at
work on Dimitrov, in Bulgaria. I daresay they are wise to try
these things on satellite heroes before operating on their own.

At an appointment he had with Gromyko, the other day,
Dad asked if there would be any special festivities for the
anniversary tomorrow, but the Minister said he had no information. There was some rumor of a diplomatic reception
but, so far, we have received no invitation, although such
invitations are rarely sent until the day before the party. The
Russians take no chances on their guests, and lists must be
checked and doublechecked. I had hoped that this time we
might be asked to the Kremlin itself, but suppose that honor
is now reserved for the faithful.

Some say that General Mao is staying on for the birthday,
prolonging his visit, but aside from a cautious announcement
of his presence in Moscow, and posters showing the solidarity
of Soviet and Chinese youth, there's been no other publicity
about his presence. We did hear that a special performance

of the ballet, *Red Poppy,* would be given at the Bolshoi to-morrow night with all the Party great to do honor to Stalin and the ruler of his newest outpost of empire.

Red Poppy is a story of the opium traffic and the wicked machinations of the American and British imperialists. It's not a new ballet; there was an original version emphasizing the decadence and degradation of the Chinese people, but those who have seen both old and new say that it's been considerably revised. The Americans are now the villains and the Chinese their victims; and to the opium traffic is added that of gun running, with wooden cases marked *"Made in U.S.A."* carried in by coolie work gangs.

Even in the opera *Boris Godunov,* a final scene of the People's Triumph has been added to allow the waving of pitchforks and flaming torches by an embattled peasantry while frightened boyars huddle behind even more frightened priests. In spite of any ideological additions, *Boris* is magnificent; and the production as given here in Moscow is one to end all others. The coronation scene is incredible, a blaze of light, gold, jewels, clanging bells, processional chants. Many of the costumes are authentic vestments taken from the imperial and church treasures, and the Russians wear them well. Beards and boots, tiaras and flowing robes, suit them admirably.

We've one more personal triumph chalked up now. The Gromykos came to lunch with us last Saturday. We'd meant to ask them some time ago, but waited until Gromyko told Dad that Madame was quite strong again after her cure in Carlsbad. I wrote a polite note to her, suggesting a choice of dates and saying that it would be quite a small party, our own family with the Minister and First Counselor, and we hoped that they would bring anyone with them they chose, from the Foreign Office.

Days passed without response, then the Foreign Office rang to say that the Minister and Madame Gromyko would be pleased to accept for Sunday, and that anyone we chose to invite from their Foreign Office would be quite agreeable. Dad decided to ask Pastoev, the pleasant-spoken young man who had come with Vishinsky and acted as his interpreter. George Morgan telephoned the invitation, adding that the Ambassador and Mrs. Kirk hoped that he would bring his wife. Pastoev thanked George and said he would let him know. Word came back that Mr. Pastoev would come alone.

We set the hour for one-thirty, and the guests arrived very promptly. We received them in the blue sitting room, where there was a bright fire, with cocktails, sherry and tomato juice on a table against the wall. Only Pastoev took a cautious glass of sherry, the Gromykos sticking severely to tomato juice. Pastoev was in Foreign Office uniform, Gromyko in a dark suit, while Madame Gromyko wore a small astrakhan fur hat and carried a little muff with her dress, which was carefully and expensively made of a style and cut reminiscent of my Great-Aunt Fanny, who died in nineteen hundred and twenty at the age of eighty-seven. It was plum silk, encrusted with medallions of embroidered velvet, the cuffs and neckline piped with the velvet, the whole relieved by a jeweled pin in the form of a gold-and-diamond bee. Gromyko, seated on my right, ate very little, no doubt because he was due at a Kremlin banquet for Mao an hour later, but she tucked in a good lunch and seemed to enjoy the party very much.

Conversation was a bit strained, but very correct in tone and subject. We spoke of the Gromykos' son, just Roger's age, who had been with his parents in the States for several years. I asked his mother if he kept up his English.

"That is very hard for him," answered Madame Gromyko. "Sometimes he locks himself in his room, just to talk English to himself. You see he has no one to talk with here."

What a foolish situation. Normally, one could have said to her, "But send him here to us. Roger would so like to meet him and talk with him." At every turn, however, one has to remember that it's impossible to say or do the natural normal thing—and that's hard for friendly folk like ourselves.

THERE WAS A
reception last night, after all, a full dress affair even more
formal than the one of November 7. I really enjoyed myself;
at least I felt more relaxed about it—I knew what to expect,
and could appreciate all the sights and single out the personalities. The party was held in the same house as before, the
Foreign Ministry's reception house.

This time, Vishinsky, having returned from New York,
received with Madame. She looked as unhappy and as ravaged
as ever and had a dress made of the same bolt of material as
Madame Gromyko's luncheon costume—a mistake, considering she dyes her hair mahogany. But she wore a fine string
of pearls, a lovely old diamond spray pin, and magnificent
earrings. She greeted me most cordially and I presented the
other ladies of our Embassy who had been invited to the party.
It appeared to be her one outing in the *haut monde,* and she
seemed to be quite excited and enjoying herself immensely.

The rooms were filled with Chinese—Mao himself was not
there—and there were hordes of plainly dressed men and
women who must have been delegates from the satellite countries. Late in the evening, someone pointed out Rakosi, from
Hungary, a man who looked like a toad and reminded me
of Streicher, the Nazi Labor Chief, whom they hung at
Nuremburg. I shook hands with a Slovak lady in elaborate
peasant costume; all the others wore European dress.

I met, too, the Bulgarian Ambassadress, and inquired so-
licitously after her health. This seemed indicated, as she had
kept us waiting for an hour at a dinner at the Italian Embassy, and then had never turned up at all. I said we had
missed her and hoped she'd not been too ill.

"Not at all," she answered. "There was a misunderstanding
about the invitation."

As that happened to be the day Rostov came into court in
Sofia and took back his confession of guilt, I daresay she had
been summoned to the Kremlin to do a little explaining.

All the Marshals were trotted out again in their blue-and-gold, and it was altogether quite a glittering affair. This time, Dad made no speeches, one such being enough for the winter, and the general tone seemed confident and cordial all around. Of course, these people feel confident; things are going well for them, and they still expect the West to crumble into economic decay; meanwhile all China is falling into their lap, and, with the exception of Jugoslavia, the Balkans are being tidied up to suit their taste. Right now, they can afford politeness. The Politburo members do not attend such functions as last night's. Undoubtedly, they had their own show, first, at the Bolshoi, where there was a big meeting, and later on a banquet at the Kremlin. It would take a Foreign Ministers' Conference to persuade them to mingle with us, and that's probably our only chance of being asked inside the Kremlin.

As we drove home, we swung around Red Square to see the illumination and the immense portrait of Stalin, which was suspended over the Kremlin by an arrangement of barrage balloons, floodlit from below. On a raised stage just in front of the Embassy offices, vaudeville turns were being run off and a man was leading a tame bear through his tricks. There was street dancing in Mokhovaya Square, mostly girls dancing with girls and men dancing with men. Luckily, Spaso House is far enough away so we are out of the celebration area, for the music was relayed by immense loud-speakers blaring out all through the middle of the city. Was Stalin even here for his birthday? We don't know.

Postmarked Moscow   *December 24, 1949*

THE DAY BEFORE
the Night before Christmas. The house is in considerable excitement, and so is the Embassy. Roger promised me a new typewriter ribbon, as this one is in shreds; but that must wait, like all else in the way of presents, for Christmas morning. At

the moment, he is entertaining his workmen at a yard party
—strong un-iced martinis, the nearest approximation to vodka
we can manage, sandwiches and cigarettes served up to them
in the courtyard of the Chancery. It should be quite a sight.

I believe the charwomen are also being invited, to supply
the ladies for the occasion; only the duty chauffeurs are excepted and they are to have their tot after work. The chauffeurs
are on call today, as the Christmas mail was delayed coming
through Helsinki and we expect seventy-five pouches late tonight. The couriers were held up by the press delegations
coming to celebrate Stalin's birthday.

Just yesterday, it occurred to me what a skilful substitution
these people had made of one birthday for another, Stalin
for the Christ child, and I am wondering if the man was really
born on the 21st of December, or if the date was picked
arbitrarily. Anyway, his picture and acres and acres of red
bunting vie with the Christmas trees in the shop windows,
and high over the Kremlin floats his portrait, a Soviet conception of the Star of Bethlehem.

We wrapped presents all yesterday afternoon. The situation
about presents is extremely complicated, as these myriad
servants, including the five laundry women in the basement,
must all be treated alike—any differences must be adjusted
in secret. This also goes for their children, and there are seventeen of these under thirteen. I had prepared for eleven, and
now Ellen Morris is out shopping for six more toys. We've
presents for our own Embassy children, in addition, and it's
taken yards of wrapping paper and sorting out to get names
and ages straight.

Then there are odd bits to think about, such as the books
entrusted to me by an old beau of Lady Kelly's, these to be
wrapped most tenderly; the *chers collegues* to be considered
—a card, a bottle of American whiskey, a toy for Chantal's
baby; cables to be sent; the new Turkish Ambassadress to be
telephoned to—she'd asked to call; I suppose, being a Turk,
she forgot about Christmas—two American lady chess champions, here for the Soviet tournament, to be invited to the
Christmas Eve supper and carol singing.

One of the hams from the deep freeze turned out to be bad and another had to be popped into the pot. An old cook, a pensioner, showed up in the kitchen, thereby throwing out the present count altogether; and, what's more, she's produced a thirteen-year-old daughter.

Dad telephoned from the office to say we'd received cables from the most unlikely people, and that he was snowed under with Christmas cards, which, having been held up and thoroughly examined by the Russian censor, were now released too late for us to send any back to people not on our list.

Our supper party is at eight-thirty tonight, lasting until eleven-thirty so as to give time, for anyone who wishes, to attend the midnight mass at the Catholic church. The tables are all set in the Great Hall, with provision for a quick shift so that chairs for our own church service at eleven tomorrow can be set up in the morning. Dad is to read the lesson. Brown sherry will be served to a select few in the Blue Room afterward, and then we will open our presents before lunch.

Postmarked Moscow   *December 27, 1949*

OUR CHRISTMAS

Eve party was a real success. We had a hundred and eight people; all the Americans in the Embassy; one lonely American fur buyer and his wife; the five press correspondents; and the two lady chess champions—in other words, the American colony of Moscow. The menu was ample—hams, baked beans, mounds of spaghetti, salads without lettuce, which is unobtainable here in winter, apple and mince pies and cheese. Dad made a good white-wine punch, and there was a flood of cocktails, before.

I wore a new red skirt and black blouse I bought in Paris, and strung Christmas tree balls into a necklace and put tinsel stars in my ears. The boys thought I was wonderful. I don't believe I've worked so hard or given out so much since my Red Cross tours. But it was all worth while, and I think everyone had a good time and for a few hours stopped feeling lonely and forgotten. One of the young Air Force Attachés played the carols, and we sang for an hour or so until a large group left to go on to the midnight mass. After it was all over, we went to work on the Great Hall, clearing the room and switching the chairs about to prepare it for church service next morning.

It looked swept and decorous when we came down, at ten-thirty, to dress the altar with our silver candlesticks and my best tea cloth. The congregation arrived promptly, a hundred and twenty-five, all nationalities. Our young friend who was to play the hymns overslept, so the Dutch Ambassadress obliged at the piano, and the British Counselor's wife led the singing. The clergyman, an earnest young man down from Helsinki, where he is chaplain of the English church, gave us a good simple sermon and was most gratified at Dad's reading of the lesson, which he did in admirable style. Altogether, it was a dignified and pleasant service. The brown sherry was duly offered to the Reverend and the various distinguished guests in the Blue Room, after church, and everyone left in quite a glow.

Our Christmas dinner was very nice. Afterward, we had great fun unwrapping our presents. Dad had ordered made for me the most beautiful palek box, coated with the lacquer that is a traditional Russian specialty, with a picture of the churches of Zagorsk on the cover. George Morgan gave me a book on Russian architecture, Roger had found me a marvelous book full of Russian illuminations, and the Morrises and John Keppel gave me six lovely old Dresden plates. It was a good Christmas, though we missed home and family. We'll hope for Christmas home leave next year, so that we can celebrate all together.

Tomorrow is our children's party, sixty, including our own, those from the other Missions, and the children of the Spaso servants. We have pieced together a movie program of animated cartoons, to be followed by ice cream and cake. Then, on New Year's Eve, there will be a big subscription ball. You can see how thoroughly this house is used, and perhaps you can guess what it means to our own Embassy personnel and to all the diplomatic corps.

Postmarked Moscow   *January 8, 1950*

THE NEW YEAR'S
Ball was like many New Year's balls, but with an added Moscow feeling. It was very very gay. The ballroom was decorated with swags of colored streamers, and a huge revolving glass ball in the middle of the ceiling; the punch brewed weeks before was excellent; the women wore their giddiest frocks. We managed to forget how far away from home we all were, until they opened a window at midnight to let the New Year in, and no sound came through—no bells, no singing, no whistles, only a draft of chill Moscow air. But we had a fine time, all told, and Dad and I went upstairs to bed leaving the party in full blast below, going on for another hour or more.

I was glad we had the prospect of our Leningrad trip ahead, for packing and going off somewhere gave us a real holiday feeling, although the weather turned bitter cold and only sheer determination made us persevere. Dad and I, Roger, John Keppel, and the two Morrises made up the party.

We started off on Tuesday night, Dad assuring me that I would find the promised "International sleeping car" most comfortable. Comfortable it may have been in 1903, which was the date of its construction—"new" international cars are of 1913 vintage—but in 1950 it creaked in every joint. I can well understand why Soviet trains proceed at fifteen miles an hour; greater speeds would be dangerous. The first station we passed was Klin, where Anna Karenina threw herself onto the tracks. I've not been yet to see the play in Moscow, for they give the role to a fifty-five-year-old actress and I almost prefer to remember Greta Garbo cuddling her face into a sable muff, in the movie version.

Most Russian stations look alike and the landscape did not change all the way to Leningrad. The country was flat or very gently rolling, there were large forest tracts, pine trees deep in snow, villages of log houses running down a single street, and sprawling factory towns whose wooden construction made them look like pioneer settlements in our northwest.

We had three compartments for our party; and Dad's four Little Men had two more, so we filled the car except for two of our couriers at the far end and a nervous looking Red Army Colonel next to them. Dad's guards had new fur hats, and warm collars to their coats. They looked very pleased with us, for they enjoy going about and welcome any excursion offered.

Each car has two attendants, one of whom seems largely to concern himself with keeping the samovar going at the end of the car. This is a most useful idea, as boiling-hot water for tea or coffee is always available. Tea they bring you in glasses set in metal holders; coffee we made by adding soluble powder to the hot water. There is no restaurant car on the train so one has to make provision for breakfast next morning, taking bread and butter and fruit juice. Sleeping wasn't too good, as we were hermetically sealed in and the car was steaming hot, the mattresses were thin and couldn't have been really comfortable, even in 1903, and I had an uneasy feeling there might be bugs about. However, the night passed and morning came, but not the dawn. The sun did not rise till ten-thirty, just before we reached Leningrad. Actually, on one day we were there, it rose and set between late breakfast and lunch. Truly the frozen north!

There was a large motor car and an Intourist guide waiting for us in the station, and our rooms were ready in the Astoria Hotel, a most impressive suite filled with more atrocious furniture than I dreamed existed even in Russia. There were plush-covered sofas, ornate tables, huge vases and bronze statues in each corner, a desk with an immense desk-set of carved wood set with deer and chamois horns, and a cabinet filled with dreadful knickknacks. The bedroom was much the same, the two beds covered with huge soiled satin quilts, the bathroom was large and cold, and only one hot-water tap worked, the one in the tub, and that gave out a brown trickle. For these elegant accommodations we paid some thirty dollars a day!

Dad's Little Men had a room next to ours, and one of them kept watch outside our door day and night. In the train, also, one remained on watch in the corridor, usually the same one, the junior of the lot, whom the others make do the dullest work.

We ordered lunch sent to our room for everyone, and then made our plans for the day. After an hour's drive around the city, which left us congealed, we went to the Hermitage for a quick look, planning to go back next day for a longer visit. It's a huge picture museum, one of the greatest in the world, and it was interesting to see that the pictures were all in place, hung in the same order and in the same rooms marked in our 1910 Baedaker. The museum is connected with the Winter Palace and with the old Hermitage Palace of Catherine II. It goes on, room after room, gallery after gallery, filled with the most astonishing treasures, more Rembrandts than one sees in Holland, a lot of Rubens, Italian masters early and late, all the Spaniards, the French, and a marvelous collection of Poussins. Only the so-called formalist school has been removed—from Manet on down, they've all gone. I believe there was once a fine collection of French Impressionists. I asked our guide about them and she answered vaguely:

"Those rooms are closed off. They are under repair. I'm sorry I don't know where the pictures are stored."

The Soviets have declared them decadent, and unfit to be seen, just as they did the superb collection of French paintings in Moscow, the Morosoff collection. We know they've not been sold abroad; they must all be packed away in cellars, waiting for later generations to find them politically acceptable.

Wednesday night, we went to the ballet to see *Red Poppy,* the Leningrad version of the propaganda ballet Roger and I saw here in Moscow, the week before. Dad had not felt he could go in Moscow; but so few people would recognize him in Leningrad, there seemed no objection. He enjoyed the dancing, and both Roger and I thought the production quite as good as in Moscow. The setting and costumes were less elaborate, because Government subsidies are not as big as those given the Bolshoi, but the corps de ballet was excellent. Actually, many of the best ballerinas, Ulanova among them, are graduates of this Leningrad school.

Thursday night, we saw the Pushkin play of *Boris Godunov* at the Drama Theater, and it was interesting to contrast it with the opera taken from the same story. The acting was remarkable, although here, as at the Moscow Art Theater, it's done in strictly classic tradition and makes me think of the Comedie Francaise, in Paris, as I knew it thirty-five years ago.

Friday noon, we saw a holiday performance of the Nutcracker Ballet that was enchanting. Many of the pupils from the school acted in it, the audience was filled with children, and it was a very gay, pretty affair.

Between theatrical events and return trips to the Hermitage, we went book shopping and came back with any number of prizes. The appetite for old books is not great enough in Moscow to have quite emptied the Leningrad shops, whereas the antique and commission shops are looted of goods, most of which have found their way south. It was amusing to see how we were followed on our expeditions by furtive, shabbily dressed individuals, poor cousins of Dad's Little Men, who hid behind pillars and in doorways in the most obvious manner. As the streets were empty and shelter scant, they had a chilly time darting behind us. When Dad came along, his own four rode the others off. We took most of our meals in the hotel, but dined one night in a small Caucasian restaurant, where we feasted off *shashliks* and caviar. I'm very glad I went, and I'm very glad I could see the place in the company of pleasant and enthusiastic friends.

Leningrad is a handsome city. I wish I might have seen it before the Revolution, for now one misses the *troikas*, the bells, gay shop windows, and people in the streets. It's a ghost city now, cold and deserted. The great churches are empty and shut, the palaces are vacant. The government offices closed. It's a dream, frozen in space, and like dreams, a little blurred around the edges, but with now and then a gilt spire rising distinct and bright against the sky. Built within a period of a hundred and fifty years, it has the integral quality of a super stage set.

There was great vision in the planning of the city, with its broad avenues, noble squares, and picturesque canals, and the river running through like the theme of a song. It took genius and daring, and faith in one's people and their destiny, all of which Peter must have had. It's a curious contrast with Versailles, which is the monument to the vanity of one man. There's vanity here, too, but of a different sort and of different inspiration. Louis XIV's vanity consumed him and his people, Peter's lit a torch for them. Leningrad may no longer be Petrograd, but even the Soviets claim Peter as one of theirs, and, while they may have abandoned his city, they've taken to themselves his dream of empire.

On another visit, we will hope to drive to Peterhof and Tsarskoe-Seloe and walk more about the city itself. This time it was too cold, one could stay out for only fifteen or twenty minutes without freezing toes or fingers. But I'm very pleased that we came in winter; I'm pleased to have seen the frozen Neva and the snow lying white on the roofs, a most convincing picture of what we imagine Russia to be like.

Postmarked Moscow   *January 21, 1950*

WITH THE THERmometer at a mere five above, we feel that spring must be on the way. It's been hovering between twelve and twenty below zero for the past two weeks, one night it plunged to thirty-five below, and that's cold in any language. The Indian Ambassador's nose was frostbitten the very day he was summoned to call on Stalin, a blow to his vanity, for he reported it very red and swollen. Ray Dayal, the nice Counselor of the Indian Embassy, told me that as the Marshal advanced to greet the Ambassador he extended his hand saying, "I am Stalin," as if the Ambassador might have any thoughts. Only Sir David Kelly, Dad, and the Indian have been received by the Marshal. The Indian Ambassador is a distinguished philosopher, a righteous man with strong principles and the disapproving attitude of a vegetarian saint. The contrast with Stalin must have been great and their mutual interests limited.

Yesterday, Ellen Morris and I went to see the Stalin birthday presents, assembled in two large museums that have been emptied of their contents to receive them. The presents are interesting, not only because they represent the workmanship of the people who sent them, satellites as well as Russians, but because the whole makes up a general impression of bad taste and sheer ugliness. Even in the case of the Czechs and Germans, people capable of such fine craftsmanship, the result is mediocre and uninspired. Only the native costumes, the occasional bits of porcelain or handwoven textiles, and the old embroideries showing special skills in folk handicraft, were pleasing to look at. The rest is mere vulgar display and it's discouraging to note that lower bourgeois art of the turn of the century seems to be the instinctive choice, not only here, but in all the countries into which the Soviets have penetrated and laid their hands upon.

From the eastern provinces there were rugs, exquisitely woven, the borders and backgrounds showing traces of old designs, used, however, to surround portraits of Stalin or symbols of the Party. Stalin's face was stitched into needlepoint; into panels of lace; carved in wood and stone—it was everywhere. Among the portraits, I was interested to see two of him with his mother, and this tied in with the dominant religious motif, for he seems to be taking on all the attributes of godhead. Even Lenin's personality dwindles beside his. In both pictures, the mother was looking in adoration at her son, much as another Mother is represented.

One of the favorite gifts seemed to be a desk-set, and there must have been scores of these in every possible material, marble, wood, malachite, gold, silver, crystal, every shape, every size. As Ellen said, you came away determined to keep your Parker 51 in your top drawer. There was a seven-hundred-piece set of china from the Heeren factory in Hungary, beautiful china sprawled with a loud gilt and crimson design. There was a massive casket from Latvia, so like a mortuary urn we thought the Letts must have sent it with that in mind. There were immense vases, etched with the pictures of the Politburo, from faithful Czech glassworkers.

There were garments of all kinds, furlined leather coats from the furriers' unions, wadded dressing gowns of brilliant satin bordered with sable, embroidered shirts, shoes of every description made to the measure of his suprisingly small foot, gloves, hats, walking sticks, umbrellas, and enough brief cases and hand luggage to outfit the entire Cominform. There was furniture, most of it pretty terrible, of the sort that used to be bought by rich bootleggers on Ninth Street in Washington.

There were monumental lamps with bright silk shades, crocheted bedspreads, a vast chest of linen, complicated machinery models, more complicated than impressive to any Western World's Fair visitor. There were shotguns, revolvers, knives, an entire arsenal of weapons, even to bows and arrows, spears and hatchets. The Finns had very cutely sent a model of a worker's flat, fully furnished with doll-house-size reproductions. Visitors were five deep around it, and we almost wondered that it was shown, for the contrast with what is offered the Soviet worker was striking. It was not luxurious by our standards, but by theirs it was stupendous.

All the while we were in the museums, there were parties of people being guided through the exhibits, and Ellen heard one woman explaining in the Korean section that every man, woman, and child in Korea had signed the pledge of loyalty in the bound books displayed. Each section had its collection of these books, with thousands of signatures, and you may be sure all those names are duly noted in the Kremlin files, even though they may represent but a small proportion of the populations involved.

Today we are going to a Soviet social function, only the fourth to which we have been invited, the others being my tea party with Madame Vishinsky; two receptions for the displomatic corps; and now this, a cocktail party in honor of the lady chess champions. It will be given in the lounge of one of the hotels, at seven-thirty in the evening. Afterward, we are going with Wally Barbour to dinner in the Uzbeg restaurant to eat *Shashliks,* roasted mutton on long spits. They are fond of giving the names of their various republics to the restaurants, but I can't see that the food differs at all. It's none of it very good, greasy and vaguely Near Eastern; only the caviar is really superlative.

The Georgian restaurant, the Aragve, where we last dined, is considered their largest and finest. The setting is white tile and the general effect is that of the ladies' washroom in the Pennsylvania Station. The Aragve head waiter is a sinister old man, with long hair parted in the middle and brushed straight down along his cheeks; his eyes are crossed with a nasty leer that is distinctly unappetizing. We hope tonight's experiment may be more successful than the last.

Yesterday, Ellen and I had an odd encounter on the street, odd only because it's rare for Soviet citizens to speak of one of us of their own accord. We were walking along Gorki Street, the broad avenue that leads through the center of the shopping district, down toward Red Square. A pleasant-faced woman came up and spoke to us in Russian:

"I heard you speaking English, but are you by chance Americans?"

Ellen answered that we were.

"I used to listen every night to the Voice of America and to the BBC; now I can no longer get either on my radio. I am very sorry for they were good programs."

She walked along a little way with us, and then said to Ellen:

"I read of your wonderful new drugs. Do you think there would be any possibility of getting some streptomycin. I have a brother, he is very sick, dying of tuberculosis. The doctors think he might be saved if we could give him the drug."

Ellen told her that unfortunately we had no way of helping

her. We were sorry, we wished there were something we might do, but surely her doctor must have his own supplies.

"I understand," said the woman. "It doesn't matter, some day perhaps better times will come."

She shook Ellen's hand and turned away. It was all very tragic. We'd no means of knowing whether or not the woman was sincere, and we couldn't have done anything if she had been, for such a gesture would have been too dangerous both for her and for us. For all we know, we were followed, and she took a risk even in speaking to us.

When we got back to the Chancery, we met our doctor and asked him what the situation was about new drugs such as streptomycin. It's not readily available in Russia, he told us; he'd heard it could be bought on the black market at a hundred rubles a gram, but that as much as forty grams would be needed for effective treatment. At the present dollar exchange, a hundred rubles amounts to twelve dollars and fifty cents (now $25.00). Four thousand rubles would represent a fortune to a Russian, and it's hardly possible that forty grams could be bought by any one person even if he had the money. In the ordinary way, you may be sure rare drugs are reserved for the fortunate few, and, the better your political standing, the better your chance of recovery.

Postmarked Moscow   *January 26-27, 1950*

THE PROSPECT OF a vacation ahead is truly exciting. I hope the world doesn't burn up before we start off. Certainly the Asian situation is none too good.

The weather has grown warmer, muggy in fact, and the snow needs recoating, for it's black now, and the city looks dingy. I'll be glad to be away during the period of thaw. No wonder these people yearn for color—they've so little of it in their lives—color and warmth.

In the opera of *Boris,* there's an extraordinary song sung by a halfwit beggar who comes on at the end of the Coronation scene, and again at the end of the last act. He sings in a strange, reedy voice—the song is almost a thin chant—telling of the sorrows of the Russian people; how sick and miserable and starved they are; no matter who their masters, it's always the same, their lot is misery and suffering.

So it seems, through the ages, and yet the race has remained strong and virile. They are a tough people, and their very capacity for suffering has given them strength, and infinite patience. When Dad had his last interview with Gromyko on the Austrian treaty, he asked him:

"How long, Mr. Minister, before we can hope to reach an agreement. This has gone on now for some time."

"That depends," answered Gromyko, "on the value you place on time."

Truly, this is the Russian attitude, and it is one we must recognize in all our dealings with the people.

Postmarked Moscow   *January 31, 1950*

I WATCHED WOMEN
at a new job today, loading garbage trucks. Garbage cans are high, with heavy covers, all alike, so I suppose they are issued or rented by the city authorities. I've rarely seen more than three in front of even the largest apartment houses, perhaps, as I've remarked before, because there's so little garbage in the Soviet Union. A sad sight, this winter, has been the occasional rubbish-picker one sees taking bits up off the street and stuffing them into sacks. Left-overs in Russia are poor enough. I've seen garbage pails, but never any trash cans. I can't think what they do with old papers—burn them probably for fuel in their *petchkas,* the stoves one finds in old houses.

It's interesting to check the housing of this city by counting the names listed over the doors. This morning, for instance, I passed a one-story house, eight windows across and five windows deep. There were thirty-two names on the board tacked over the front door; and, farther along, a smaller house of the same character, only five windows across and three deep, had twenty names. As these are old houses, and have obviously had no money spent on them since the Revolution, plumbing must be rudimentary, probably not more than one bathroom, at the most two, for the whole lot and, of course, one kitchen.

The housing situation is a definite factor in the marriage plans of the young people. Many prefer not to enter into formal marriage, for they have no possibility of setting up a home of their own, certainly not until they have a large enough family to justify so much living space. But they do marry, and somehow manage to get on with in-laws and their in-laws' relatives. It even happens, so one of the servants told me, that a man's divorced wife simply retires behind a curtain in the same apartment when he brings in a new bride. As she has no other place of residence assigned, she cannot be evicted.

Divorce is growing less frequent in the Soviet Union, and all the newspapers and magazine articles, even the new laws, stress the family's unity and its significance in the upbringing of children. As parents and children are now products of two generations of Communism, it's not so necessary to educate the children away from the parents, for they share the same experience and standards.

Early schooling—that is, a nursery and kindergarten schooling—is provided for workers' children but it's not required for those who can be cared for at home. For the little ones there's usually a *baboushka* available and, then, once out of swaddling clothes Russian children run about quite freely. Social restrictions are few, and any organized activities are arranged by the State, not by the parents. It's the State that decides, as the children grow older, which of them shall have dancing lessons, which will learn French or English, what children will wear to school, which of them shows enough promise for Komsomol training, which will go into technical school, and which to secondary school and to the universities.

137

Small children look happy and unconcerned. Later, their faces become one with the Russian pattern; one sees the difference at twelve or thirteen, in both boys and girls, for it's then that the State really fastens itself upon their lives.

Postmarked Moscow   *February 3, 1950*

VACATION PLANS

are coming along. Meanwhile, we must continue with the business of life here in Moscow. We have two lunches, a good-by party for John Keppel, who leaves for duty in Germany, and a more formal affair for the Turkish and British Ambassadors and their wives. The Kellys are going home for the elections. They stayed over to receive the Gromykos for lunch, the same kind of intimate function they attended here. Sir David told me that Gromyko left his coat and hat in the Embassy outer hall and their doorman, a loyal Soviet type, remarked on the fine fur and good Russian cloth. One of the young British secretaries looked at the label inside, and had the satisfaction of showing him the New York tailor's mark.

Clothes are fabulously expensive here, and for the average citizen the purchase of an overcoat is as serious as the buying of an automobile is for us. The whole family gathers at the shop and the matter is discussed at length. The same with shoes. A pair of better-grade, leather-bound, felt overboats, which men and women alike wear, costs what amounts to a month's salary for a stenographer or a clerk. It's hard to give exact prices in our dollars; it's more to the point to balance the prices against the income of the purchaser. The shoe problem is easier, now that supplies are coming in from Czechoslovakia, and the same is true of many other consumers' items, but this country is still pitifully short of what we would consider the barest necessities.

Average kitchen equipment consists of two or three iron or

tin pots; roasters do not exist, as there are so few ovens, and there are no broilers, all cooking being done on top of the stove. As flour is available only two or three times a year, bread is bought from the Government bakeries. Meal can be had to make *kasha* or porridge, and this, along with bread and soup, is the staple diet. Even black pepper is a precious commodity, and one of our sewing women asked for, and received, payment in kind, the kind being three bars of Ivory soap and a tin of pepper. She had done more than a day's work, but felt herself well paid. The average worker is always given one meal on the job; but again, this meal is bread and soup, quantities varying according to whether the work is manual or otherwise. The streetcleaners, all women—for men can't be spared for that work in Russia—are issued wadded cotton coats and felt boots. The coats do not come below their hips, and many wear thin cotton skirts. In this costume they are out from five in the morning, chipping ice off the streets, with the thermometer at from twelve to twenty-five below zero. Certainly a hardy race!

There are other regions in the world where conditions are far, far worse than in Russia; other parts of Russia and Siberia where the conditions are far, far worse than in Moscow. I don't mean to say that those I see here are as bad as those in China, India, the Balkans; what I do resent is that the Soviets claim that conditions are perfect. The Soviets claim this country to be the greatest and best in the world, and their people the happiest and best cared for. It's the hypocrisy and cynicism of the whole business that revolts me.

Postmarked Moscow   *February 11, 1950*

JUST TWO WEEKS
before we leave on vacation. It's snowing hard today, and I hope we have a spell of clear weather to follow so there will

be no trouble in our getting away, by plane. It's not so much the taking off, it's bringing the plane in here, as they've no proper ground-approach system.

John Keppel and the Service family left on Thursday, at five A. M., only to come down a few hours later at Vilna. They were in a Russian plane bound for Prague. No Russian pilot likes instrument flying, so he simply comes down if the weather gets thick. Any of us might enjoy coming down in one of the forbidden cities, forbidden to us, that is, if they let the passengers into town, but foreigners are always shut into waiting rooms or escorted, almost under guard, to a hotel and left there.

We were sorry to see the Services leave, but it's obvious that this post is not one for families of more than one child—and even then! The health, school, and recreation difficulties are insoluble. We have a small class of Anglo-American pupils, using the Calvert School method taught by an Embassy wife, and housed in one of the British Embassy buildings. It's not ideal, but it's the best we can do, as the Russians have now refused to accept any of our children into their schools, or even into their kindergartens.

The apartments available for our personnel have no more than two bedrooms, many only one, and there is no play space for children around any of the buildings, except the crowded courtyards, most of them more like car lots than playgrounds. The Service family lived in a house, the last single dwelling we have been able to rent, on the other side of the river. They met with disaster after disaster, ending with a fire from an overheated stove, the insulation for which they discovered to have been sawdust! The youngest child contracted dysentery, the eldest had a badly infected ear. No servants would come and go, so far away, and there was no room to house them on the premises. Altogether, it was an impossible situation and is typical of what happens outside of Spaso House and the big Chancery building, Mokhovaya. But, as there are three children in the Service family, they simply couldn't fit into one of the usual apartments. I think it was a wise decision on their part to take the children home.

We have asked Dick Service to come here to live. George and

Roger like him very much, and the Chinaboys are delighted, as he speaks fluent Chinese and can cope with their special and particular problems.

Yesterday I made my first subway trip with Ellen Morris. The Russians boast loudly about their Metro, and I must agree it's quite impressive. It was originally constructed by English engineers, from the Vickers Company, who brought in the machines and plans. The Russians have gone on to extend the system, lines are now being linked up, and eventually the whole city will be quite adequately serviced. It's a very deep subway, reached by long escalators that move very fast and are pitched very steep.

The stations are of gleaming marble and stone, super-lavatory architecture but lavishly ornamented with columns and lighted archways, bas reliefs, and bronze statues, all very dazzling, and calculated to be so, but clean, and efficiently run with obvious disregard for cost of upkeep or equipment. The trains are roomy and well-lighted, not too crowded at any time. The whole effect is good, and the authorities have reason to be proud of it all. No national organization at home, nor any private enterprise, could afford such lavishness, but it's an excellent psychological investment on the part of the Soviet Government: it's a promise of things to come in a brave new world that is very convincing.

Within Moscow itself, all public transportation is pretty good. The trolley-busses are numerous and well run, and they have replaced streetcars wherever possible. Private automobiles are rare, but there are taxis for those who can afford them. For most practical purposes—family outings, funerals, weddings, delivery, and moving, the Russians hire one-and-a-half-ton trucks, open trucks with slatted sides, sometimes with chairs and benches, oftener without.

Only twice have I seen a hearse on the streets, usually the funeral party sits or stands around the open coffin in the truck, riding with it through the streets, sometimes followed by another truck with mourning friends, plus a brass band. Many people are still buried in cemeteries, though the usual method and the cheapest is cremation. Embalming is reserved for the greatest of the Party great; the average Soviet citizen receives home attention of the most amateur variety, with a coffin brought back from the cash-and-carry store.

One very cold day, as I was walking back to Spaso from the Chancery, I saw an old man pulling a coffin along on a sled, bumping it up and down the curbs, no one taking any notice of him but me. When I arrived home, I asked Mike, the doorman, about it—I thought the body might have been inside. "Oh, no, Madam," said Mike, "he'd just been to buy the coffin at the furniture store."

"Can anyone go in and buy a coffin, Mike?" I asked. "Suppose you wanted to get rid of your mother-in-law—could you just quietly dispose of her and cart her away?"

Mike thought you had to present a certificate to buy the coffin, but I think it all sounds very chancey.

Postmarked Moscow   *May 26, 1950*

BACK IN SPASO,
after nearly three months away, to the Near East and home through Rome and Paris, where I left Dad and Roger to fly on to Moscow; a month in the States with two new grandchildren, one born on Palm Sunday and one on Easter day; a trip back to Europe by boat, very restful after such intense activity; then a journey by train from Paris to Stockholm; a flight to Helsinki, where Roger met me; and two nights more, by Russian train, to Leningrad and down to Moscow.

Here things seem to have changed very little. Chin has had the house cleaned from top to bottom—not perhaps to the very bottom, where feeble attempts were made to evict odd Russian lodgers, such as our doctor's chauffeur and wife, an old tailor and his family, and an upholsterer who works for the Embassy, not to speak of the steam laundry with its five gossiping laundresses. The tailor and the upholsterer have been moved

to American House; the others stay. It's a job keeping the
Spaso basements clean and tidy, and harder yet with Russians
living down below. No matter how thoroughly the place is
scrubbed and whitewashed, the insects manage to hide out
during the process, and they and the mice return next day.
In New York, I telephoned my shopper at Bloomingdale's
and asked:

"Do you carry mousetraps?"

"I'll find out," she answered. "How many would you need,
four or five?"

"Oh no," I replied, "let me have three dozen."

She was horrified, but produced them, and they met me at
the ship along with elegant presents from kind friends, baskets
of fruit and orchids. The Russian mice seem very resistant to
Russian mousetraps. Anyway, traps are hard to get here and
very expensive! I hope ours will do the trick.

It was good to see Dad on the station platform, looking very
cheery and so obviously glad to have me back. He and Roger
managed very well while I was away, but it's heartwarming to
have such a cordial welcome, not only from the family, but
from all the staff lined up to greet me in the hall.

It was a good thing I'd had my share of rest, for, the night
I arrived, Dad had a dinner of forty for the Brewster Morrises,
who leave for Germany this week, a terrible loss for us and
for the Embassy. Brewster's work is excellent, and Ellen's un-
failing enthusiasm and thoughtfulness for me and for others
has meant a great deal. The night after our dinner, there was
another at the British Embassy, and Saturday our armed services Attachés gave an evening reception for three hundred at
Spaso, loaned them for the occasion.

Exactly two Russians attended, a Lieutenant-Colonel and a
Commander. Other Russian military were invited and, true
to form, never responded and never came to the party. The
Polish military Attaché and his wife came, also the Czech, but
none of their Foreign Service personnel, nor did any of the
other satellites appear. As a party, it looked quite brilliant, with
all the uniforms, and white ties, and gay gowns. As usual at
such affairs, the ranking guests—heads of diplomatic Missions

and principle service Attachés—were shepherded aside and Dad and I gathered up assorted colleagues, ranging from the Indians to the new Dutch, the last Ambassadress quite pale with fright and confusion over the shock of Moscow life.

The new ruble exchange, now six to the dollar instead of eight, and by July to be four, is disastrous and prices are more fantastic than ever. I've been out this morning to nose about the shops. Swiss cheese—a Russian version of Swiss cheese—is $4.50 per pound, all first grade meat $4 to $5 a pound, and so it goes. A loaf of white bread will cost us 75 cents and, as for luxuries like caviar and vodka, they will be almost out of reach.

None of this affects the Russians, it's only the dollar exchange that suffers. Russian prices remain stationary but the result is the doubling of those prices for us. We suspect that the maneuver is designed to force foreign governments to cut their staffs, and to make life as disagreeable as possible for us all. It would be nice if we could retaliate but that seems difficult.

It's exasperating. In fact, my feeling in coming back to this benighted land is one of violent indignation. At Leningrad, the Intourist people were so blatantly rude, and the charges for accommodations so monstrous, it was maddening. Roger and I were there from six o'clock in the afternoon until eleven in the evening, just five hours. We were met by a car which took us and our hand luggage to the hotel; only three bags were carried upstairs, where we had a room and bath for those few hours; our bill did not include our dinner, for which we had purchased tourist meal tickets in Helsinki; we spent nothing extra during the evening and simply rode back to the station with the bags—the cost was $54.00. I was furious, but Roger said it might have been more.

The hotel room was dirty, of course, and there was no hot water, but the attitude of the people at the desk would lead you to believe the Waldorf was a roadside inn compared with their magnificent establishment. I got into the train and went to sleep, exhausted by sheer rage.

Sunday, we persuaded Dad to go on a picnic, and started forth in caravan with two cars following, filled with his Little

144

Men. With Wally's car and our own, we made quite an imposing party. We journeyed out along the edge of Moscow, where the landscape is reminiscent of the Newark flats, and turned into the grounds of an old monastery, the birthplace of Peter the Great. Not that he was born in a monastery, but there was once a huge wooden palace there, since burned down. We found a grassy slope, removed from a factory worker's picnic on one side and a herd of goats on the other, and installed ourselves, with the Little Men deployed, keeping watch, above. They stood at a distance, quite silent and respectful, but it does give one an odd feeling to munch sandwiches under their eyes.

It's good weather now, and I suppose Russia looks as well as it ever will, but even the spring has a hard time with this landscape. It was our last outing with the Morrises, and we felt very sad indeed. We left early, but rejoined them later on in Wally Barbour's apartment in Mokhovaya for a last supper of *blinis,* pancakes with caviar and sour cream, then left at nine for the station, Ellen clasping Vlady, her Siberian cat, in her arms. As she said, Vlady is the only Russian citizen in recent times to have obtained an exit visa for the United States! The station platform was crowded with friends. Leavetakings occur often here, but this one in particular was hard.

Now we have a quiet week. Preparatory to putting them away, I'm airing the woolen clothes, from which moths fly forth in an alarming manner. Soviet moths are very indifferent to camphor and sprays. The French Ambassador told me he found three in a box full of iron keys. They are a voracious lot. Outside in the garden, Theodore, the yardman, has been scattering plants and seeds with drunken abandon, so much so that I think there are bound to be turnips coming up amidst the petunias. That, some might say, is the charm of Russia!

We are putting the outdoor badminton court in order and hope to play, if the wind ever stops blowing. It comes in such gusts across the steppes, there are very few still days. In the Square in front of the house the school girls have put white pinafores over their smocks and the *baboushkas* sit, sunning the babies. The winter is finally over.

SATURDAY, WE

drove to the Dacha, the small country place, outside of town, which the Embassy hires for the use of the personnel. Our Information Service group had optimistically planned a picnic tea, which had to be abandoned, as it rained dismally. The hosts were discouraged, but it was pleasant to look at green trees, and I was glad to see the place had been put into some kind of order, for last year it reminded one of a deserted Catskill Mountain summer resort.

The road is very bad indeed and the drive takes nearly an hour, as we have to fight our way down one of the big industrial highways to get out of town. There is still some forced labor at work in the factories along the road, and there are high fences strung with wire around them, and guard towers every so often. Dad thinks we have a good chance for useful propaganda by exploiting the Russian statement that all their war prisoners have been returned. Certainly in Germany and Japan the poor families of these men know better.

As we came back into town, the road was jammed with hundreds of trucks going in the opposite direction—big, small, open, closed, most of them filled with furniture, though we saw one with a cow standing in the middle, the family sitting around it on chairs, and another with a horse. I thought it must be one of the mass migrations we hear about, but no, school was ended and fortunate Muscovites were moving to the country. There they will live in as crowded quarters as in town, and certainly in very primitive conditions, one water pump to a whole village street, little or no electric light, but anything to get out of the city for a short while, and out they go, bag and baggage.

Russians have so few possessions, a two-and-a-half-ton truck will take care of the family and the furniture—and the neighbors besides. Some of the trucks were obviously of American make, left-overs from our Lend Lease days, some still carrying American numbers on the rear. One of our men told me that we sent an entire assembling plant over here during the war as well as a great number of finished vehicles. The Russians might forget to paint out the numbers, but they would never acknowledge where the trucks came from. Right now, they are manufacturing trucks, themselves, in good quantity. They do this in preference to making private cars, for, trucks are the chief means of locomotion for their entire populace.

The British Ambassadress, Lady Kelly, was at the Dacha tea. She was just back from a trip to Vladimir, an old cathedral town, and looked a little haggard, for it had been a rugged journey. She is very keen on architecture and archeology, and anxious to see whatever she can of Russian churches, especially the early ones, so went off with her son, another woman and two young secretaries. She told me they rode all day and all night in a none too soft "soft car," made out fairly well at Vladimir itself, but, coming back, were put out to change trains and wait several hours at a town along the way.

Lady Kelly asked if she could go to a hotel in the town.

"Very sorry," the Intourist people replied, "this is a forbidden area. You will have to stay in the station."

Whereupon she was offered a bed in a kind of women's dormitory, a peasant was awakened and shoved off it, and there she stayed with a dozen others. The toilets, she said, were beyond anything, even the floors so deep in filth the smell stuck to your shoes and clothes when you came out.

"To be quite technical, my dear," said Lady Kelly, "I'm told the Russians never use a toilet seat but stand up on top of it, with the results that may be imagined."

For Westerners, it's the sanitary problem that's the chief drawback to travel in Russia! Again, we wouldn't criticize it so much if they weren't so smug and self-satisfied about it all.

Roger and a party of our young people have gone off to Novgorod by train, to fly back tomorrow from Leningrad. All of them speak Russian, and it's trips like this that give them their only opportunity to talk with the people of the country. Being young, they put up with rough travel conditions, but they do go armed with sleeping bags and their own food, plus halizone tablets to purify the water en route. They come back very soiled around the edges, but very pleased with all they have been able to do and see. It's true they are usually followed, once they arrive at their destination, but just the same they feel freer than in Moscow.

The latest story spread throughout the Russian and satellite press claims that Americans have scattered Colorado potato beetles over eastern Germany, in order to destroy the crops there. As our statistics show that the beetles were prevalent in Poland during all last year, it's an unlikely tale, but the Russians are playing it up full blast. They've even put out match boxes with pictures of the beetle on them, warning people of the danger and of what the wicked Americans have done.

They have their own insect problem. I'd hate to think that I would take away any Russian moth eggs in my things when I leave here, for the native species are violent. Already last winter's fur hats seem to have lost most of their fuzz, and I suspect the worst. Speaking of vermin, Chin is delighted with the Bloomingdale mousetraps. He made up a batch of tempting cheese sandwiches to put into them—result, eight mice in the traps this morning. He is triumphant.

Postmarked Moscow   *May 31, 1950*

R A I N   S E E M S
wetter in Moscow than any place else. Gutters are almost non-existent, and there are floods at every street crossing. The side streets are a mass of mudholes, and rusted, broken drain pipes spill water onto the sidewalks, so you need rubber boots for your morning stroll.

I think that every roof in Moscow must leak, for even the newest ones show patches on the tin. It's true the winter is hard, and snow and ice leave damage behind, but these people have no idea whatever of upkeep or maintenance. They let things go until repairs assume such proportions it would seem cheaper to tear down the buildings and start afresh. But they just slip on a little plaster and whitewash, throw a few shovels of gravel into the holes, splatter some waterpaint on the walls—for which there seem to be just two colors, yellow ochre and deep blue—and the job is done. A month later, it looks as bad as before, but no matter. Only snow can hide the horrors of the courtyards, but nowhere have I seen any efforts made to make these spots clean or attractive. And yet the children must play around the buildings; and their elders must look down on this squalor every time they go to a window or walk out their door.

With all this, the two newspapers, *Pravda* and *Izvestia,* carry long articles on the sad conditions of Western slums, and on buildings in America where hundreds of people must live on top of each other without light or air, the streets dark caverns below, where the sun never shines!

Two of our American Embassy families and a number of our junior colleagues are moving into a new apartment house, a kind of Diplomatic Ghetto which the Russians have been building for the past four or five years, and which even now is only partially finished. I've been to look at our apartments, the largest has two bedrooms so presents the same problem for families with children as Mokhovaya. There is no hot water in the kitchen, and none immediately available in the bathroom where a geyser is installed over the tub. This, mind you, to Russian eyes represents the ultimate in de luxe housing. They insist they are offering us their best. Any young couple living in a modern development at home, such as Peter Cooper Village in New York, would find the Russian version very uncomfortable.

The price, under the new ruble rate, will come to about four hundred and fifty dollars a month for the two-bedroom flat—two bedrooms; a small living room; same size dining room; bathroom; and a minute kitchen, with cupboard space almost nonexistent and no pantry or store closets; heat and light to be paid for in addition to the basic rent. These outrageous rents are set up for us, as we know that Soviet citizens, in comparable buildings, profit by some arrangement that enables them to obtain low-priced living quarters along with their jobs. The allotting of housing space is very carefully regulated by the authorities involved; various ministries and state factories control whole sections of town; and the ordinary citizen has trouble finding anything on his own account.

When he does get a place to live, he guards it jealously and will fight to the last for his few meters of living space, since loss of lodging can be worse than loss of a job. While we have no proper data on medical statistics, there do not appear to be great epidemics of disease due to this constant overcrowding. For us Westerners, the sanitary aspects of such living would be intolerable, but the Russians are a hardy race—and a patient one!

Postmarked Moscow   *June 1, 1950*

WE ARE HAVING visa trouble. Dad is going to see Gromyko tomorrow to ask about our Junior Counselor, Ed Freers, who will be George Morgan's replacement. He and his wife have been kept waiting ten weeks in Stockholm, sitting on their luggage. Then there is Mrs. Cannon, wife of our European Air Force Commander, and her friend, Jacqueline Cochran, the aviatrix, also waiting in Stockholm to come in to pay us a visit. Other Missions with more interchange of tourists and travellers put the squeeze play on the Soviets, when it comes to visas, but we have very few going and coming—only United Nations Russian personnel, who are special cases.

I asked Dad if he saw Trygve Lie when he was here. Only informally, he said, when Lie crossed the room at the Norwegian Embassy reception to speak with him. A space was cleared, and they were able to chat alone for a quarter of an hour, under the eyes of the Russian guests. Dad said that he found Lie sincere, and felt that he wished to make an earnest effort to straighten out the knots in the UN situation.

Our AP correspondent, told me, however, that Lie was never given the top VIP treatment by the Soviet authorities. He was met on arrival by Gromyko, not by any of the Politburo, his suite at the National Hotel was the second-best, instead of the best; and no effort was made to publicize him or to exhibit him in the honored-guest category.

As Lie came with the announced purpose of talking with the Russians, our own people and the rest of the Western Missions did not think proper to stage parties for him, with the result that the visit fell a little flat and, the last night, he was seen dining alone with his Secretary in a corner of the hotel restaurant, spending the rest of the evening picking up a few post cards in the lobby and waiting for the time when his plane left. None of this is by "happenchance," for every move the Soviets make toward foreigners is a calculated one.

If Mrs. Cannon and Jackie Cochran do manage to get in, we will arrange some gay functions for them and a few sightseeing tours. I would like to go back to the Kremlin, as I feel I know more than last year about Russian history; besides, I'm most anxious to see if any of the churches are open. Roger reported that those he saw on a trip to Novgorod had been very carefully repaired and restored. It's a pity they've let so many of their best ones go in Moscow. The little church in our square, once the parish church of the aristocratic quarter, grows worse every week, yet it's crowded as an anthill, and the lines of washing in the yard show how many families must live inside.

Wash lines in any country are pretty indicative of what is being worn at any season. On Moscow wash lines you see colored cotton knit undershirts, which must be used indiscriminately by men and women; women's knee-length colored knit bloomers, brown, bright blue, brick-red—no other underwear; a row of squares of thin cotton, cheesecloth or such, unhemmed, which must be either diapers or dishcloths; a few patched sheets; a tablecloth or two, and now and again, a coarse cotton lace curtain. That's about the lot, along with a few colored shirts and men's or women's jerseys.

Actually, there's very little underwear displayed in the shops, aside from the cotton knits, the rest being luxury items. And even the cotton bloomers cost 28 rubles, $7.00 now, in our money; and a slimsy rayon jersey slip, nile green or bright mauve, was priced at 80 rubles, or $20.00. Certain of our more observant young men tell me that the latest in chic is a black bra, especially noticeable when worn under a sheer blouse or light dress. Nightgowns I've never seen in shops; pajamas occasionally, but these all appear to be designed for lounging purposes or for use on train trips. I know men wear theirs on such occasions, for one sees in them in the sations; bold, multicolored stripes seem to be preferred.

Yesterday I went with Lady Kelly and Dad's Secretary, Margaret Sullivan, to the Soviet Fashion Show, something to which I have looked forward for many months. Each time I asked about it, I heard that the building, the headquarters of Mod, the ladies' garment center, was being "remonted," the collection was not ready, the public showings had not begun. Finally, a date was set, and off we went, first buying ten-ruble tickets at the door from a little old woman in rags. Thirty or forty Russian ladies, who looked as if they might have just stepped away from their streetcleaning jobs for an hour's recreation, were there before us, seated in a fine, big room which might once have been the salon of a pre-Revolutionary *couturiere,* with its white-and-gilt walls, mirrors, and a central platform surrounded by chairs in dirty dust covers.

We were placed in a front row, and waited some fifteen minutes before the room filled up and the show began. A blonde young woman in the ubiquitous short-skirted blue tailor suit, with a row of cellophane-covered campaign ribbons, came out from behind yellow plush curtains at the rear of the room and took her place on the platform. She first delivered a lecture on this season's trend in Russian fashions, emphasizing the longer lines, less sleeve padding, and the handwork details in embroidered motifs and buttons.

The first model appeared, a lady of fifty in a tan suit, definitely the mature matron's ideal. She was followed by a younger, stouter model, and two others less stout but hardly the Jacques Fath, Christian Dior silhouette. All four wore slightly soiled white kid shoes; one changed hers, during the showing, to a squeaking pair of black patent leather. With tailored suits or coats they had black or brown kid gloves, carried in the hand, not worn. Coats were on the tent style, all full length, with shoulders which, may not have been heavily padded, by Russian standards, but were square in the manner of ours of five or ten years ago.

Materials were shoddy and thin; but Margaret, who does dressmaking, herself, said the workmanship, the finish of the buttonholes, bindings and seams were carefully done. The designs, however, were all bad and the fitting, as applied to the women who wore the clothes, deplorable. Russian women wear their dresses very loose, as a rule, especially about the waist, which is generally belted in, showing the dress to be the same width at shoulder and hem. Numbers of the models were adaptable for various sizes, so that one pattern could serve an entire family of women and be changed by the addition of collars, sleeves, and curious peplums, which tied like belts round the waists. There were only two long dresses shown, formals, though neither had a décolleté neck, and both had elbow-length sleeves. The most striking and original costume of the collection was a maternity garment, worn by the youngest and most coy of the four models. This was a skilfully designed affair of printed silk, cut amply enough to permit the waist and skirt to expand by means of a series of small loops and buttons. But the unique feature of the dress was explained by the directress, who said:

"This garment can be worn before and after the birth of the baby. It is equally smart for street and house wear, and is especially adapted to the young mother's needs."

Whereupon the model demonstrated a flap pocket over each breast which unbuttoned to permit the necessary—"either on the street or in the home." Truly, the latest of many great Soviet inventions!

Unhappily, none of these dresses was for sale, only the patterns, so we had no way of knowing what were the prices of finished garments—very high, I imagine, as many had hand-embroidered collars and belts, cuffs or hems. The colors were disastrous, the plums and browns and purples we have seen all winter, varied with pale greens, dull blues, and confused all-over patterns of the summer materials. The skirts were longer than one sees in the street, the stockings worn with them were of medium color, nylons, but of thick, service weight. The hats were hard-felt casseroles.

Actually, the turn-of-the-century costumes one sees on the actresses doing Chekov and Gorki plays are by far the most attractive women's clothes to be found in Moscow. Some are of such fine cut and material they must be old dresses plundered, during the Revolution, from ladies' wardrobes. No one in the Soviet Union today could have cut them, and no one could be found to do the lace and embroidery, make the parasols, the feather boas, the chiffon cloaks, all a very far cry from the creations of the Soviet Garment Trust.

Postmarked Moscow   *June 6, 1950*

JUST SIX YEARS

ago today, Dad made the invasion of Normandy. Tonight, we drank his health and that of the Free World at dinner. As he sailed from Plymouth, he scarcely thought we would be toasting him in Moscow, six years later. Life rolls around in a surprising way.

The visas for our two lady guests have actually been granted, and we are waiting to hear if they have been received in Helsinki. There's always the old Russian game of slipping betwixt cup and lip: "So sorry, the visas must be in the office, but the Consul in charge is ill today and unable to sign the necessary papers." "So sorry, our consular office is closed three days a week. Naturally the visas will be issued as soon as the office opens again." As Gromyko said to Dad, "It depends on the value you put on time," and patience is the first thing one learns in dealing with the Russian people.

I've tidied the guest rooms as best I can, hung some pictures over last winter's leaks on the walls, robbed other rooms for tables and chairs. It's so long since a guest has appeared at Spaso to spend the night, it's difficult to remember how easily they came and went in Brussels, where it sometimes seemed as though we kept a wartime routine of one checking in as the other went out the door.

As luck would have it, the plague of annual vacations for the servants has started, one of the worst problems of Russian housekeeping, as each employee receives thirty days a year, and invariably and understandably wants these thirty days in summer. Result, we are always short some essential cog in the domestic wheel. I hardly dare bring up the servant question right now, lest Dad fly into a rage. We have been passing through the great Bread Crisis, which is still unsettled. Eighteen to twenty-two people eat three meals a day in Spaso —a veritable army, champing away on great quantities of food.

In addition to his meat, soup, potatoes, cereal, sauerkraut, and the rest, each individual used to receive eighty rubles a month for bread money, and he or she bought his own bread. At the new July ruble rate, this amounts to twenty dollars a month per person, for bread alone. It was bad enough when it was ten dollars at the old rate, but now it's impossible. We therefore decreed that bread should be made in the house. This is all very well, and the cooks are willing to do the work, but you can imagine how much flour it takes—or perhaps you can't. In order to issue the daily ration of one loaf per person, per day (and that's a very ordinary ration for a Russian), it takes one hundred pounds of flour per week. The flour that we buy from the Army in Germany costs us only five cents a pound, if we can bring it in with us.

But how to get enough flour, how to bring it in month after month? It's all very complicated, and completely exasperating. We have tried very hard to get rid of the laundry, but no Russian laundry would accept our trade, so the little women stay on, grumbling and muttering away in the basement, making no end of trouble, and always full of gossip and complaints. What they would like best would be for us to dole out the flour to them, instead of the bread. This they could always sell on the black market, flour being such a precious commodity, and a new book would be written about the iniquitous black-market traffic of the American Embassy. I must say, I have renewed sympathy for Marie Antoinette these days. Let them eat cake, indeed!

It's true, of course, that we must make every effort to hang on to the old servants, and to do what we can to compensate for the risks they run in working for foreigners. None is allowed to stay too long in our service, lest they be corrupted. Mike, the old doorman, has left; and the other doorman, Vassili, is leaving this month. The Russians never permit an employee to remain until he reaches retirement age and might therefore be entitled to a pension from our Government. Once gone, they are swallowed back into the Russian mass, and we hear no more of them.

The weather is uniformly bad, these days. This morning, Chin said, "Moscow summer all over," a discouraging remark, considering it's only the 6th of June. We did have two or three brief days of sunshine when I first got back, but it's dreadful to think that's all we can hope for. I haven't yet shaken out my cotton dresses. What a benighted country this is! The Kellys went on a picnic on Sunday and stuck fast in the mud, hub deep. With great generosity and considerable condescension, David Kelly's MVD guards turned to, seven of them—the eighth was covering the Ambassador at his tea—and they heaved the car out by main force. They do have their uses.

I was amused to have Dick Service point out to me that both the Kellys' and our guards use American and German automobiles, not trusting their own; ours have a Plymouth sedan and a small German car, the others a Chevrolet and a German car. They are taking no chances on Russian equipment.

I can imagine the Little Men's excitement when they hear about Dad's projected trip to Siberia; four of them at least are bound to go along. Dad, Roger, and Dick Service hope to get off soon after June 16, to be gone over a week, most of the time spent coming and going—six days and six nights on the train going out, a night there, three nights and days back halfway by train, and the rest of the way by plane.

THESE HAVE BEEN busy days. The guests turned out to be undaunted sightseers, especially Jacqueline Cochran, who assures me that world speed records, heading the Women's Air Force, being awarded the DSM, mean nothing compared to two weeks in Soviet Russia. It's true that a visit here is unique today. One forgets the initial impact Moscow makes on newcomers, and it's great fun to see the picture through fresh eyes. Jackie is a remarkable woman. I like her immensely, and admire her energy and determination. Mrs. Cannon, who is with her, is a delightful person, very wise, very serene; we are more than happy to have her here, as General Cannon has been so unfailingly helpful to us.

The Freers got their visas at the same time Jackie and Mrs. Cannon got theirs; they have come as far as Leningrad, but are stuck there. The Russians commandeered all the trains, to transport the delegates to the meeting of the Supreme Soviet, to which Dad went this afternoon, flanked by two interpreters. I would like to have gone with him to see the show, held in the big Kremlin palace, but they have refused tickets to anyone but Ambassadors. Nothing much happens, to be sure. Stalin usually attends the opening session—comes in and takes his seat with the rest of the Politburo on the platform. There are speeches, new laws are read and voted on, but never a dissenting voice is heard or a dissenting hand raised. The diplomatic gallery is at safe distance from any of the Soviet big shots, and you need opera glasses to see their faces at all clearly.

Our three men are greatly excited about the Siberian trip, but I must admit I hate to see them go so far into the interior of this vast land. I'll be glad when it's all over and they are safe at home again. The Freers will stay here in the Embassy with me. He speaks Russian and can cope with any emergencies, as this is his second tour in Moscow; and she is a gay, pretty young woman, great fun to have around. I can't help feeling it's going to be an uncomfortable sensation, seeing one's husband and son off for Siberia, under the care of the MVD; certainly it's not a sensation I ever thought to experience. Roger laughed as he received an invitation to a ball in Washington on June sixteenth. He though of replying, "Mr. Kirk regrets he will be unable to accept, as he is leaving for Siberia that evening."

Tonight we have a dinner for the new Dutch Ambassador and his wife, and I have my head done up in pins and combs. Jacqueline Cochran cut, washed, and set my hair. I told her she couldn't have given me any present I would rather have had, for I've never dared try Russian hairdressers, for both sanitary and esthetic reasons. One of our girls went, one day, and said they put a wave in with a string, had her hold both ends for some minutes, then moved the string up to the next wave!

Until the visitors came and exclaimed about the smell of Russia, I'd almost grown to ignore it. One gets used to it, but, when reminded, I tried again to analyze the odor, a kind of stale sweetness, the dead sweetness of decay. The odor and the color of Russia are the same, a dull yellow brown or the dirty gray of age-old cobwebs, the smell of rags left long in corners, of food that has rotted and dried, of clothing worn month after month in heat and cold, sun and wind. It's indescribable and unforgettable.

Yesterday, Sunday, the town was full of people, some of them here for the big meeting, others because these summer Sundays bring all manner of folk on holiday to Moscow; soldiers on leave, factory groups, school children, and vacationers of all kinds. Moscow is the Mecca for them all, and you can see, by the rapt reverence on their faces, what standing in Red Square means to each and every Soviet citizen. This is literally the center of their world; between Moscow and the sky shine the red stars of the Kremlin, beyond there is nothing.

Postmarked Moscow   *June 15, 1950*

DAD IS PACKING
as many warm clothes as when he went to Leningrad last winter with the thermometer at twenty-two below. He's probably right, for it's cold enough here in Moscow, and I dare say Siberia is worse. All he's leaving behind is his astrakhan hat. Six days and nights on the train bound for a place called Sluydianka, on the edge of Lake Baikal!

All this was Dad's own idea. He proposed it the last time he had an interview with Gromyko, who asked why, when there were so many other places to see, Dad wanted to go to Lake Baikal. Dad explained that he had always had a curiosity about that body of water, the deepest on the earth's surface; that the journey was as long as any permitted foreigners in the Soviet Union, and, in brief, that he simply wanted to go. Now word has come from the Foreign Office that they see no objection to the trip; it will be up to Intourist from now on.

They won't get away on the sixteenth but, with luck, they should leave a few days later. There will be a diner on the train, and they are promised compartments in an International Car; but they are taking no chances and will go equipped with a case of food supplies, complete with canned meats, hard-boiled eggs, butter, cheese, jams, and corned beef hash which Dick Service volunteers to cook on a primus stove in the lavatory basin.

Our lady visitors leave on Sunday night, and the Freers move over to Spaso to keep me company until the men return. Meanwhile, we hold a solemn church service here at eleven on Sunday, when the Anglican Bishop of Fulham and Northern

159

and Central Europe comes to officiate. He is making his Episcopal rounds, but can minister here only to a congregation within the Diplomatic Corps. The British Chaplain from Helsinki comes down with him, the same young clergyman who celebrated our Christmas service. Perhaps we can persuade the Bishop to say a prayer for those about to go to Siberia. Dad says I'm foolish about this trip, but it looks so very distant and so severely geographical when laid out across the atlas page.

Yesterday, I saw a dead man, I believe, being dragged along the street. Two militiamen had him by the arms, pulling him down the gutter. Fortunately, I was in the car and, fortunately being near-sighted, I couldn't see too well, but the back of his head had been crushed in and he must surely have been dead; in any case, he couldn't have lived long after being dragged the length of the block. No one on the sidewalk seemed disturbed or even curious. One of the British Secretaries told me he saw a poor man fall or jump into the Moscow River one day, a couple of months ago. He ran over to see if he could do anything, and was horrified to watch a boat put out through the broken ice, and a man lean out and tie a rope around the poor fellow in the water, who was then pulled to shore. Once landed, he was tossed to one side like an old sack, no effort at artificial respiration being made. It was probably too late to do much for the man, especially after his rescuers had towed him back under water, but the callousness of the whole proceeding was shocking to the Englishman. Human life means very little in this country. It may always have been like this, but it never ceases to revolt Western sensibilities.

Just up the street from Spaso is a large house labeled "Sobering-Up Station No. 9." That's the literal translation of the name. To this place are brought all the drunks picked up in this section. As I passed there last week, I saw a man being heaved out of a truck—heaved out like a bale of rags and carried through the door. What treatment is given the poor creatures, we can only guess at, but on the warmest summer day there's a cloud of steam coming from a basement window, so I suppose they must have some baking-out process, as they keep a big boiler going all the time. Drunkenness used to be traditional in old

Russia, and harmless drunks are tolerated by the police, but the penalties for drunken driving or any damage or injury done to others have been increased and now carry a prison sentence, rather than a compulsory steam bath.

We passed several forced-labor gangs yesterday, on the Zagorsk road.

The roadbuilding was going ahead very slowly and the main idea seemed to be to lay broken stone in the middle, a very narrow middle, and gravel along the edges. As it has rained a lot this spring, the gravel washes away and the little women must shovel it all up again, for it's usually women who do this sort of work, sexless-appearing creatures without shape or features. At one crossroad, a girl engineer was bossing a group of men, obviously enjoying herself. She looked harder-faced than the men themselves, harder than the MVD guard who stood behind her with his rifle. It will be interesting to hear if Dad and Roger see any prison camps along the railroads in Siberia.

Our cook has finally heard from her son, a post card, the first in nearly four months. The poor boy has another five years to do up north, and when he does come away he can never work in Moscow again. That in itself is a terrible punishment for a Soviet citizen. When prisoners are released, they go first to probationary towns or villages, where they must work under close supervision; then, if their conduct is satisfactory, they may go elsewhere, but never back to their own homes or to Moscow. To their families and former acquaintances, the majority are little better than dead. Bare existence is the only thing restored to them when they come out, and always there is the shadow of trouble—trouble for themselves and anyone with whom they live or work. The new crime of guilt by association is a terrible one, and accusations are easily made and very difficult to refute.

The departure of our three travellers for Siberia was most impressive. The travellers themselves were greatly excited, their excitement equalled only by that of the four MVD guards who had been chosen to go along, the first team we called them. Those left behind looked quite forlorn. I asked Dad's Secretary,

Margaret Sullivan, to interpret for me and I shook hands with the head man, the one Dick has nicknamed Salmon Shirt, and told him to take good care of the Ambassador. He gave me what was meant to be a reassuring smile, and a hard, horny hand.

Our men had two compartments; all the luggage was piled in with Roger and Dick Service, and Dad was left to ride alone in elegant and solitary splendor. The cooking, they planned to do in the washroom; and they prepared menus of corned beef hash, stew and baked beans. The car looked comparatively comfortable and clean, painted bright blue, with Moscow-Vladivostok lettered on the side. They were to stay in the same carriage all the way, the only "International car" on the train, the others being the usual "soft" cars with four-berth compartments and the hard cars with their tiers of yellow wood shelves. Besides a man attendant, there was a porteress decked out in a small white apron like a tea-shop waitress. I wondered if the latter had been provided for the Ambassador's benefit.

Other passengers in Dad's car included military men—Generals and Admirals, lesser ranks usually being assigned to the soft cars—and one stout gentleman who had already donned his travelling costume of vertical-striped cotton pajamas.

So far, we have had three telegrams from points along the journey, and one from Sluydianka, their destination on Lake Baikal, saying they were "having a wonderful stay." The head of the Intourist, who came to see Dad off, again asked him why he had chosen that small town as his objective. "Because it's the farthest you'll give me tickets for," answered Dad. Speaking of tickets, Dad's didn't come until an hour and a half before it was time to leave, but that's the usual thing. It makes one feel a bit uncertain; there's no question of going to the station or sending someone there to buy the tickets, these are delivered to the Embassy by Intourist, and in Intourist's good time.

I wonder what sort of accommodations they have found at the other end. Of course, the Russians are quite capable of ordering people out of an entire house, cleaning it up, and putting it at the disposition of Dad and his companions for the night. Anyway, they went prepared with sleeping bags and safari equipment, so they should be all right. The Freers, who are staying at Spaso with me, made the trip to and from Vladivostock three years ago, at the time when we still had a Consulate there. They said it was a rugged journey, but Ed was then a young Third Secretary and they were travelling without the special privileges accorded to Dad.

In the time of Catherine the Great, when her favorite Potemkin was Prime Minister, the Empress announced that she intended to make a trip down the Volga to inspect the villages and public works she had ordered erected along the river. None of the villages or works had even been started by Potemkin but, nothing daunted, he had false fronts put up along the shore, and, as Catherine sailed by, she admired the silhouettes of towns and churches and factories, little realizing that they were mere stage props.

The Potemkin village idea is typical of Russian thinking, and such maneuvers go on all the time. Our people tell us that they believe we may be restricted to the four roads outside of Moscow because these roads are the only ones that are properly paved, and the only ones showing a start of housing developments and factory projects. They assign the foreigners to these roads, not to rout them around military objectives, but simply to convince them of the great and peaceful progress going on in the Soviet Union. It seems very far-fetched, but one has only to go back to Potemkin; and, anyway, we've all learned that nothing can be too much trouble or too devious for Soviet reasoning.

Such machinations could hardly hold true all the way to Siberia, however, and it will be most interesting to hear what the men have to tell when they get back.

I've not been too lonely since they left, although I was sorry to see our two lady visitors depart, going out again by Leningrad and Helsinki. Two such nice women, I miss them very much.

The weather has turned to summer, the sunshine is warm and pleasant, though there's not much we can do with it. Moscow streets are unlovely except in winter, the parks unkempt, and the trees and flowers untrimmed and scrubby. A favorite kind of tree is a sort of cottonwood that blows fluff all over the city —dusty gray fluff that sticks to your hair and clothes and gets up your nose.

The famous twenty-six-story skyscraper on the boulevard, near Spaso House, comes along slowly. Layers of brick and surface stone or concrete are being applied over the rusted steel beams which they never even painted but, inside, things cannot be proceeding very fast.

One of our foreign colleagues who has had engineering training has made a study of this magnificent edifice, through the months. When they first started setting the upright beams, he walked around the lot to see if they were using instruments to line them up. Not at all. After a few weeks, the Russians realized something was wrong, so applied great vises to the beams to bring them into line. This, our friend said, would never work, as the beams were too heavy. Sure enough, they finally decided to heat the steel and cut into the beams to set their vises. Result, when the vises came off, the beams were really wavy.

Now, says our friend, they will run into real trouble with their elevator shafts, as these cannot be laid against the walls, but must be blocked out an eighth of an inch, a quarter of an inch, etc., all the way up the twenty-six stories. This may not yet have occurred to the Russians, but, when the horrid truth dawns, it will take them years to finish the job!

Across the street from the skyscraper, a large brick building, seven or eight stories high, is under construction. The bricklaying is all being done by women, none of whom look very expert. I walked past there the other day and, even with my bad eyes, I could see that the side of the building leans out, while the doors and windows are all askew. And still they go on, the little women, piling brick on brick, like children building a fort in the backyard, and using about the same technique. But, with all this seeming inefficiency and waste, the buildings do go up. People live in them and work in them. If a building falls down, they rebuild it. No one seems to care. That's the frightening thing, the power of the mass. It's what crushed the invading forces of the Germans, the skilled technicians of the modern world, who had to give way to sheer numbers and space.

The individual counts for so little in this country, his needs and aspirations being sacrificed to the needs of the state. The cripples are an example. You might think that a society which boasts of its social consciousness would care for the infirm and the aged. Instead they swarm about the streets; and, to the best of my knowledge, I've never seen a man or woman fitted with anything but wooden stumps in the way of artificial limbs.

One might even understand their ignoring the old as unfit and unproductive, but surely the young war veterans could be returned to useful occupations. The worst of these young cripples I saw was a triple amputee, begging in a courtyard of one of the big new apartment buildings. He had no legs, and his right arm had been torn away from his side. It was a cold day, but he was in rags, with his right side exposed to catch the sympathy of the passer-by. At Zagorsk, another young man with amputated feet was crawling across the ground on hands and knees, big pads being attached to his trousers.

All monasteries and churches are crowded with these people, plus the poor old women who look as though they might have stood for ages on the steps, grown as much part of them as broken statues. Pensions given to war veterans and to industrial victims are very small, depending more on length of service than on the injuries. Death itself would seem more merciful.

It can never be emphasized enough to Westerners that *human life is cheap in Russia.* It is a commodity to be spent like any other, conserved only when it is to the interest of the State to conserve it, but without compassion or human feeling. Between individuals, between families, there is human feeling, of course, but there is also an acceptance of authority and a submissiveness to fate. All this shocks and repels us, but it's been part of the Russian character for centuries, and the men in the Kremlin know this and have taken every advantage of it.

Much of what we see might be excused on the grounds of ignorance, of lack of trained personnel, of hospitals, of social service centers, of education itself. These people have passed through years of revolution, of transformation from an agricultural to an industrial society, of a terrible war fought on their own soil. One gives them credit for all that,—but their claim to being better than anyone else, to having better hospitals, better social laws, better trained personnel—that is what exasperates us and kills our sympathy.

Postmarked Moscow   *June 27, 1950*

THE FIRST LESSON
we learned on Sunday, September 3, 1939, was that totalitarian states are no respecters of the Sabbath. Even so, they still manage to fool us, and statesmen and soldiers are too often happily week-ending while these single-minded people start wars.

Sure enough, the Korean Communists marched into South Korea yesterday, Sunday, June 26, attacking from ten or twelve different points. Someone arranged to summon the Security Council of the United Nations in order to meet by nightfall, and strong words are now flying about. Last evening, echoes of them reached us which Wally, as officer in charge, tried to pass on to responsible Russian officials here.

None could be found, not because it was Sunday or because they were off on country jaunts, but obviously because they didn't want to see him and were carefully hiding out behind the Kremlin walls. Here they speak of Sunday as "our day of rest," and the duty officer whom Wally finally aroused at the Foreign Office told him, in reproving tones, no one was there and no business could be done that day. Our men have expected something to break sometime, somewhere, in the Far East, but this Korean invasion looks very serious and no one is happy about it.

Dad had heard nothing on the train of the Korean attack, so was greeted with the news on his arrival at dawn this morning. He and Roger and Dick flew in from Novosibirsk, a long fourteen-hour flight, but they reported it to have been a smooth one and the pilot very competent. The Russians had probably laid on a special flight, as there was only one other passenger in the plane besides Dad's party and the four Little Men. The latter enjoyed a triumphal progress all across the country, as the fellow members of their club, the MVD Comrades, met them at all the stops.

At Omsk, Roger said, there were twelve of the "local brotherhood" gazing into the air, with happy faces, as they came down. Introductions were made, great hand shakes all around, and much interest. Headed by "Salmon Shirt" four of the Little Men went with Dad and the same four came back. One, the junior member. was detailed to the dirty work of carrying bags and holding tickets—that is, their own bags and tickets, for they never volunteer such services for our people.

Altogether it was a most carefully chaperoned trip. Dad knew it would be, but I was just as glad to have such expert help on hand, and am certain the authorities would not have allowed it under other circumstances. It's quite different, of course, from the gay jaunts that Roger has made. He travels second-class with a party of our girls and young men, and, with their holiday atmosphere, they are much freer than on one of Dad's de luxe voyages.

I think our three travellers were glad to climb into bed for a few hours this morning, after their night in the plane and all the preceding nights on hard lumpy mattresses. Dick came home with a cold, but otherwise all remained in good health. Roger said the train stopped every hour or so at stations, where they walked on the platform. In some of the larger towns, they stayed as long as half an hour. The nature of the country varied, though birch and pine trees remained constant. The towns, however, were all alike—wooden houses, brick and wood factories, just more and more of the same—few roads, just land, then more land, a vast, vast country. Altogether, they travelled three thousand miles to reach their destination.

Lake Baikal, they said, was very handsome indeed, and, as they were not in a forbidden area, they were able to drive along the shore of the lake and even to take a rowboat out onto the water. I would so love to have had a picture of that expedition on the lake. It appears Dad, Dick, Roger, and two of the Little Men got into the boat, the two men taking an oar apiece, while Dad rowed two oars and set the stroke. That would certainly have made the "Picture of the Week"—the American Ambassador with his two MVD guards in a rowboat on Lake Baikal, in the middle of Siberia.

Speaking of pictures, a magazine representative sent Wally a cable saying that, while they realized it might be impossible for the Ambassador to write up his trip, perhaps his son Roger might be induced to do so. Wally replied that unfortunately Roger was also an employee of the United States Government, so would be unable to accept any such offers. That would surely have been the end of a promising young diplomat's career.

At Sluydianka itslf, they were lodged in a private house belonging to the wife of an engineer whose husband was away, and whose two children were off at school. It was a small unpretentious four-room cottage, built of wooden logs like the rest of the village, but it had been freshly painted, in spots, and there were not only enough beds but clean sheets and blankets. A telephone had been installed obviously the day before and there was a new radio on a table neither of which the owner knew how to work. As the weather was hot, and the lady had a variety of barnyard life in her back garden, the flies were so bad that Dick let loose a bug bomb. It killed the flies, but nearly gassed the three men and considerably startled their hostess.

The MVD guards lived in a house across the street. Three motor cars were provided, imported for the occasion, they seemed almost as much a curiosity in the village as the American Ambassador. That night, all the shutters of the house were carefully battened down, probably as a protective measure, the landlady giving the unconvincing explanation of an expected hurricane. The weather gave no sign of it, the sun shone the day they arrived, the night was calm, and the slight ground fog next morning did not more than obstruct their last view of the lake.

They are lucky to have landed here early today, for now it's pouring torrents and the flying must be very bad. A murky afternoon to spend arguing about Korea with Vishinsky. That's what Dad has gone to do, although he was not too hopeful of obtaining satisfaction.

Postmarked Moscow   *July 2, 1950*

EVENTS SEEM TO have taken hold this past week. Dad and Roger got back from Siberia on Monday morning, and notes and telegrams have showered like raindrops ever since. For some days, there was no response from the Foreign Office. Almost immediately after his arrival, Dad asked to see Gromyko, to tell him officially of the Korean "incident" and of the action of the Security Council. No answer. This was followed by a further request to see him, as Dad had a note to present, informing him of the second resolution of the Council and of President Truman's order. As there was still no answer, Dad sent Ed Freers to the Ministry, with instructions to deliver the note to whomever he found in authority.

On Friday, Dad succeeded in seeing Gromyko, as the latter was ready with his response. This was a categoric denial of the legality of the Council's action, and a denial of North Korean aggression, along with a refusal to interfere in the matter as being the business of a sovereign power, it being "a well-known fact that the Soviet Government made it a practice never to intervene in the internal affairs of other countries!"

Dad had this note read to him by Gromyko, but there was no discussion of its contents. Soviet ministers, even high-ranking ones, receive orders which they cannot question or even explain. The only discussion was one quite beside the point, about the million rubles which the Soviet Ministry of Finance was to have exchanged for our dollars last winter. This money is used within the country for the running of our Embassy and for meeting rents, salaries, etc. Quite openly, the Soviets put off the transaction until it must now be done on the new ruble rate, thereby costing the United States twice as much as before.

Dad told Gromyko that he only regretted he could not reciprocate and instruct our people to double the rent of the Soviet Embassy in Washington. Unfortunately for us, that building was ceded to Russia when we restored to them the property of the old Czarist regime. "Would you really do that?" asked Gromyko. "I most certainly would," Dad answered.

One encouragingly aspect of the Korean mess is that the Indians have gone along with the Security Council, even so far as to instruct their Ambassador here to go to Gromyko with a protest. This, Dad says, is most important, as it prevents any development of an all-Asia alignment against us. Meanwhile there's a lot of rough talk going on, and the radio fairly sizzles. What it will amount to in the end, no one knows. Right now, we can only hope MacArthur knows what he is doing, and that he has enough forces at his disposal to do it, for any Western defeat would be disastrous.

As if the Korean situation weren't enough to bother us, the Russians have lodged another formal protest on the Colorado beetle plague. It would be ludicrous, if they were not presenting the matter in such a serious way. Of course, the authorities know this is a lie, and we know it's a lie, but as they have hammered on it for the past six weeks and are now giving it official backing, a lot of ignorant folk here, some in Germany, and the satellites will believe them. Anyway, Ed Freers is spending his whole Sunday translating the note from the Soviet Foreign Office; and Dad is at Mokhovaya now, looking it over, and drafting a reply when he's not checking on the Korean situation.

Yesterday, all the servants in the Diplomatic Colony were instructed to appear at the big Trade Union Hall to listen to speeches about Peace and the Soviet efforts to maintain it, after which they were made to sign the Stockholm manifesto. That is the way that paper has been signed. It's a wholesale fraud, but a clever one. How we let the Soviets get away with the Peace slogan, I can't imagine. It would seem as though any good advertising man could have told us that Peace is a term to hang on to for our own use. Of course, all of us are in favor of peace, but poor, ignorant folk all over the world sign Soviet-inspired appeals about it, little realizing on what terms that peace must be bought. Anyway, it was funny to see all the diplomats rushing away from the cocktail party at the Canadian Embassy yesterday afternoon. We'd all been warned we must get home for early dinner so the servants could go and vote against us.

Meanwhile, life goes along quietly and cheerfully. We are getting ready for our Fourth of July ball, and expect three hundred and fifty guests. It would have been three hundred and seventy-five, but we think some of the satellites may be ill that evening! We hope the weather will turn warm again so we can use the terrace and garden. I'm going to wear my best satin frock, Dad and Roger their white ties, and we will dance in the Great Hall, decorated for the occasion with the biggest American flags we can find.

Postmarked Moscow   *July 5, 1950*

THE AMERICAN

flag, flying in the very face of the Kremlin, was a welcome sight yesterday. It was a fine, windy day, and Old Glory waved about in great style. Dad had asked them to send him a big new flag for the Chancery, and it arrived in the nick of time, brought in yesterday morning by Stuart Warwick, the Assistant Air Attaché. He also brought us another, just slightly smaller, which we thought of hanging between two of the columns of the Great Hall. We tried it, but the effect was a kind of "convention in Madison Square Garden" look. Dad said it reminded him of Admiral Dewey's homecoming after the Spanish war, so we compromised by using it at the far end of the supper room, where it did wonders for that odd bit of architecture.

It seemed just the day to wave the flag, for Gromyko's speech was anything but cordial, timed we think, as a Fourth of July greeting to us all. It was an absurd document, a lot of it made up out of whole cloth, and what wasn't made up was distortion of fact. While it was intended for home consumption, and designed to bolster the morale of their own people, it's a false and cynical statement from a man who obviously knows much better. We wondered if he or any of his Vice Ministers would come to our party. Dad put up a bet they would not—and he won.

About seven or eight Russians came, minor officials, stayed half an hour, took nothing to drink, and went off, after stiff handshakes. They were a scrubby lot, definitely the second team, so it was almost more insulting to have them come than none at all. Actually, it shows how unsure and naïve these people are; for any of us, under similar circumstances, would have attended the party in our best clothes and swept in as befits representatives of a great nation. They don't know enough for that—not yet.

The real mark of Soviet displeasure is the withdrawal of Dad's right to turn left in Moscow traffic. This is something that only he and the British Ambassador have enjoyed, and it may have been due to the protection of their Little Men. But it was the Little Men themselves who told the chauffeur he must henceforth conform to the accepted regulations, and it seemed quite clear they had received the orders from their higher-ups. The final touch would be their own withdrawal, but I hardly think that will take place, not while we are still here and they can keep legitimate watch and ward over us.

It's a job to put on a big party such as we had last night— that is, it's a job in Moscow, for one must contrive and imagine what would be easy to arrange in more civilized spots. Chantal Goffin and I went to market on Monday and bought masses of flowers. Our scheme was red, white, and blue, and we were lucky enough to find delphinium, red and white peonies, and red sweet william. We made smashing great bouquets, for those are the only kind that are at all effective in this huge place. Chantal's masterpiece for the main dining table was just three yards across!

Our soldier and sailor boys looked very smart last night, their medals pinned up and down their chests. Our ladies were in their best clothes, the diplomats were strung with decorations, and altogether it was a very gay sight. Just at first, it was a job to handle them in the big room and get dancing started, as they had been conditioned to using the ballroom, and to eating their supper on arrival. But we stuck to it that this was a ball, and a ball it was. In the end everyone enjoyed themselves, the drinks were good and plentiful enough, and these vast rooms looked very lovely when the dancing really began. The crystal chandeliers reflected on the floor, carefully polished that morning by Chin and his charwomen; the orchestra fiddled away in fine form; and the stately folk withdrew into the blue dining room where we had put chairs and sofas. It was altogether a handsome affair, of which, we hope, our people could be proud.

We received with Wally and General and Mrs. O'Daniel, the General wound about in his yellow cavalry sash, and clanking more medals than a Soviet Marshal. Dad bolstered us with a little champagne upstairs, so we got through quite nicely until midnight and time for supper. We shepherded the VIPS into the blue dining room, where Chin arranged their buffet, and I even corralled the Jugoslav Chargé d'Affaires, a tall black-mustachioed gentleman who demurred at first—but I got him there—and the ladies all made a fuss over him.

Madame Brosio, the Italian Ambassadress, wore a pink-tulle dress that seemed all spun sugar; Chantal Goffin had a kind of "Marie Antoinette at the Trianon" summer model; the Dutch Ambassadress wore the most exquisite and exquisitely complicated Paris creation, the Swiss Chargé's pretty wife was lovely in a wide-skirted yellow brocade—we all did our best to maintain the tradition of the wicked capitalist world.

The Ambassadors came looking like Ambassadors, with stars pinned to their pockets, and ribbons across their fronts. The Swede had a most distinguished decoration—a black moire ribbon with a big cut-steel and diamond Maltese cross and star. He said one South American foreign minister who paid a visit to Sweden asked particularly if he might be awarded that decoration, as it would come in so handy for funerals! I don't think we had any satellites at all. I must check, but I think this time they all stayed away. Dad tells me they did, every one of them.

Toward half-past two, the light began to come in through the open terrace door, and from the big skylight above. But the dancing went on, and we finished off toward four-thirty with a spirited series of Russian folk dances. Roger performed a solo dance in white tie and tails, much to the delight of the guests and the servants, who crowded the floor to see the Posolchek, or "Little Ambassador," do his stuff. He is very popular with all of them, and there was loud applause. All in all, it was a good party.

Postmarked Moscow   *July 7, 1950*

THE SOVIET TEMPER

seems to be growing worse as time goes on. Perhaps that flag flying in front of the Embassy the other day, really annoyed them. In addition to the absurd claim about our dropping potato bugs all over East Germany, they have now had the audacity to say we sent in all sorts of harmful germs and insects along with UNRRA and Lend Lease supplies. That's gratitude for you! They would never have won their war if we hadn't helped out; and now for them to say we peppered our charity with microbes is a bit tough. But there's no possibility of our making denials that they would accept; denials would, in their minds, give some credence to the allegations.

In spite of the VOA, the general public hears little from the outside world, and there are few ways of our reaching the mass of the people or shaking their belief in what their Government puts out. Any point that the Soviet authorities want to plug is repeated over and over again, with the good old advertising technique, until sales resistance is worn down.

No medium is neglected. Even the circus, a favorite form of entertainment with all classes of Russians, is riddled with anti-American propaganda, so much so that none of our people find it comfortable to attend. Roger went with a pal, but he could pass in the crowd. Some of the acts he said were excellent, the best being the performing bears, one of which rode a motor cycle. We agreed this was symbolic of the entire Russian people—performing bears on motor cycles is about what they are.

I'm going to start a half-day job in the Embassy library next week, as sitting at home these days is tiresome, and social life is at a minimum. As mentioned earlier, the endless vacations for the servants, one month with pay, have begun and that cuts down the parties—not to speak of the ruble exchange blight.

For example, when I went shopping for flowers, the other day, I longed to bring back some of the fresh vegetables I saw; but, with tomatoes at three dollars a pound and strawberries the same, I could only look wistfully at them. We buy nothing we can help in the Russian shops, as, even with the raise in our cost of living allowance, prices are prohibitive. The Russians must love to see us squirm, and I only wish there were some way we could have a "Soviets Only" counter set up in a central A. and P. Store in Washington and force them all to buy there at comparative costs.

One jolly item from the French Embassy, to confirm our ideas about Russia, old and new: The Ambassadress was out driving in the outskirts of Moscow, when two odd-looking dogs, young ones, ran across the road. Baby wolves, the chauffeur told her. So you see this country never changes.

Postmarked Moscow   *July 12, 1950*

DAD WENT UPSTAIRS
after lunch, very purposeful, and came down in one of his

neat dark suits and a stiff collar, thereby indicating that he had an appointment at the Foreign Office this afternoon. We gather there has been a period of "diplomatic activity," these last few days, and the dispatch about possible negotiations between Sir David Kelly and Gromyko offers some clue as to Dad's collar. But it's hoping too much if we expect the Korean war to be quickly finished. It's a real war now, and not an incident. All we can pray for is that the Soviets don't start up somewhere else.

As if to make matters worse for those of us who live here, the Soviet Air Force is over us night and day, practicing for their show on Sunday. Jets scream overhead, with a line of heavy bombers off to the side. It seems as though they choose to fly across the chimneys of Spaso House. The first dawn I heard them, I jumped out of bed in a panic, and even now the nasty things give me cold chills.

Roger will go to the show, but we think we'll stay away. Our people who have looked in on the rehearsals say it will be almost the same as last year, and it seems more fitting that the American Ambassador absent himself. Actually, one sees very well from our terrace roof, and there's no need to give the press here the opportunity of printing pictures, as they did last year, with the caption, "American warmongers out to spy on the Soviet Air Force." Just as if they hadn't asked us to the party.

One of the girls from the Canadian Embassy who came to dinner the other night reported that someone had thrown a large hunk of hard bread at her in the street. This is the first time such a thing has happened, and we assured her it must be a Soviet "wolf call," but she said no, it was aimed at her and thrown very hard. When the Korean thing first broke, the guards at the gate and the policemen on duty outside of Mokhovaya stopped saluting Dad's car, and did not speak to Roger or Dick as they walked in and out. Twenty-four hours later, the saluting was resumed. But Dad is still required to obey ordinary traffic regulations, and he fumes as he has to turn right and right again like other, lesser, folk.

All over town, on all the billboards and in shop windows,

there are great posters with "Peace" written across them. One of the most popular shows a clenched fist against a red banner, and Truman and Churchill cowering in the corner below. Such a convincing bit of Peace propaganda!

Dad was calling, after all, not on the Foreign Office, but on the Indian Ambassador. It was he who went to see Gromyko, to protest the North Korean attack, and now I dare say he is anxious to promote any possible negotiations. Anyway, Dad came home after a conversation of an hour and a half at high level, and two cups of scented tea, both conversation and tea somewhat divorced from the realities of life. It seems useless to make spiritual appeals to these people, who interpret Peace as an active force—the force of the clenched fist they've put on their posters.

Many of the radio commentators hint at Ambassadors, on both sides, being withdrawn. There's been no indication whatever of such a thing happening.

To show you that Dad is not too alarmed, he's letting Roger go with three other young people to Tiflis next week. They go by train, a soft car—four berths in a compartment—and come back by plane. One of the Britishers who is just back reported the Caucasus at its best now, and the people very cordial. One Georgian gentleman, an obvious agent, had made himself most agreeable, asking the Englishman if he knew Mr. ——, such a nice man in the American Embassy. The comical part about this was that the nice man, Mr. ——, had been in those parts last year, had had drinks all evening with the fellow, had finally put him to bed, and, in doing so, had discovered notes of their conversations in the man's shoe. These he read and returned, but naturally passed on the name and description to subsequent friends who might be staying in the area. The Britisher recognized the agent at once, and filled him full of every kind of fascinating misinformation.

Our people receive fairly ready permission to make certain trips out of Moscow. They must ask permission, of course, and word is sent all along the way, but the provincial Secret Service boys are not as alert or as competent as the local crew, and many are so downright curious about life in the great outside world that they are eager for information and will grant small favors in return.

A State trip, such as Dad made to Siberia, is all very interesting but it's so carefully supervised there's no chance for what might be called independent action. The only way to get that is to travel as Roger does. Russians themselves often cannot travel far without presenting papers, to obtain their tickets. It's as if you had to show identity cards at Union Station, in Washington, every time you bought a ticket to Chicago, or asked for rooms in any hotel.

The Britisher who made the Caucasian trip said that his two companions came down quite promptly with dysentery. Our own people are more careful. Having a wholesome American regard for germs, they go armed with halizone tablets to purify the water and sulfaguanadine to purify their insides. They take most of their food with them, and peel the rest.

Postmarked Moscow   *July 17, 1950*

WE ARE ASKED TO the Polish Embassy reception for their National Holiday, on the 21st, but do not think we will attend. None of the satellites came to our Embassy on July 4, so we are to take a haughty line in return. Actually, I'm sorry, as it's our one chance to look at Russian society. Last year, they swarmed at the Poles' reception—Marshals, ballerinas, the entire lot.

The former Polish Ambassador was a nice enough man, though he had just lately been given the sinister job of Political Director of Education for the Polish army. His wife was a sweet-faced woman who would like to have been friendly, and who seemed quite overcome by the invading hordes at her party, last year. Now there is a new man whom none of us have met, and who has not asked to call on Dad, so I fear we won't see the Marshals and ballerinas again. The

Hungarian who was to have called on Dad yesterday after-noon, rang up to put off the visit, and so it goes.

None of the new satellite ladies have come to see me. At the French party, last week, they all sat in a dismal group by themselves, along with three or four very mussed-up-looking Russians. Bogomolov was at the French party, but we avoided each other. In fact, no Russian spoke to me, except Vlasov, the Consular Director, who arrived a little "tight." As at our party, the Russians stayed exactly half an hour, and then left in a body.

The weather has been foul most of the month, cold and wet. Three British bachelors, who live in a *dacha* just outside of town, gave a gallant party last Saturday, complete with rather damp Japanese lanterns strung around the verandas. Like all Russian *dachas,* this one looks like a cross between a Swiss chalet and an Adirondack camp, but the Embassy ladies had trimmed the house with all manner of flowers and greens, and the effect was quite gay.

There was a good supper, with plenty of champagne, and all went well until the Ambassadress, Lady Kelly, got locked in the lavatory and stayed there for half an hour before at-tracting attention. She got a window open and waved her handkerchief at the *dvornik,* or yardman, who was parking cars outside. Of course, everyone thought of the old song about the three old maids who were there from Monday to Saturday. They sang it, and Lady Kelly joined in the chorus.

Roger is off, this afternoon, for Tiflis with a group of young people. He will certainly be a travelled young man when he leaves here. They hope to take a bus over the Georgian mili-tary highway, a scenic drive that looks very frightening in the pictures, and I hate to think how uncertain Russian brakes may be. They are coming back by plane.

We've sent a telegram to Germany, asking for a plane to take us out on August 12—only as far as Wiesbaden this time, to deliver passengers and collect food supplies. It's a disap-pointment not to go farther, as I'd looked forward to those two weeks away, but it hardly seems the time to venture far from base.

Though not anticipating any sudden developments here, I am sure the Russians have been surprised by the world's reaction. I only hope it has frightened them. We note a difference as we drive about with Dad in the car. When passers-by see the flag, they look, point, and generally take far more notice than before. One amusing incident happened in front of the Chancery yesterday, when a passing drunk came up to the militiaman on guard and asked, "Is this where the warmongers live?" The militiaman tried to wave him away, but the drunk fell on his knees, kissed the guard's hand, and said, "Thank you, Comrade, for protecting us!"

To read the daily papers and magazines, it's a wonder we're not stoned in the streets, for we must all appear to them as devils with horns. So far, except for the piece of bread thrown at the Canadian girl, we've had no real trouble. And she is pretty and plump enough to suit the fancy of any Russian "wolf."

The news of the Korean battles seems to have crowded most other things out of the newspapers. I was electrified, on picking up my *New York Herald-Tribune,* to see written large across the page the signature of the American Ambassador to Holland, former Minister to Hungary, my brother, Selden Chapin. There has been a series of articles by two Hungarian handwriting experts who forged the Mindzenty trial papers, the same two who manufactured several notes from Selden to the Cardinal, attempting to prove the latter had guilty communication with the Americans.

No doubt there's a fine set of false specimens waiting in the Kremlin basement to be released on order and A. G. Kirk will one day be sprawled across a courtroom table—the signature, I trust, not the gentleman. It may be, as they say, that our response to the Korean aggression has put war off for another ten years, but listening to the broadcasts and reading the notes and dispatches makes me very uneasy, as it sounds as though the tempo were speeding up more and more, the "symphony" of the spheres growing faster and faster, until one day we must all dissolve into a nothingness, a chaos of destruction. I can only hope that, if it does come, it will be general and not leave a few of us to drag about a ruined earth. But truly what a stupid, useless business.

And all that great war machine set in motion again. We read the President's speech this morning, a good one I thought, but surely we might have had a few more years' respite. Calling up reserves, taxes, rationing, lady welders, A cards, B cards, queues for sugar, air-raid defense, the whole dreary works. And yet there's no other way if we want to live as we believe, and to allow others the same right. No silver-tongued orator, and no living Buddha, can touch these people or turn them aside from their resolve to conquer the world and remake it to their own deadly pattern. . . .

Postmarked Moscow   *July 25, 1950*
                                      July 27, 1950

WE DON'T SLEEP
too soundly these nights. First, because it's hot and the sun streams in from 3 a.m. on, and then because, once awake, there seems a lot to think about and that lot is not sleepmaking. The news from Korea is distressing, and it's bad to visualize what the fighting there must be like.

Here, the propaganda so long poured into the public mind seems to have had its effect, and the generation growing up today is even more convinced than their parents of the need and the possibility for Soviet world conquest. They are promised this conquest under the guise of world peace, and they have no chance whatever of knowing how false that is, nor what real peace could be like. It is a very cruel and cynical hoax that has been perpetrated, but it's an effective one. These miserable, ignorant people seize on the idea just as they seized on the idea of immortality in the Middle Ages. Then it was the one thing that made life bearable on earth; now it's the same.

181

Last Sunday, I went with one of our Russian-speaking clerks to the service in the Old Believers Church. The Old Believers sect is a curious one, and its members are very devout, having survived persecutions throughout Russian history. Peter the Great shut hundreds of them up in their own church and set the place on fire. He disliked them very much for they seemed to represent the very essence of old Russia; and certainly the priest holding the service last Sunday looked like Saint Nicholas himself.

This Moscow church has some of the finest ikons to be seen anywhere, but they are mixed with a lot of gaudy trash and it's hard to examine them closely. The church was crowded with worshippers, most of whom carried peculiar rosaries, flat beads sewn close together, with two triangular tabs at the end. The Old Believers make the sign of the Cross differently from the Orthodox. They raise the second and third fingers, holding the thumb against the other two, whereas the Orthodox religion prescribes the thumb and first two fingers to be held together as symbolizing the Trinity. The vestments of the priests are a little different, and the order of service varies, from the Orthodox.

The congregation numbered men as well as women, and there was a surprising percentage of young people. Many women with small babies crowded up around the priest, so it may have been a special kind of Mothering Sunday. Certain of the ikons were especially venerated, and on one side of the church there was a long queue waiting to kiss a holy picture hung about with wreaths of paper flowers. The singing was very fine, although the voices were untrained. Women took the place of young boys in the choir, and they were an orderly, decent lot, with white kerchiefs tied neatly over their heads.

When the priest began his sermon he stood on a low platform and the people clustered round him, almost as though he were preaching from a soapbox on a street corner. Just below, a lesser priest held a silver crucifix which the faithful came forward to kiss, and be blessed with, as he made the sign of the Cross before them. In a side chapel, before the altar lay an open coffin containing the body of the deceased, whose friends had come to pray, and to listen to a priest, who intoned the prayers for them to follow. As they left, they kissed the forehead of the dead man. There seems to be a lot of ceremonial kissing in Russian churches.

Originally, the property on which the Old Believers Church stands was part of a special community comprising a smaller church, used during the winter months, an old people's home, and a hospital. Another building may have been a school, and just beyond the wall there is still the old cemetery. The graves here are fairly well cared for, and some had strings of paper flowers laid on them like those placed around the ikons.

The smaller church is now an Orthodox chapel, and services were being held at the same time as those in the other church. There were a number of women, with infants in their arms, waiting in the porch; and, as we watched, an old priest came out—was led out, rather, by a fat old woman, who seemed to take matters in charge. She lined up the mothers and babies, plus two shamefaced-looking fathers and odd grandmothers, poured water into a large font, placed a surplice around the shoulders of the priest, and handed him his book so that he could read the baptismal service.

He mumbled away for a few minutes, put the book aside, and took the naked, squalling infants, one by one, and immersed them in the font, then handed them back to the mothers or godmothers. The old man was very shaky indeed, and it seemed a hazardous process, but he got through with it, and the old woman helped bundle the babies up again, shooed the people all out of the porch, and put the baptismal paraphernalia away, for the next time.

The people look sad, and sorrowful. Most of them are of the poorest, and it would seem as if they turned to the church to compensate for their own misery, to bring some ray of color and light into their lives. The gown of the old priest was very dirty and spotted under his surplice, and he himself looked even dirtier; but the gold shone bright, and he smiled very sweetly when he handed back the baptized, regenerated babies.

WE READ IN THE
dispatches that the Korean front has been stabilized, an indication of that may be the fact that the militiamen salute Dad once more, and that Chin and Tong were given their Russian work permits yesterday.

One of our colleagues has just lost an old butler who had been with their people some sixteen years. He received a paper saying he was no longer eligible to work for foreigners—no reason given. As he is very old and quite friendless, this means starvation. He cannot hope for other work, because of his past record, and there are no private charities to help such people.

He brought his two most precious papers to the Ambassador and asked him to burn them before him. The papers were a testimonial from some dead and forgotten Prince as to his service as footman in his household; and a birth certificate of his son, born on that same estate—a son who died or disappeared in Germany. Then he shook the Ambassador's hand and walked out of the house with a very small bundle over his shoulder, perhaps to stumble and fall and be run over like the man I saw dead in the Arbat gutter.

BY THE MOST
insidious of all methods, the Soviets have succeeded in harassing foreign Diplomatic Missions in Moscow. They sabotage our servants. Whether bitter and long experience in the United States has taught Gromyko and Company that he has a sure-fire weapon against which there is no possible defense, or whether it's just devilment on their part, it's effective and will

probably go further toward reducing the size of our Missions than any one other thing.

The constant propaganda in the Soviet press has begun to react on even the old retainers, and the material benefits of better lodging, food, and clothing, if they work for us, cease to be all-important. These people, even the best of them, are very ignorant, very credulous and they are now afraid. They have reason to be. Already a number of the older ones have been turned out of their jobs—no explanation given except that it was no longer desirable they work for foreigners.

The servants who remain are a pathetic lot, flotsam and jetsam, whose frayed nerves lead them to drink and quarrels. To replace them is almost impossible. They know this, and take some consolation in knowing it, as that puts us somewhat at their mercy. At home, in simpler, more easily run households, any of us could manage, but here these cumbersome places require a small army of people, and not one of whom will do another's work. As if they were not stirred up enough by all that is happening, the Government Union, to which they must belong, holds weekly meetings where they are lectured to, where problems are discussed and instructions given.

All servants must attend these meetings, and a certain number from each household constitute the Communist cell in that household, with one individual at its head. Dictums go out, and this one individual is responsible to the Union and to the police for his group. Two weeks ago, it was declared that chauffeurs should wear caps only when their Ambassadors or Ministers were in the car. If they did not wish to go bareheaded, they could wear a cloth job or felt hat, but official caps belonged only to Heads of Mission, along with the flag flown on the front of the car. As the Ambassador's wife, I get neither flag nor cap.

Any so-called overtime the servants put in is claimed, and their fellow-servants tell tales on those who do not insist on their rights. The tale-telling is one of the worst features of the whole business. Every one is jealous and suspicious of everyone else. This is characteristic of all Russians. In the case of the servants, however, it reaches such proportions that I cannot give a cotton dress to my own maid without the yard boy looking hurt because I didn't hand the same to him for his mother, who is eighty and weighs three hundred pounds. In the small Chancery apartments, where there are only one or two servants to a family, this can be handled, but here at Spaso it's a nightmare.

Yesterday and the day before, we had no hot water. The furnace man was home, drunk, having gone off in a fit of temper. Ordinarily, we could have sent him away, but that's risky now, and so back he came this morning, looking a bit green, but otherwise very pleased with himself. The gardener, who should be in control of the men on the place, is frightened to say much, as he has a son doing ten years in Siberia. The young *dvornik,* or yard boy couldn't speak out, as he is working here without being registered and is afraid of being reported.

Right now, as far as the servants go, the British are down to a second-rate lot, except for their Belgian chef, who gets up and goes to bed with a bottle of cognac to console himself for ever having come to Moscow. Maids who had been with the Embassy for twelve and sixteen years were told to leave overnight. The same is true of the Turkish Embassy, where they run a small household, but lost two of their Turkish-speaking Russians within a week. The Dutchman has lost his old *maitre d'hotel,* who had been in his post for sixteen years. The Belgians are continually losing people; they have no chauffeur, nor can they get one. The Egyptian Minister is doing his own cooking. So are the Luxembourgers. The Italians have been unable to get visas for servants to come in from Italy. He is the *doyen* of the corps and Burobin has sent him Russians, fairly good servants, but he is paying what amounts to $250 a month to each maid.

Our own Embassy officers are very badly off, many families having no help at all. Both our old doormen have left, one or two of the maids, and now Morris, the rascal who has done our buying for years. The latter is no loss, but, as he is cleverer than most, it's obvious he's sliding out to save his own skin.

If we could only bring in Americans and shut the gates on all these Russians, that would be splendid, but it's not so easy. The poor creatures would lead lonely lives, or else the Russians would try to get hold of them and that would make for greater trouble.

Postmarked Moscow   August 11, 1950

OUR PLANE CAME in yesterday afternoon, and it was good indeed to see our old pilot, Captain Young, and his smiling crew. It's most reassuring to know they are here. I only wish we might be going for good, but even five days is better than nothing, and the breather will serve to remind us that there is a free world outside, and new faces to look at, and new voices to hear.

We are taking seventeen people; ourselves and Roger, who returns to Princeton; the O'Daniels; Margaret Sullivan, Dad's secretary, who goes home for reassignment; plus a whole group going on leave and two slightly pregnant ladies on their way to consult doctors at the Frankfurt hospital.

The plane will be unheated, so I am shaking my old fur coat out of moth balls and will take stadium boots, as at ten thousand feet it will be chilly.

This has been a week of crowded social activity. It's a job eating your way out of town—everyone wanted to give Roger and Margaret and the O'Daniels good-bye parties. There was a champagne lunch, one day, with so much champagne my cataloguing of the library books looked very hit and miss. I have Father Brassard helping me now, an energetic young priest who was sent over here by the Catholic Church and has little to do, as the Russians will not give him a permit to hold services.

He and the French priest, Père Thomas, are the only friendly Catholic clerics left in the country. Père Thomas still holds serv-

187

ices, in the French Church of St. Louis, but has been told his sermons can no longer be in Russian. There is only one Protestant church left in Moscow, a Baptist one, where foreigners are hardly welcomed. The British get a Chaplain down from Helsinki or Stockholm, two or three times a year—that's about the limit of our churchgoing, so prayers must be said at home.

An encouraging note in the midst of considerable gloom about the house is that the servant situation seems quiet for the moment—so much so that a number came back from vacation to help with a buffet dinner of sixty the other night. We had a gay evening and Roger performed his Russian dances in fine style. We sang various raucous songs, and I'm told there were sore throats and heavy heads at Mokhovaya next morning.

Postmarked Moscow   *August 19, 1950*

BACK AGAIN IN
Moscow after five very hectic days, four of which we spent flying. I said I felt like an air-circus party. But even those five days did us a lot of good and we feel refreshed. Dad, especially, looks a different man after his talks and discussions with the men outside. On thing that gave me new courage, and strengthened my wabbling resolution, was the confidence people showed in the job we are doing, and their genuine sympathy and understanding of many of our problems and difficulties. Of course, Germany is also close under the guns, but our people there live in a very American world, and the atmosphere is gay and free compared to anything behind the Curtain. We brought back seven tons of supplies, and even have our Thanksgiving turkey nestling in the deep freeze. This time, we concentrated on as much meat as possible, fresh oranges, grapefruit, eggs, etc. One egg today in Moscow is 27 cents!

OUTSIDE MY WIN-
dow, little Russian women are scraping away at the porch
floor, preparatory to re-laying the cement. They've finished the
job downstairs, where they spent days carrying very small
buckets from the farthest point of the garden. The request to
Burobin for this work to be done was made months ago, as
soon as frost was over. Typically, they have chosen the only
fine weeks of the summer, so that we cannot use the porches
until frost sets in again. And, typically, the work is done halfway. Noticing the new front veranda pavement, I had someone ask the forewoman, "Why do you lay it this way? It would
be better to slope it toward the outside edge so that water can
drain off." She and her helper looked astonished, and explained there was no necessity. "If any rain comes in, you can
sweep it away!" The common-sense approach never occurs to
these people; and, as for ingenuity, one wonders how they have
been able to invent all the scientific marvels they claim so
loudly.

Looking at these girls of twenty to twenty-five who did the
work here, it's hard even to remember they are women. They
are without shape or color—their faces, their clothing, all of
a piece. They wear faded jerseys; a length of stuff made into a
tight skirt; coarse stockings; and broken shoes. Their heads
are wrapped tight in another bit of cotton cloth. They work
silently; and even when they are resting under the lilac bushes,
they scarcely talk to each other. They go about their work with
great patience, but with no apparent enjoyment. Even the rare
sunshine we are having these days brings no response, and they
neither speak to any of us nor answer us when we speak to
them.

The lot of them seem to prove the explanation of labor re-
cruitment in schools. The stupid are sorted out and put at
trades, with no hope of advancement, a kind of robot group
perpetually condemned to forced labor. They don't complain.
They never will complain; they simply accept. This acceptance

does not minimize their force. Stalin himself has said, "Leaders change, but the people remain. Only the people are immortal. All the rest is transient." The very passivity of the people is a positive force, and the Soviet leaders have learned to use and control this force for their own ends. Whether, as Stalin suggests, those leaders will give way to others, we cannot tell. For our own purposes, we must deal with the present lot.

The inefficiency and poor workmanship we meet on every hand is discouraging. Our porches are examples of it; but, worse yet, are the repairs being done at American House, where the enlisted personnel live in drear discomfort. For over a year we have been asking Burobin to send people to repair the roof, the washrooms, to repaint the building. The washrooms were especially bad, and the kitchens were disgraceful. We had the money from home, but could get no action out of the Russians.

Finally, last month, they sent a crew in who puttered about in wet plaster, and installed new American plumbing fixtures with long nails and screws which went through into the next room, breaking into newly done-over walls. Pipes were so badly laid that, no sooner finished above, they dripped into the washrooms below. Paint was put on over damp surfaces. Altogether, it looks very little better than before, and has cost the United States Government thousands of dollars. We went to see the place ourselves, and decided our building inspector had been quite right in refusing to accept the job. Since then, the Russians have simply called their men away and sent no others. Our people have been without hot water for ten days—and so it goes.

If we really wished to retaliate, we should contrive so that the gas main in front of the Soviet Embassy in Washington would be shut off without explanations; their telephones would stop working during rush hours; street repairs would go on in front of their driveway, barring all exits; newly arrived staff members would fail their driving permit examinations; and the brakes on their motor cars would be declared unsatisfactory. There are dozens of ways in which we could quite politely and quite correctly annoy and harass our enemies.

The weather is fine at the moment and, as a result, we are

having an "epidemic" of serious stomach trouble among our employees. Waking to see the sunshine, they immediately telephone to say they are too sick to come to work. Careful searches through the Parks of Culture and Rest would find them happily picnicking with their families. But we must accept the fiction and welcome them back with solicitous inquiries as to their health.

We now have a willing young American, of Polish parentage, from our Information Service Office, who has taken Roger's place as house manager, and he reports he cured two of the sick—the furnace man and yard man—by administering strong doses of black coffee, as they had spent the day before drinking vodka under the trees. Hence the stomach-aches.

He is having his troubles with the laundry women, those five ladies whose tongues clatter away like those of the *tricoteuses* at the foot of the guillotine. They had a terrible fight over two yards of white cotton left over from re-covering the ironing boards. Each wanted the material for herself and finally it had to be removed from their clutching hands. These same ladies were in a frightful temper because, when Mrs. Cannon and Jackie Cochran were here, and left small presents for the maids who waited on them, they were not given an equal share!

Coming back from the *dacha* the other day we were stuck behind a truck. Our chauffeur pooped his horn, with no result. The Little Men following behind pooped even louder. We finally passed, and looking back we saw one of them lean out the car window, shout at the truck driver, and wave his revolver at him. We thought what might happen if we tried that on the Baltimore-Washington Highway some crowded Sunday afternoon.

Postmarked Moscow   *August 30, 1950*

ALREADY THERE'S
a feel of autumn in the air, and the days grow short. The

nights also grow longer, which is a comfort, as Russians have not yet invented window shades. The sun streamed into my bedroom all summer, from three o'clock on. Our vegetable garden is dried and withered; only our celery beds, our chief prizes, are still intact. Celery is an almost unknown plant in Russia, so we nurse it carefully and store it after picking. The tomatoes have had no chance at all and remain hard, green balls. The squash have just finished flowering, with no possibility of bearing fruit. It's all very sad, especially when we read that other parts of Europe have rejoiced in hot luxuriance. Perhaps, if we'd had better weather, it would have exasperated us all the more to have to remain cooped up in Moscow; but the endless cold and damp is not a cheerful prelude to the long winter ahead.

One explanation of the early demise of the garden may be that Theodore, the gardener, took his vacation in August. His replacement is not too sympathetic, and fighting Russian arguments is no easier than fighting Russian weeds. They are very tenacious and voracious plants. I did my feeble bit, but had to resign when I found nettles mixed in with them. Even very small nettles defeat me.

On Friday we went to the last mass to be held in the French Church of St. Louis by the French priest, Père Thomas. This church was founded before the French Revolution, and was at one time a very prosperous community with hospital and school attached, ministering to all the needs of Roman Catholics, foreign and native, in the city. The Czars gave it their support and, since the enactment of the Litvinoff Agreement, a French priest was permitted to hold services there and to care for the faithful. About a year ago a group of parishioners demanded the church keys from Père Thomas, saying that they had constituted themselves a committee in charge, that a Polish-Russian speaking priest had been sent for, and that henceforth the church and its affairs would be in their hands. Père Thomas could still say mass for foreigners at specific hours, but that was all.

The poor gentleman had no choice but to give in, and things went on like that until last week his residence permit was cancelled by the Russian Foreign Office and he was told he must make ready to leave the country. The parishioners, aside from those enrolled in the church Soviet, were distressed. They are a pathetic lot, mostly Polish, very old, very poor, with no hope left here on earth, so that any in a life hereafter is especially precious to them.

Père Thomas told me one story of a sick woman who sent him three hundred rubles, wrapped in a dirty paper. She had saved it for her burial. Now that he was leaving, however, she realized she could not hope for a decent Catholic service, so she sent the money, asking him to say three masses: one for the Pope, one for the dead of her own family, and one for her own soul's salvation.

Curiously enough, the date of Friday coincided with that of the Feast of St. Louis, the patron saint of old France and of that particular church. The mass was at twelve o'clock, and we went from our Embassy, sixty strong, our service men all in uniform. As these last arrived, passers-by and workmen from buildings opposite guessed something unusual must be up and they stopped to watch. Quite a crowd gathered as the cars drove into the courtyard.

There were four Ambassadors in the front pews, along with several other ranking representatives of Missions. The British, French, and Italians are all Catholics. Most of us were not, but we followed the mass as best we could. There was a handful of poor old men and women shuffling about the side aisles, looking in astonishment at the pews filled with well-dressed foreigners. Dad's four Secret Service men, along with Sir David's, stood glumly against the back wall. Père Thomas said the militiamen outside rang up for an extra Security Police guard as the congregation gathered, and it's true I saw some familiar and sinister figures lurking about the yard as we came in. The MVD are all alike in aspect, their overcoats being as much a giveaway as the felt hats of FBI men.

Père Thomas was visibly affected as he celebrated the mass; and the choir, directed by the American priest, Father Brassard, had to lend support to his rather shaken voice. He read us an edifying homily on the life and holy example of Saint Louis, and we all joined in the prayers. The occasion certainly called for a warrior saint, and I trust he heard us in heaven.

At the conclusion of the service, Père Thomas walked down the aisle with the French Ambassador, and we followed to shake his hand at the door. Later he came to lunch, and seemed very grateful for the support that had been given him, realizing we had done so to show solidarity against one more example of unreasoning persecution. Father Brassard will stay on, but he must say his masses in a room of his flat, in what he calls the modern Catacombs.

Meanwhile the Polish priest, who looks more like Erich Von Stroheim than any cleric, will continue to run the church. Père Thomas thinks he may not be a priest at all, but simply a stooge brought in. He pointedly walked in front of the altar the other day, and his aspect is more that of an executioner than a minister of the gospel.

Père Thomas' mass was usually served by a pious young man of Polish descent, otherwise employed as a chauffeur in one of the Embassies. As he's not always available, the good Father asked the church handyman to help him one morning. Afterward, the Polish priest took the man severely to task and had him brought before the authorities of the Cult, the Soviet officials who deal with religious matters. Why had he served mass for the foreign priest? He replied that the priest had asked him, as it was a special service for the mother of one of the clerks in the French Embassy. This lady had died in Paris, and her son wished prayers said for her.

"Not at all," said the Polish priest. "If you had listened closely you would have heard Père Thomas say, 'Viet Nam.' The mass was said in honor of that nation, and you were tricked into collaborating with enemies of the Soviet people." What the Father had really said were the words, "Vita Eternam!"

A pack of Russians have asked for passport visas to go to the General Assembly in New York. We wish we could keep them waiting. We wish they did not have to go at all, but, as Dad says, what would be the use of closing out our Embassies and leaving them to roam about New York in large groups, taking notes on everyone and everything? Panyushkin, their Ambassador in Washington, left here last week, having been in Russia since May. He never made a move to call on Dad or to offer any of the polite gestures which protocol requires. This year, there will be no luncheon given here for Vishinsky.

What a farce it all is. The only Soviet citizens we have contact with are the servants and shopkeepers. Even the latter are very careful to confine their conversation to "Eighty rubles, fifty kopeks, and thank you." Those who speak French or English are afraid to do so in front of the other shoppers, and even guides in museums prefer us to come with an interpreter so they will not be accused of fraternizing.

Right now, our servant problem is more acute than ever. Chin was quite ill before he went on holiday, and the Doctor is fearful for his heart. Tong had a cold yesterday, and I dosed him with pills. Today Claudia, the fat scullery maid, asked me for pills for her stomach. I told her that I was no doctor, and that, while I could help Tong's cold, stomach trouble was much more difficult to treat. She was greatly hurt by my refusal, so I prescribed a diet of *yoghourt,* a Russian variety of which can be bought in the dairy stores. An hour later, one of the laundry women wanted a poultice for her wrist, and so it goes. Actually I try to keep away from the lot of them, for they are as insistent as children, and as jealous of any small favors.

All of Moscow has been decorated with posters announcing a fine new motion picture, *Secret Mission,* which purports to show how England and America attempted to make a separate peace with Germany and get her to fight with them against the Soviet Union. The picture has received a Stalin prize, and is playing now in twenty-five of the city theaters. Eisenhower and Bradley are shown plotting against their Russian Allies —two "would-be soldiers" who had to rely on the Soviet armies to fight their battles. There is a fine pure-minded young American who sees the light in time to renounce his allegiance to a nation of warmongers and seek a new home in the glorious U. S. S. R. This is the picture of the year, and the people must believe it.

DAD GOES TO SEE
Vishinsky at one today. About the plane incident, I assume.
Until he read that Austin had announced the fact in the Security Council meeting yesterday, Dad was prepared to refuse
to receive any communication on the subject. Now, it seems
certain that we shot down an attacking Soviet bomber over
Korean waters. Malik, of course, says that the affair was staged,
and staged over water so that no evidence could be found.
Evidence has been found, far more than we had to go on in
the Baltic plane incident, and I should think the Russian case
would be prejudiced by their attitude at that time.

As luck will have it, we have the Indian Ambassador for
lunch today. I've just been down in the kitchen, ordering a
special plate prepared for him, as he is a strict vegetarian and
will not even help himself from a dish that has had meat or
meat gravy on it. We asked him today because he is leaving
soon, having taken as much of this harsh atmosphere as his
philosophy can endure.

It will be interesting to see what the Soviets make of the
plane business. Of course, they will play it up in all their
papers, claiming that we massacred an innocent bystander—
"by-flyer," rather. Right now there are most inflammatory
articles appearing in the Soviet press, retailing every sort of
atrocity our troops are alleged to have committed in Korea.
The language is more violent than ever before, and one wonders if the articles are designed to work their people into a
war frenzy.

Certainly these are anxious days, and I admit I am glad,
for that reason, that Roger is away and safe home. We have
numbers of women and young children in the Embassy. Too
many of them, perhaps. Housing and service become every day
more difficult, and it is not right that the men should be
bothered by domestic crises when they have political questions
heavy on their minds.

Our own domestic crisis is the illness of Chin, who was taken off to hospital three days ago. After an intercession on the part of our doctor, he was admitted to the Polyclinic, the hospital reserved for foreigners. As the Russians believe in keeping a patient in the hospital until he or she is able to return to work, the bill will be large. But the poor little man is so grateful, and, after all, he has been a most faithful servant.

Lunch should have been at one-thirty. The Indian Ambassador arrived at one-fifteen, and I sat him down before a bowl of nuts, as I feared Dad might be very late. The others came: the Australian Chargé; de Limairac, the Counselor of the French Embassy; Dick Service; and Bibs Thurston. We drank sherry, ate nuts along with the Ambassador, and finally went in to lunch at two. Fifteen minutes later, Dad and Ray Thurston, now Acting Counsellor, came in.

Dad had been with Vishinsky for forty-five minutes, during forty of which the Minister endeavored to force a protest note into Dad's hand. Dad refused politely, but very firmly, to accept it. The Minister insisted that such action was contrary to all diplomatic procedure, but Dad replied that the matter was one concerning the United Nations and could not be discussed between the U. S. S. R. and the United States Government. The Soviet Government, Dad reminded him, had its representative on the Security Council in New York, and that was the proper place for any discussions of the event.

Vishinsky, through his interpreter, Pastoev, repeated over and over again the necessity for Dad to take the note. Dad folded his arms, and finally, still very politely, said, "Mr. Minister I do not think this conversation can be profitably pursued."

In the end, Vishinsky said, "Mr. Ambassador, for the third time I pray you to accept this note."

Dad refused once more, and the interview was over. Both Dad and Ed Freers, who went with him to the Ministry, reported Vishinsky as completely astounded by the refusal, actually rocked by it. As our two men turned to leave, they asked him if he intended starting soon for the United States.

"If you will grant me a visa," answered Vishinsky.

"I signed one for you yesterday," said Dad, "and I presumed you had already sent for it. Mine took ten days to be validated when I went out to Germany last month."

The Minister apologized, saying there must have been a mistake, as his office had strict orders to honor immediately any application from the American Ambassador.

Dad smiled politely, accepted the apology, and said, "I hope Mr. Minister that you will meet with the same courteous treatment in the United States that has always been accorded me here."

All this story we got after the guests left. Dad went back to the office and I sat here, waiting and wondering what the results of the whole business would be, for this was independent action on Dad's part. Although we hoped it would be approved by Washington, one is never sure they will look at things with the same cold realism we acquire here.

At seven fifteen, we tried to get the regular Voice of America news bulletin in English. On the radio, lately, there has been jamming all over the dial, so nothing clear came through. We had dinner, and at nine-thirty one of the American press correspondents called to say BBC had reported the note's rejection, monitoring the news from a Tass despatch over Radio Moscow. At ten, to our surprise the Voice of America simply reported that a note had been given to the American Ambassador. Dad was quite discouraged; but later, when we went to the Chancery to pick up any message that might come in, there was a special news flash from the State Department over Voice of America, reporting the refusal.

Dad went to bed in a cheerful frame of mind, and this morning a message came in from the Department, starting, "We commend your action," and going on to say, "For your information, a note was delivered to the Department in Washington which was promptly returned to the Soviet Embassy." Everyone here was pleased and some of us felt very proud, in addition.

WE HAVE BEEN
dining out with various colleagues this week. The weather has
been so bad I think everyone felt the need of cheering up. The
Swede is going to the UN sessions in New York, and gave a
party on Tuesday to say farewell. I sat on his right, Madame
Brosio being away, and next the Austrian Minister who is really
a very funny man. An old-time hussar, he has handlebar moustaches and a sweeping manner. His political opinions are
original, perhaps because he has fought two generations of
wars in Central Europe, never twice on the same side.

Brosio, the Italian, is a fine man whose principles and pa-
triotism remained unshaken and unquestioned throughout the
war. He is from Turin, a lawyer, and much respected by his
Government. His wife is exquisite. We like them both very
much. We lunched with the Austrian yesterday, a party arranged in order that Dad might sample a new shipment of
Burgundy he had received. Dad thought he had received it
too recently to drink. The French Chargé, a nervous, sensitive
man called Brionval, thought the wine should have been more
chambrée, but it proved pleasant enough and warmed Brionval
sufficiently so he told me the sad tale of his family chateau in
Lorraine, looted by the Germans of everything he loved.

Both he and his brother were on service abroad, at the time.
His old mother watched the Germans tear the tapestries and
pictures off the walls, watched them burn her books—then took
to her bed, and died. A pathetic story, typical of modern France,
where so much that was beautiful has disappeared. We can
only hope that the essential richness and vitality of the country
will bring regeneration and produce a new race of hardy men
and women to face up to the challenge of the new enemy.

Last night, we dined at the British Embassy. Now that win-
ter is upon us, they draw the curtains across the view of the
Kremlin. I miss it, for it's the finest in Moscow. This was the
Kelly's last dinner before the departure of their Belgian chef.
The substitute sent them by Burobin is quite worthless. Lady

Kelly is looking for another, but gets no offers under a monthly wage of 2000 rubles, $500 a month in our money.

One of our people, just back from a trip to Leningrad and beyond, said he heard talk on the train of the ruble returning to the prewar rate of two to the dollar. There is no reason why the Soviets couldn't make it one if they wished to. It's a purely arbitrary matter and affects no one but foreigners living on the dollar rate.

Just recently, all the rents of Diplomatic properties have been doubled—no reason given, no appeals listened to. This, along with the wages we must pay, makes the Moscow budgets so big for our Governments that many of the smaller Missions have folded altogether, and others are cutting their staffs. It's a skilful maneuver, designed to oust us all, but Dad feels the United States must meet the expense, even if it's considered part of our Defense measures. Looked at from that angle, the sum is small.

Tonight, our thirty-second wedding anniversary, we have a select group dining here to drink toasts with us. I reminded myself last night that never, in any one of those thirty-two years, have I been able to know or guess what the next would bring. While it's been a lifetime of uncertainty, there's also the cheering realization that it's still one of anticipation.

Postmarked Moscow   *September 23, 1950*

ALL MONTH, THE thermometer has been in and around the fifties, and as yet we've no heat in the house. Burobin has sent a team of men who have torn up the basement and torn out the radiators from each room, taken them outdoors, and forced water from the garden hose through them to clean out the rust and muck. Russian radiators have no valves to release steam or air. Any repairs must be a major effort. With the radiators all spread out across the lawn, we've no real assurance that we will have heating next month, though our engineer says cheerfully that the job should be finished by October 2nd.

I hope so, for it's growing chill in the house and the two open fires, one in Dad's room and one in the blue sitting room downstairs, are hardly enough to keep us comfortable. On the other hand, we dined at the Norwegians' last night, and I saw Dad mopping his brow furiously because of the heat. I tell him he will be desperate when he is home this winter, and has to put up with American central heating. He agrees, and is ordering some tropical-worsted suits from his London tailor.

We've just had a visit from our inspector. He said that, of all the Chanceries he's seen in Europe, Asia, and Africa, Mokhovaya takes the prize. I'm sure he's right. It's a fantastic building, first designed and constructed in 1936 by the Soviets as musicians' and artists' studio apartments. Its exterior is florid, its interior badly planned and constantly in need of repair; but its location, on the big open place whence avenues lead into Red Square, is good.

Just across are the Kremlin wall and a long line of buildings, once convents or barracks. From the windows we sometimes see people peering out with spyglasses. That is, we can see them if we use our own spyglasses. But, at so many hundred feet distance, there's no danger of their looking through the windows to read the papers on our desks! They've repainted the Kremlin buildings a lurid egg-yolk yellow, and now they are doing the same to the ornate riding stable which fills one end of Mokhovaya Square.

Once the Kremlin walls were whitewashed. Now they are pinky red, and the tower brickwork is newly pointed up, the only tidy job in all of Moscow. Their bricklaying is slapdash, mostly slap, the kind we use when buildings are to be plastered over and the mortar left rough to hold the plaster. Here, they often omit the plaster, and wind and weather eat into the mortar so the whole business crumbles. We dined at the Australians' the other day. Their Embassy had just been "remonted" and a new doorstep laid three days before. Already a piece had fallen off the front, and the new paint on the stairs had started to flake.

Just down the street from Spaso House, they are building a new block of apartments. There is a high fence around it, and guard towers at the corners. I walked past, the other day, and, sure enough, there were armed Security Police in each tower, showing that it was a forced-labor project. Other buildings and bridges have soldiers from the Red Army working on them. What a curious system it is!

Our first attempt at the ballet this year was unsatisfactory. Everyone complains the standard has deteriorated. That's a pity, for it's one of our chief entertainments. Now we plan to see Ulanova on the 29th, in the Prokofieff *Romeo and Juliet*. It's my favorite, and if the spark has gone out of that perform-ance, it's all over. Last year, I remember, we were all so en-thused that seven Ambassadors signed a program and sent it back to her, with their compliments. There was no response, of course, and I fear Dad's dream of seeing a ballerina dance at Spaso, under the chandelier, is *only* a dream.

Neither of the two new première danseuses, Placetzkaia and Strutchkova, can equal Ulanova or Lepechenskya, both of whom are forty or over. The wartime star, Semonava, danced the other evening, and—owing to a life of dissipation and fif-teen pounds' overweight—fell down on the stage. Awful scandal! The Russians take their ballet very seriously, and a fallen ballerina is as much in disgrace as a fallen general.

Speaking of the ballet, we were quite concerned the other night to see one of the women clerks from another Embassy, an unattractive female, nestled up against two Russians. One of our people pointed her out, and inquiries have been made. The poor creature was approached by a Russian lady at some concert. Very flattered to have someone take an inter-est in her, the girl responded eagerly. The lady then introduced a gentleman to her, and since then she has been to the theater and ballet with them several times. The gentleman makes speeches to her about the sympathy of true minds—as opposed to the sexual approach—a line of talk the pathetic girl warms to at once, and, unless her Embassy rescues her, I should think she is a lost soul.

It's by such methods that the Russians seize on people. It's no longer a question of money bribes. They learned a more subtle approach from the Germans, and they are even better at it, for, where the Germans preyed on human lust for power, the Soviets prey on human weakness, fear and insecurity. They are good at the game. That is why we have a policy in our own Embassy whereby any officer or clerk may be instantly detached and sent home, on either his own or the Embassy's request.

Last year, one young man, after he had been here two months, came to our doctor and said his nerves were such he couldn't take it. The doctor reported the matter to Wally Barbour, and the boy left within the week—left with Wally's and Dad's commendation for his courage in admitting his difficulties. This is no place for scratchy nerves or irritated complexes. It's not because any of us are in danger, for we're not, but it's the indefinable pressure that lessens, only to increase.

Dad's great regret at the moment is that he has no occasion to call on Gromyko, for he aches to ask him what he thinks of the war news! I must say it's encouraging to hear the radio reports, and now we are wondering what the effect will be on these people, and whether they will merely continue their support of North Korea or attempt to force the Chinese into the fight. At the ballet, the other night, one of our men sat in the midst of a Korean delegation, all of whom looked very crossly at him. Obviously, the Koreans were being given "the treatment" by the Russians. Front seats at the Bolshoi are the first indication of favor.

Postmarked Moscow   *October 8, 1950*

OUR AUTUMN
vacation is in sight. The plane comes in late this afternoon—Dick especially is excited, as his wife, Helen, arrives to spend a month with him. The separation has been hard for them both.

I had my men all set for their beauty sleep last night, but the Embassy Duty Officer rang to say Mr. Gromyko wished to see Dad at eleven forty-five. It was then ten forty-five, and I'd tucked him into bed with an asthma pill and a dose of cough medicine, to make sure he would be well for the trip out on Thursday.

Quite rightly, Dad declined to get up and go down to the Foreign Office. He sent Wally—but you can imagine we stayed awake to hear what it was all about. When Wally came back, he said he'd rejected another note, this time about an alleged strafing of an airfield in Soviet territory, somewhere near Vladivostok. Following Dad's lead of last month, he declined to accept it, insisting that the matter be referred to the United Nations.

He said he had the impression that Gromyko expected a refusal, and that that was the only thing that made him hesitate whether or not to take it. But, while the translation was going on, he determined to refuse the note just as Dad had done the earlier one, this procedure having been approved by the State Department. As before, the Soviets sent the note around to the Embassy and, as before, we returned it to them without comment. What a silly business!

Of course, we had to get Dick up, as he is the Far Eastern expert, so Helen will not find him quite as fresh as I had hoped. He went down to the Chancery, afterward, with Wally, to send off a dispatch to the Department, and then stayed to listen to the last Soviet news bulletin. Invariably, the Russians put anything like this onto the radio before we have a chance to comment on the event, or even to translate any notes that may have been exchanged.

Wally said he thought, from Dad's description of the interview with Vishinsky, that Mr. Gromyko was a far smoother operator; and some of our people believe that he is actually the man in charge, and that Mr. V. takes orders from him. In any event, he showed none of the dismay or embarrassment that the latter had demonstrated.

I am greatly relieved that the incident does not seem too serious, for I should hate to see our trip put off.

While we are away on holiday, the Freers, Ed and Elaine, will move into the corner apartment here in Spaso, and will stay on through the winter. I am very glad, as we like them both and it will be good to have a woman in the house during the two months we are gone on our Christmas vacation—one who can direct the establishment, and run the parties, and keep peace among the servants, as the latter job becomes more and more complicated.

Postmarked Moscow   *October 4, 1950*

JUST AS I WILL
never forget the blackout in England that first year of the war, so will I never forget the blackout of Russian radio jamming. No matter where we turn, up and down the dial, whenever there is news, or the hint of news, distasteful to these people, on goes the roar. Here in Moscow, it's very bad; and the noise is so unmistakable that any unfortunate Soviet citizen attempting to listen to BBC or Voice of America gives himself away by simply turning his radio knob. It's maddening, exasperating, and desperately discouraging. That noise seems the very negation of freedom.

These last few days, there's been no getting through to the VOA or the BBC, even for English-language broadcasts, and the operator who takes down our Embassy daily radio bulletin sent word to Dad that there had been constant jamming all night. Imagine a country where the people accept this kind of thing as right and proper. Imagine a country where they never question the Government's privilege to tell them what they should hear and read.

The concrete evidence of Government interference is there, every time they turn their radios on. After all, even if they are not going to believe what we talk about, at least they've the right to hear it! Last evening, as we were searching for radio news, a French voice came in quite clearly, Radio Moscow in French—one of their foreign-language broadcasts. We listened, only to hear the lady announce that a dispatch from the United States gave the horrifying details of a compulsory sterilization program for the poor, now operating in twenty-seven states. Both Dad and Dick said they were reluctant to go home if that were the case. The Russians put on their own foreign-language broadcasts, but, if that's a sample, it doesn't seem as though they could be very convincing to civilized Western audiences.

We are still without heat in the house, and it grows steadily colder. They promise some for the end of the week; but, when our engineer went to look over the work, he discovered that they had omitted to repair a large leak in one of the boilers and that the oil tank had never been cleaned. Our hot water is fed from a small emergency tank, but, as that is getting low, he's got to put the oil in the big one and not wait for it to be cleaned. All this is so typical of the Russians. They never quite do a job right, never quite finish it.

When Dad gets angry about it all, I tell him it's hopeful for our cause and he must not complain. Another of his exasperations is the way the two Russian chauffeurs treat our beautiful Cadillac car. They think it beneath their pride to shift gears, so strain the motor around every corner and up every hill. Like most Europeans, they are great horn-blowers and rely on noise rather than on brakes. Granted, the pedestrians are a real menace, as they have no more traffic sense than geese, and jaywalking is a national pastime.

The other night, as we were starting up the side street near Spaso Square, suddenly a man loomed up in the middle of the road—a pathetic figure with ragged clothes and empty, staring eyes. We stopped just in time, and one of the Little Men behind got out and led him across the road. He was not only blind, but crippled. This is the kind of poor creature that wanders everywhere along Moscow streets, but it's awkward to meet one in the dark.

I wish that I might visit some of their hospitals. As I've said, I applied to the Foreign Office, last year, and again this year, but have heard nothing from them. Yet every Peace Delegation that comes to town is trotted around to a selected number. It's just one more frustration.

While medical treatment is supposedly free to all Soviet citizens, also dental treatment, our doctors judge, from stories told them by our Russian employees, that there's as much kill as cure about it, and that legs come off and teeth come out whenever the patient is deemed expendable. The patient has no choice of doctor—it's socialized medicine carried to the *nth* degree, so it's largely a matter of luck. Some of their physicians are excellent, the same for the nurses; but techniques are fairly primitive, and aftercare of any illness or operation is very sketchy. The individual in Russia is unimportant; only his contribution to the State matters, and he will be looked after according to that contribution. We ourselves are always assigned to what is called the Polyclinic, where a wing is set aside for the use of foreign diplomats. I asked one of our medical men how he rated its equipment. "Like that of a second-class English nursing home," he said.

We have a new MVD team on duty, these days. I suppose even the Little Men need time off, now and again. There was an impressive showing at the Bolshoi Theater, last week, when our seats were next to those of the British Ambassador and Lady Kelly. Dad's and Sir David's men were banked solidly behind us, eight of them in a row! And what a good time they had, peering through the windows of the Italian Embassy, the other evening. The Brosios have started a Russian folk-dancing class. A very select group has been invited to attend, and you should see us lined up on each side of their big ballroom. We've at least three Ambassadors, plus Ministers and other distinguished gentlemen of the Diplomatic Corps, the whole flavored with enough of our prettiest young women to make it interesting for them. The teacher is Russian, a rather coy lady who speaks a certain amount of French and makes eyes at the ranking guests. Occasionally, she lapses into Russian, and then Ed Freers does the interpreting, making a dash to find himself a partner after he finishes. As numbers are sometimes unequal, he's often left with a choice of the Austrian

Minister, a large hearty gentleman or, Brionval the French Counselor, who weighs all of a hundred and fifteen pounds. The ladies are taken in the first grab.

The funniest sight of all was the classic afternoon, when Dad and Sir David walked hand in hand for the Grand March. I'm told Dad's language became very nautical when he missed a step; and both he and Sir David, who is an old soldier, were furious at the teacher's insistence on their starting with the right foot first. "It would take the Russians to think that up," said Dad.

Speaking of dancing, we went to the Red Army Chorus the other night. The singing was as loud and booming as last year, the dancing more astonishing than ever. This time, the program was given in Tchaikowsky Hall; and, even though the interior decoration is a touch on the pretty side, the design of the auditorium is interesting and the acoustics are excellent. It's obviously a product of the '20s or early '30s, as Soviet architecture has taken a dip since then. The same tall announcer officiated. The Russians are great on these masters of ceremonies.

The accordions, dozens of them, whanged away, the balalaikas strummed and behind them the brass blew great blasts, especially in the March from *Faust,* which the Russians seem to have adopted as one of their national songs. There were the usual tum-tums to Father Stalin, the Democratic Youth, the Glorious Consomols, and a new orchestral horror entitled Moscow-Pekin. As always, this huge men's chorus was at its best in soldier songs or folk songs, and it seemed too bad they afterward chose to embark on classics, such as Schumann, which they hummed a hundred strong.

There were the soldier dances we remembered from last season, all based on friendly competition between branches of the Services: airmen, sailors, soldiers, with a little fellow bringing down the house when he whirled around the stage, turning handsprings that were literally handsprings, his feet never touching the floor. Dad's Little Men applauded loudly, and were very pleased he had chosen to attend this performance, it being straight down their alley. They are quite wistful about

Dad's indifference to football this year, but one can hardly say the weather has been propitious.

The other day, I took a special tour of the Moscow department stores to see what progress had been made. The Mostorg, of which I have spoken before, used to be the Altman's of Moscow and, before the Revolution, was owned and managed by two Scotchmen. In addition to supplying palace guards for nervous royalties of the Middle Ages, the Scotch seem to have specialized in setting up department stores in foreign cities, the chain of Old Englands in Paris, Brussels, Madrid, etc., dates from the same period as this store in Moscow.

Now there is little left of the original aspect. Every aisle and counter is crowded with Russian workers, and ice-cream vendors are stationed on the stairways and just inside the doors. Both the crowds and the ice-cream vendors—not to mention the merchandise—spoil what was once an elegant effect. Astonishing how the Russians eat ice cream at all times, at all seasons! Someone told me it satisfies their craving for fats, and that it is the most economical way the Government has discovered for supplying milk fats to the people, ice cream being easy to transport and to keep.

With some difficulty, I forced my way up the stairs; the elevators, of course, ceased functioning years ago. By the time I had toured the second floor, given over to wearing apparel for women and children, I needed fresh air and understood why all museums and theaters require outer clothing to be checked at the doors. But it was worth while looking around and shoving between those dirty, wadded coats. The poorer Russians do not own two coats, one light, one heavy; they simply own a coat, and must put that coat on or none at all.

I was greatly interested in the infants' and children's departments, as I wanted to see exactly what Russian children wear. First the babies. The women were packed deep around that counter, and all were buying the same things. Nowhere did I see any woolen underwear—no strips of flannel, even. There were little muslin shirts on display; no knit shirts, no dresses or nightgowns, were shown. I gathered that the infants are simply wrapped in a square of cloth, unhemmed, anything the mother happens to have, and the same must be true for diapers, as I saw none of these on sale.

The main wrapping of the child consists of a tan or gray part-wool or, more likely, cotton blanket; over that, a thick cotton quilt, pink, blue, or green; and over that, for those who wish their babies really dressed up, a white cotton cover, edged with a machine-embroidered frill. When the bundle is complete, it's tied with broad ribbons. Gorer, the English anthropologist, in his book, *The Great Russians,* has an interesting study of Russian characteristics due to this swaddling. His conclusions may be exaggerated, but the custom of swaddling remains very general. There did not appear to be any other form of infant outdoor clothing for sale in this big store.

Nor was there visible any woolen underwear for older children. Here again, there were cotton shirts and bloomers and drawers—dark blue, purple, bright green—made of knit rayon or cotton. These last were quite expensive and, as no one could afford to buy very many, it's understandable they had to be of a dark and serviceable color. Dresses of rayon, cotton or shoddy wool were of poor quality and workmanship, boys' suits a little better. Children's coats were of thick stuff, often lined and padded, but again very expensive.

The women's underwear counter was almost impossible to get close to, as just as many customers crowd in to look as to buy. But I finally managed, and concluded from the purchases made that the average female wears a garter belt, again colored deep blue, yellow, or green, plus rayon or cotton knit shirts and bloomers. There were brassières for sale, all the same model—obviously made by countless thousands in a state factory—white or pink cotton, buttoned in the back, the pockets for the breasts being perfectly round.

This accounts for the astonishing shape of the Russian ladies. No matter what the nature of their bosoms, they must be shoved into these dome-like pockets and held high, almost under their chins. I say Russian ladies, for brassières seem to be luxury items and most Russian women one sees are block-shaped, anything else being of artificial creation.

The satellites' 1950 gift to the Soviet fashions is millinery.

There are far more hats worn this year—real hats, not just fur ones. These hats are of much the same pattern, untrimmed felt creations, reds and blues and browns, looming out beyond the wearer's forehead with no regard for becomingness or suitability. The fortunate possessors of these creations combine them with straight-hanging cloth or, less often, fur coats, the shoulders squared to the point of dislocation.

The best of the fur coats are of astrakhan, the rest are pretty anonymous. All are amply cut, with no attempt at style or fit; most of them have full collars which can be brought up around the face in cold weather. Separate fur collars are on sale in many shops—fox, wolf, any long-haired fur—usually black or dyed black. Fur hats are almost invariably mouton or astrakhan, black or gray. Little children are also bundled in fur, any old kind of fur, often pieced together like Jacob's coat. In the parks they look like packs of little animals playing about with each other.

Postmarked Moscow   *November 2, 1950*

AS ALWAYS, COMing back to Moscow comes as something of a shock after a glimpse of the outside world. Once away, it's all a dream; once back, it's reality. I was interested to see Dick Service's reaction after his first trip out in a year. Like mine of last spring, it was rage. He told me today that he had walked back from the Chancellery along the Arbat Street. It was Sunday, and the narrow sidewalks were crowded, supposedly with people in their good clothes, people walking for leisure. Dick had just returned from his holiday in Italy.

"Nowhere," he said, "not even in Italy, where slums are really slums, did the mass of the people have that look of sodden, accepted misery. I think it's the acceptance that most shocks a Westerner, that and the fear one reads on their faces. At the door of the subway, in Arbat Square, I saw a little girl; a peasant woman stopped her, probably to ask directions, and put a hand on her arm. The child turned in terror. Only some memory of fear, or some present sensation of fear, could have brought that look to her face."

It's true that the clothes of the public this year are better than last, but better only by comparison and better only for the few. I'm speaking now of Moscow, for, outside of the capital, things are not the same. Much of the improvement is due to what the Soviets have brought in from the satellite countries, but now that the weather is growing cold, the shoes from Czechoslovakia, which seemed so smart in the summer, look worn and shabby. Not any of the goods imported are of what we would call first-class quality. Jackie Cochran commented that they look like the kind once sold to the Negro laborers in the turpentine-mill stores in the South, in the United States. In a year and a half, I have never seen any really good material except in the military uniforms.

People at home ask us about furs. What we see for sale here are usually second hand, and even the new are badly pieced and badly cured. The best furs are kept for export, and are sold to foreign dealers at the annual Leningrad Fur Auction. None are offered to us or to the general public. Last year, when we could still visit a Government export store, on application, we were told no furs were available. Actually, there was very little available in the store beyond a few rugs, some lacquer boxes, and a little embroidered linen, all of which could be bought more cheaply outside the Soviet Union.

November 7th, the great Soviet holiday, the anniversary of the Revolution, is nearly here. Already, red flags have gone up all over the city, and portraits of our Father Stalin and his friends are plastered over the fronts of buildings. Nagosky, our house manager, the Russian-speaking employee of the Department, is doing an excellent job for us. He is very competent, and the servants all like him, so our house runs as smoothly as possible under prevailing circumstances.

He tells me that the staff have asked for their bread ration in flour for the holiday. They would like it in flour every day but that's not possible, as their own Government allows them to buy flour only twice a year and, if we gave it out daily, they would be tempted to sell it and thereby make a huge profit on the black market. We make our own bread in the house, out of flour we bring in from Germany or Finland. Russian bread, both the light and the dark, is excellent; but our own is even better, and costs only a tenth as much. As each employee, house servant, yardman, and chauffeur gets a loaf a day, this means a great saving. November 7th is one of the two occasions on which the Russian people may purchase flour, about five pounds per person, so, not to be outdone by Father Stalin, we supplement his generosity with that of Uncle Sam, and each employee will have his ration without the long standing in queues we see on every street corner.

High policy decisions have had to be made as to whether we are to attend the big mass meeting in the Bolshoi Theater, on Monday night, the 6th. This is the same one to which we went last year, the traditional gala affair honored by the entire Politburo, with a speech, by the chosen orator of the year, which is an official pronouncement of Soviet policy. Last November, it was Malenkov who spoke; the year before, it was Molotov. Stalin is rarely present for this November celebration; his winter resort, Sochi in the Crimea, offers a more salubrious climate for a gentleman of seventy.

The reason for our hesitation about attending the ceremony is that it is bound to be even more than usually anti-American and anti-Western in tone. Last year, it was bad enough, and Dad took me out directly the speeches were over. Unfortunately, the best part of the program comes late in the evening, when the top ballerinas and other artists perform, but one's resistance is considerably lowered by that time. Another reason for not going is that Dad and I are the only ones from our Embassy to be invited, and we would have no one to give us a translation, on the spot, of the remarks made. If too bad, we'd have no idea when to get up haughtily and go home!

Right now, the weather is clear and fine. I hope it remains so for the parade in Red Square. Standing two hours in cold rain would be trying. Traditionally, it's good—as one of our old doormen used to say, "God helps the godless."

Madame Chaumet, wife of the French Commercial Counselor, has just been here to say good-bye, as they are leaving for Indo-China. She and her husband have been occupying one of the apartments in the block of flats I call the Diplomatic Ghetto. Although under construction for the last five years, the building is not finished, and now great efforts are being made to get it done by the first of the year. Both front and back are covered with scaffolding, and men and women crawl about the face of the building, tacking on plaster and drilling holes for balconies.

Just yesterday, there was a splintering noise in her kitchen and Madame Chaunet came in to find one of the workmen had driven his drill straight through and there was a big hole in the rear wall, the exterior rear wall. On careful examination, this wall was found to be mere plaster, just two inches thick. It's true, what has been reported in the Western press, that there is construction going on all over Moscow but it's this kind of construction, and by next year it will be as shabby and crumbling as the cheap Czech shoes. The famous skyscraper which they are working on day and night, to have finished for November 7th, may look convincing to the uninitiated, but our experts tell us that the last five floors have been made of such thin steel that no Russian will willingly go up into them. Material ran out, and they have had to use anything that came to hand.

We see it over and over again whenever we have anything done to our own properties, and it's even visible to the naked eye as you walk along the street. There have been complaints in the Russian press about output and workmanship; and, when the Russians let those complaints go through, it's obvious there's trouble. Just now, they are rushing everything, with the hysteria of the last days of Christmas shopping, so as to make a fine show Tuesday, the 7th. I'm sure a lot of fake style will be used, more of the Potemkin-village idea.

One article in a recent American paper was lyric about "parks with shade trees and sparkling fountains," describing in particular the one around the Pushkin statue. They did move Pushkin from one side of Gorki Street to the other. They do have a fountain behind him; the shade trees have been planted and are about six feet high, some have already died. I saw no real reason for moving the statue, and was alarmed when I saw the crane at work, as I feared the poor gentleman was being liquidated altogether. But there are still streets with parks; there were more in pre-Revolutionary times, for I've seen them marked on my old Baedeker map.

Streets have been liquidated, as well as human beings and ideas. Tverskaia, the once famous Moscow shopping street is now Gorki Street, an immensely wide avenue sweeping up from Mokhovaya Square, and running into what is called the Leningrad Chaussee. Gorki Street has new buildings, each side with gaudily impressive fronts of ornamented plaster and some stone and brick, the newest and most magnificent being faced halfway up with brown stone, the kind once used on lower Fifth Avenue—quite hideous. The only really handsome building is that of the headquarters of the Moscow Soviet, which not surprisingly turns out to be an old pre-Revolutionary edifice moved and added to.

In this same midtown district, in addition to the various large hotels, there are numbers of restaurants, called by such names as the Uzberg, Armenian, Georgian, supposed to feature the national dishes of those provinces. We have tried two or three of these places, our young men have tried others, and they all offer much the same food: caviar—good caviar—and vodka to start with, or fish salad; then shaslik; kebabs of lamb or beef on skewers; Kievsky cutlets; breaded filets of chicken, stuffed with butter and fried in deep fat, or tough underdone beefsteaks. I forgot borscht, always obtainable, or other cabbage soups.

They may have a lot of other things on the menu—perhaps they can produce them if ordered far ahead, days in advance —but that's what you get, along with a little music on strange, wailing instruments and, now and again, a feeble attempt at singing by a vodka-drinking diner. This the headwaiter discourages when foreigners are present. None of it's very gay, and it costs a lot of money. A dinner such as I described, with a bottle of thin Caucasian wine, comes to from fifteen to twenty dollars per person. There are two or three night clubs, night clubs with music, not entertainers; and, quite late, they occasionally play some American jazz for dancing—that is, they play it if no official-looking Russians are about.

This, of course, is the Moscow picture. But, as uniformity is creeping over the land, not only the Russian land but that of the satellites, I doubt whether it's much different in other places. The people are really working hard, so hard they've little leisure or appetite for play beyond the stated vacations they are entitled to. Even then it's a business for them to get tickets and reservations for workers' rest homes. Life is surely real and earnest in the Soviet Union.

There are vestiges of old customs left, many of them. Samovars they still have—no brass or copper ones, however: that is, no new ones in brass or copper. The new ones are of pretty thin metal, and I'm not sure whether they are still made in the old samovar factories of Tula. We go through the latter town when we visit Yasnay Polyana. It's now a forbidden area for us, as they make metal products and machine tools there—a very busy place. It was in Tula that we picked up a third police car when we took Dad, under pressure, on a sightseeing trip to Tolstoi's home. Coming back, we still had the three cars following us and, when we stopped to picnic by the road, two motorcycle police joined, so we ate our sandwiches under the watchful eyes of fourteen MVDs.

No wonder that, when we were out last month, our jolly Belgian friends said afterward, "We didn't like to tell you, but it took you three days to lose your Moscow faces."

We really enjoyed ourselves during those two weeks away. They are fun to look back on, now November is closing around us here and the November 7th holiday must be gone through with. But we go out again on the 4th of December, so that won't be too long, and, with Christmas at home to think about, the immediate prospect is a cheerful one.

FOR THE FIRST TIME
in many years, it rained on November 7th. My feelings were
mixed. I wanted the weather to be as nasty as possible for
the Russians; for those of us who stood two hours in the Diplomatic enclosure to watch the parade, I wanted the sun to shine.
I could have compromised with a light snow; instead it rained
and fogged. The red banners hung limp; the portraits of Lenin,
Stalin and Co. were streaked, and the paper garlands around
them looked sodden and sad. We had had five days of clear
weather, but the Russians still expected it to continue over the
7th—it always had.

It started raining on the 6th while all the happy citizens
were busy putting up decorations all over town. They do a
fair job; red is a decorative color and it stands out well against
the dingy buildings. Colored electric lights were strung like
ornaments on Christmas trees, festooned and twined across
balconies and doorways. As someone said, only the Kremlin
and the American Embassy were left untrimmed. But we put
our flag out, a big one, and it waved convincingly in the face
of the paraders as they assembled in Mokhovaya Square, in
front of the Chancery. It's a good flag, and looked especially
fine in that place on that day.

All our people in all the front Embassy apartments held open
house. This was a very heroic effort, as, in order to get through
the lines, the first, and less important, guests—rather those with
pink instead of blue traffic passes—must come at half-past seven
a. m. Poor Wally had four Afghans arrive at seven-fifteen,
devout Moslems who all day couldn't eat anything he provided
and looked paler and sadder as the hours wore on. I think they
finally succumbed to a little vegetable salad and some fruit
juice.

We left here at a quarter to nine, dressed for the weather.
My one fear was that the sun might come out before noon.
I had borrowed an old overcoat with a hood and wore knee
boots. Dad said afterward I could have joined the People's

Parade at any point—I looked just like them. Dad's appearance was more "cultured," as was Ed Freers' and the military, but the rest of the women looked much like me. We were sensible as it was a very damp affair. Along with a group of colleagues and our own people who had been invited into the Square, we proceeded from Mokhovaya, leaving the cars in the courtyard there. Dad's four guardians went along and cleared the way through the crowds of soldiers already formed up. We were stopped four times by rows of Security Police, to have our passes verified; even the Little Men had to show theirs.

Our enclosure was to the right of Lenin's tomb, the Ambassadors and their families, plus high Soviet Foreign Office officials, being given the front row. I stood next to the French Ambassador and a stout lady. Her enthusiastic applause, each time Stalin was cheered, led me to identify her as the wife of the East German representative. She turned her back to me, and I mine to her.

Beyond our section, and over to the right, were other sections set aside for the rest of the privileged. The Politburo and the Moscow Soviet officials mounted to the top of the tomb, where they stood to review the show. The Square was ringed with soldiers and Security Police; they were heavily reinforced when the military part of the parade was over and the so-called "spontaneous demonstration" began. Spontaneous demonstrations were being practiced by heavily organized Moscow citizens, for weeks ahead, and I'm told the last to parade formed up, nearly ten kilometers away, at eleven o'clock the night before. It must have been a very wet night for them.

At just ten, the Kremlin clock pealed and a stout-breasted General, on a prancing bay horse, and followed by an aide, rode into the square. Massed bands on the opposite side rolled out a fanfare, and Marshal Budenny, a little overstuffed, but still a fine figure of an old-style cavalryman, his moustaches swept back, rode out to meet him. Marshal Budenny would take the review; the General as commander of the Moscow garrison would ride beside him. As they passed each company of men, and rode out into the streets and squares around where others were waiting, they were greeted by a loud cheer and the band's ruffles. Back they came into the square, and Budenny dismounted and went up to take his place with the rest of the Politburo. There was a salute, and then he read his speech, barking it out in military fashion. We heard two "Americanski Imperialisti." There was loud applause, as he finished, with a ringing "Slava Stalin" (Glory to Stalin). The band crashed into the national anthem, and the parade was on.

Compared to the one we saw last year, and the one Dad and Roger saw on May Day, it was almost a token parade. The military display was cut in half; there was no "air show" because of the weather; the tanks were old ones, painted up for the occasion; and our people had the definite feeling the whole picture was being played down. Even so, it was impressive enough and the setting was dramatic, in spite of the drizzle.

The sound of soldier's boots, thousands of them coming down on paving stones, strikes a convincing chill to anyone's heart. I still wished we might have had snow. The General Officers in the parade all appeared to be exactly the same shape, the soldiers who paraded the same height. It's remarkable how uniform this race looks when viewed in the mass. The Generals were substantial figures, their chests padded to be in line with their stomachs, all this weight in front giving them a stance like the Little King in Soglow's comic strip. In our own stand, the Foreign Office officials had on their best blues, the material of which stood up rather badly to the wet and rain. Gromyko was there, and Zorin, and Bogomolov; the latter two Vice Ministers, along with a host of others. Russian officials always manage to look self-conscious in public and watchful, as if they not only didn't trust us, but didn't trust each other.

We left soon after the civil part of the parade began. Ordinarily, this goes on for hours, beginning about eleven-thirty; it lasted on previous years until two-thirty or three o'clock. This year, the whole business was over by one—because of the weather, perhaps, though I had a feeling that, if the authorities had wanted it to go on, the marchers would have had little choice. We were a big group leaving the stand, as most of our friendly colleagues followed Dad and the British Ambassador, knowing their Little Men would get them through the crowds and across the square to Mokhovaya. It was good to get back under our own sheltering flag and to take off our wet clothes. Wally provided drinks to hand and we settled down by his windows to watch the rest of the show.

Some of the guests who had been there since seven-thirty, especially the four Afghans, looked a little tired of it all, but it was quite a sight, the streams of people with their banners and placards held aloft, feeding across the square from three sides and up the incline into Red Square. Once there, they marched ten abreast and between each lot stood lines of soldiers or militiamen. No one was taking any chances on spontaneity coming out of the "spontaneous" demonstration. The term spontaneous is a literal translation of the Russian, and hardly applies to what we would call popular enthusiasm. There were bands, and, as each group came in front of the tomb, they shouted "Slava Stalin"—led by a fellow who gave them the signal from the top of the tomb—that was real spontaneity.

Dad went to the Bolshoi gala, the night before. We decided that I'd not go, thereby marking for any who cared to observe, that he went alone, purely on official duty. He was tucked into a box along with Sir David—with two Little Men apiece —plus the Iranian and the East German Ambassador. We listened here on the radio, and counted fifteen "Amerikanski Imperialisti"—Sir David told me afterward that the British were mentioned three times. Last year, we ran up to twenty-two, but this year's speech made up in specific violence. Dad came away directly it was over. It's a curious idea of theirs to invite us to hear ourselves reviled and insulted.

The only reason Dad went was that if he had stayed home, the five press correspondents would have put the fact on the wires and made so much of it as to create an incident. As it was, they told him, next day, they had cabled back as a portentous fact that he had gone to the parade in a soft felt hat, rather than a topper. I was glad they didn't describe my costume at that event!

The diplomatic reception this year was held at the Métropole Hotel, as the official Foreign Office house is under repair. The party began at nine-thirty. We did not arrive until ten—Wally, the Counsellors and their wives, and the three military Attachés. The receiving line had broken up, and already the hordes had fallen on the supper tables, so the big ballroom looked like an overdressed version of Childs or Lyons Corner House. I took off my diamond earrings and put them into my bag—no use losing anything in that mob—held the skirts of my best dress tight in one hand, lest something be spilled on me, and made my way to as clear a corner as I could find.

There was a tap on my shoulder and a cordial greeting and it was Madame Gromyko, grown fatter than last year, and dressed in pale green, so she looked like a round, soft caterpillar. But she is a kind, rather frightened, woman and the scant encounters we have had have been pleasant. I corralled my ladies and introduced them to her, asked about her children and her health. She has a very uncertain gall bladder, which couldn't have been improved by the food she was eating that evening. Across the table, Marshal Budenny was holding court, tossing down glass after glass. Our own military Attaché spoke to him and introduced his wife, to whom the Marshal took a fancy and asked her to go riding with him some morning, an invitation she will hardly hear of again.

Dad had told us we were all to leave after forty-five minutes, the same length of time the Soviets stayed at our reception, Fourth of July. We felt like a pack of Cinderellas, but our watches were synchronized and out we went when he gave the signal. The Russians noticed it, I hope—our colleagues did —but the Soviet heads were pretty well down in the troughs. Poor Madame Gromyko must be feeling very tired indeed this morning.

Postmarked Moscow   *November 15, 1950*

PERHAPS ONE OF
the most discouraging aspects of a Westerner's life in Moscow is that we must distrust every gesture made toward us. We

must suspect every friendly look, every approach that is attempted. And we must do this for the protection of the innocent individual, but for ourselves even more It's not often, of course, that we are approached, or that gestures are made; but away from Moscow, on trains, and in the smaller cities and towns, our people have a few contacts Even then, they cannot be sure they are genuine, or that they are not reported, and they must always be on guard as to what they say and do.

One of the young British couples had made friends with a Russian couple of their own age. The English girl had lost her purse in the bus, and the Russian had telephoned and made an appointment to return it to her. In this way, the two families became acquainted and met several times, Mr and Mrs. B—— being very careful to phone, to the number given them, from a public call box instead of the Embassy. They were invited to the Russians' flat for dinner, and never at any time was there any political talk or discussion. All four were interested in music and the ballet, and the conversation remained harmlessly esthetic throughout. Then, one night, our English friends thought they were followed Nothing happened, but the next time they telephoned there was no answer, another time still no answer, and that was the end.

Such stories make us realize how dangerous it may be for anyone to be friendly with us. We dare not let them take the risk, and, if they do so quite freely, we wonder about them and question their motives. In the satellite countries, things are actually more difficult, for there must be many people who still have relations with foreign diplomats. The diplomats see their friends drop away, one by one, many of them under suspicion or under prison sentence, because of their foreign contacts. Here it's only occasionally that we have more than casual words with any Russian and stories such as the B——s' are rare.

Another diplomatic colleague, Henry. a nice man, a former History Professor, told us of the experience he had in Tiflis last month. He met a Russian on the train, got into conversation with him and his wife, and found he was a Professor of Musical History from the Moscow Conservatory. Both being scholars, they found mutual interests and became so entranced with each other's company that they remained together for the whole week in Tiflis. The Russian Professor took Henry to call upon friends in that city, he introduced him to some of the local intellectuals, and Henry lunched and dined in their houses and went on sightseeing expeditions guided by the curator of the local museum.

All this seemed to be done quite openly; and certainly, if the authorities had wished to prevent it, a word to the Professor would have been sufficient. Henry says that no mention whatever of political affairs was made by the Russian Professor or his friends, most of whom spoke English or French. All were cultivated men, but entirely preoccupied with their intellectual pursuits; they accepted Henry as a fellow-scholar, and that seemed to be all. He enjoyed himself immensely and, since his return, has been called several times by the Professor and has been invited to dine at the latter's home.

I asked Henry what it was like. The Russian Professor's salary is five thousand rubles a month. He and his wife live in two rooms, simply furnished, but lined with books. They have a kitchenette of their own and a bathroom, all of which puts their flat in the luxury class. They have no servant, but a woman comes to clean and wash up. They have no car, although the Professor said that he had thought of buying one; but the Conservatory puts one at his disposal whenever necessary. His vacation in the Caucasus was arranged by the Conservatory authorities, and he realized certain royalties from books they published for him. He was a composer, but had not written any music for some time.

Henry said that the Russian showed him some of his music manuscripts, and that they were distinctly modern in feeling and composition. This would explain why he had not produced any recent works, as all such music is highly disapproved of by the authorities and condemned as actually subversive to the Communist cause. He said nothing of this, however, merely telling Henry that he was finishing two musical histories, one of Czech music and one of Polish, and that his writing took up his whole time.

Henry was puzzled and we were, too, by the whole story. Was the man genuine? Why did the authorities permit him to be friends with Henry? If this was done with their permission, why was there no attempt to influence Henry intellectually or politically? Each time, we went back to the conviction that the authorities must be ware of what was going on, and that it must have been done with their permission.

Such incidents are so rare we are bound to question their meaning. Certainly, the Soviets could have little hope of converting Henry to their way of thinking, as he is the most solid citizen imaginable, and entirely impervious to pressure of any kind. But it's puzzling business. Usually the end is like that in the other story, about the British couple with their Russian friends. One hopes this may be different, for the Professor's sake.

We are busy arranging a program of events for the Jack Cabots' visit. They come down on the 19th from Finland, where he is our Minister, and will stay until Thanksgiving night. We have our dinner at midday, and that afternoon a big cocktail party for all the Americans: the Embassy, the five American press correspondents and the one fur-buyer and wife—in other words the entire colony.

One of the real old-timers here is the Luxembourg Minister, Monsieur Blum, who told me of an amusing experience he had which illustrates the Russian feeling about their papers, their documents. These are precious and necessary possessions, to be carried on the person at all times, and without which they feel, and are, naked in the eyes of the State and the law.

Monsieur Blum was standing in front of a bookshop window, apparently manifesting undue interest in the books displayed. A militiaman tapped him on the shoulder. "Please, *documenti,* let me see your papers." "I'm sorry," answered Blum, "I prefer not to show them." The militiaman was horrified, astonished. "Come now, Tovarich, let me have a look at them."

"I refuse," said Blum. The militiaman was more than horrified, he was hurt. The argument went on. A crowd had begun to gather, and the militiaman felt he was being made ridiculous. The crowd took sides with Blum. "That's right, why should he show his papers? What has he done? He's a foreigner, let him alone."

Finally Blum said to the militiaman. "Step over here into the corner. You've made such a fuss, I'll show them to you. You will see who I am. Of course, I could complain about you to the Foreign Office—you would lose your job, you might even be put into prison or be sent north, but take a look for yourself." The man read out all Blum's titles and began to stutter frightened apologies.

"That's all right, all right for this time," Blum told him, "but let this be a lesson to you, and don't go bothering harmless people without reason."

Postmarked Moscow   *February 9, 1951*

OUR CHRISTMAS
holiday was a perfect one. The U. S. is a good country to live in. This time it seemed harder than ever to come back, yet here we are. Leaving Berlin early in the morning, we flew through clouds hanging over Germany and Poland and out into the sunshine. And then—there was Russia below us, with its black forests and snow-covered fields. The runway at Vnukova looked scarcely swept, but the pilot brought us down without a quaver, and we taxied along to the control building, where there was gathered a large, enthusiastic group waving red flags.

In a moment, our own friends extricated themselves from the flag-waving lot and advanced to meet us. The flag-wavers were there to meet a planeload of the faithful from Poland. Our Embassy delegation looked very good, by contrast, and we were really pleased to see them again. I kissed a lot of people I hadn't expected to, my hat fell off, and I dropped bundles, but it was all very gratifying, for everyone seemed

225

glad to see us back. There's a lot of snow around, which always helps the Moscow landscape, and the city looked more cheerful than when we left.

Our trip from Germany to Moscow was uneventful. We were six passengers, one of them being Mrs. George Patton, who had gotten her visitor's visa in five days, much to her and everyone else's surprise. She is a stout little lady, stout of heart rather than of figure, and excellent company. I liked her immensely, and was sorry that her stay had to be brief. She came in to stop with our military Attaché and his wife, and will return on our plane.

She told us that General Patton had been decorated by the Russians, his decoration allowing him unusual privileges, such as the right to ride free on the subways and to occupy the front seat in all busses. His widow was also entitled to a pension of two hundred and fifty rubles per year. Mrs. Patton's trustees in Boston quite solemnly and seriously approached the Russian Government to collect this money for her, but have never heard from the claims they entered on her behalf. Perhaps the visa was given her in lieu of the pension.

Mrs. Patton told of the great banquet given to the General by the Russian High Command when they first met in Germany in 1945. Food had been sent in especially, and the table was laden with every kind of dish—but only four forks to go around for the thirty or more guests. (No wonder all our maids are taken away from us once we've trained them, and put to work for the General's wives. I daresay they conduct etiquette classes wherever they go.) After the banquet decorations were awarded. Patton had told his officers to wear the best uniforms they had with them, but that was a mistake, for the Russian aide approached each man with a small knife, slashed his tunic, and his General than stuck the decoration into the hole!

There have been a few changes in the Diplomatic Corps, not too many, but we've been here long enough now to sense the small undercurrents of likes and dislikes, personality clashes, and small scandals. There can't be any big scandals—those we avoid out of sheer self-defense—and there's a kind of team loyalty that keeps us all together, as if we were serving in the same front line regiment, or tossing about the ocean on a large raft. We share each other's joys and sorrows; and later, when we meet in the outside world, we are very glad to see each other, for we've been truly comrades-in-arms.

That's what makes coming back possible, though I confess I had regrets this time. It was hard leaving the family; my month at home made me realize how much I had missed them.

The other day, Marjorie Blakeny, the wife of the Australian Chargé, told me such a funny story about Mrs. Clark, the wife of the American *Daily Worker* correspondent. The two women crossed from England together, on a Russian boat, with their children. As they docked in Stockholm, Marjorie told Mrs. Clark she was going ashore to do some shopping. "But why?" asked Mrs. Clark. "Surely one can buy everything much better in Moscow." "I'm sure you would think that," said Marjorie, "and that's quite all right, but, as you have two small children who may be very cold this winter, perhaps I'd best tell you a few of the facts of life." The woman looked at her, wide-eyed—"Do you mean to say there's no Didywash in Moscow?"

The poor lady has found out better since then. She has two small children and, so far, they have been living in a room and a half in the Métropole Hotel, cooking over a hot plate, washing in the tub. Our Acting Consul at the Embassy told us that she came in, the other day, to register her name as an American citizen living in Moscow, and to apply for dental treatment. Bearing in mind the lady's difficulties, no wonder her fanaticism has broken down to the extent of wanting a tooth filled with an imperialist compatriot.

At the moment, life at Spaso seems one big house party. The Cummings—Hugh Cumming is our new Minister, having replaced Wally Barbour—are installed in the guest room, as their apartment in Mokhovaya is not yet ready.

The household is working fairly smoothly. We hear that the British have lost four servants this month. It seems to go in waves. The Norwegians lost a cook who had been with the

Embassy for five years. She received a notice, saying she could no longer work for foreigners, so she packed and left for Siberia on her own account. Voluntary emigration entitles the individual to keep his or her passport, and she thought she might as well make her own arrangements, as otherwise they would be made for her!

The men here worked hard over a homemade skating rink, flooding the lawn behind the house. It looks quite promising, and I think I must try it out tomorrow. The main hazard comes from a pack of crows, perching in the trees above and dirtying the surface. That was one we never thought of. The Russian yard man tells us we should kill a crow and hang it in a tree, as a deterrent to his friends and relatives. But no one dares fire off a gun.

Speaking of vermin disposal, Astrid Helgeby, the Norwegian Ambassadress, told me a grisly story. Her little girl came into her room one morning, crying bitterly. "Oh mummy, come look, see what Stasha is doing to the poor rats." Astrid got up, peered through the window, and saw that the gardener had hung in a tree a cage full of rats he'd caught in their cellar, and was spraying them with the hose, meaning to let them hang there and freeze. The gardener, she said, was essentially a kind man, but he thought this a very comical idea, and couldn't see why she ordered him to drown the rats, instead.

The British Air Force plane comes in today, with Sir David and Lady Kelly, who have also been out on vacation. Now we are all back in residence. Everyone remarks how well we look, how fresh and enthusiastic. The weather has something to do with it, for it's actually clear and bright, and not too cold—almost the best weather we've had all year. I prefer Moscow winters to Moscow summers, even to Moscow springs, for it's probably the one spot that that lovely season can do nothing for. Now the square in front of Spaso is full of children, bundled to the eyes and ears, rolling about in the snow like puppies or kittens. The old *baboushkas* are there, cradling the babies; the old men walk about with their sticks; and the little ruined church looks almost gay in the winter sunlight.

YESTERDAY, SUNDAY
the 18th, our men went into heavy consultation about Stalin's
interview with *Pravda*. It's hard to assess, particularly his insistence on Atlee's misdeeds, and later his reference to American Generals and soldiers, their fighting qualities, their lack
of enthusiasm for the Korean War, their excellent performance
against Hitler's army, and their supposedly poor showing
against the Chinese. Our people seem to think the statements
are intended to appear in advance of any Foreign Ministers
Conference agreement. The statements emphasize the Soviet
peace theme, and point us up as the real aggressors.

The paragraphs about Soviet demobilization are certainly
false, and must be known as such by their own people. The
biggest of their labor projects are not the result of free labor,
nor of demobilized soldiers; they are the result of forced
labor. The canals and engineering marvels to which Stalin
points with such pride may be more useful than the Pyramids
of Egypt, but they have been built by the same methods. A
most interesting book, called *Siberie,* has just been published
in France. It's written by Ciliga, a Serb, who served seven
years in the Siberian labor camps, and his account of the
recruiting and drafting of workers is certainly revealing.

Whenever a big project is on, the word goes out and the prisons
are emptied all over the nation. Persons awaiting trial are
hurried before judges, and their sentences are often adapted
to the immediate labor needs of the State. Off they go in
batches, men and women, the lucky ones being allowed to
practice their own crafts and specialties on the construction
jobs. Our cook's son is doing his last four years in Siberia, in
the very far north, but he is an electrician and she comforts
herself with the thought that he is working indoors all winter
at his own trade.

Our Embassy agricultural people tell us of a new policy
regarding *kolkhozes,* many of the smaller of which are to be
combined into mammoth State farms. The villages also are

to be combined, transported bodily and set up together. Each villager is allowed fifty small carloads of effects, but this allowance includes his house, torn down and loaded on carts, to be rebuilt in the new location, any overweight to be charged at so much per kilometer! One immediately thinks of the vast distances the workers must go to their fields, under the new arrangement—all right if there is motor transport available, but that is still very short in the Soviet Union. The arrangement will tend to break up the old village life, of course, to make big communities, almost urban communities, factories for agriculture.

Certainly the Moscow people are far better dressed this year than last, and they look better fed, too. I want to do another study of the clothing for sale, and the prices. The clothes are not stylish by our standards, but the coats are warm, the majority black or dark-blue wool, with fur collars to turn up around the neck, or with woollen scarves Shoes are more plentiful, but of poor quality, and the rubber overshoes worn by the better dressed seem a foolish substitute for the felt *valinkis*. That's still the favored form of footgear, and the sound of their shuffle along the streets is one not to be forgotten.

Postmarked Moscow   *February 26, 1951*

THE MAGAZINES

that came in yesterday were so vernal they made us nostalgic for crocuses, and white piqué collars on blue suits! Here it's still winter, with deep snow, and the little women are still chipping ice off the streets. I spent yesterday at the British *dacha,* lunching with Fred Warner, an energetic young man who is one of those who have made the most of their Russian opportunities—travelling a lot, striding about through the Caucasus collecting amusing experiences and a store of books and phonograph records of native music.

After lunch, the Freers went out with me and we skated on the flooded tennis court, duly smoothed and swept to receive the Ambassadress. It was great fun, and the woods looked very pretty in the snow. Soon we'll be sloshing through deep mud and, after that, comes the gray-brown dust. The people look better in winter; they have more color, even a little red in their cheeks. They are a consistently sallow race, their skin, their hair, their eyes all of a dun color. No wonder they like brilliance and gaudy show in their churches and the theater.

Saturday night, we went to the *Queen of Spades,* the opera taken from the Pushkin poem. It's a melancholy story, the tale of the old lady whose knowledge of three winning cards leads a young officer to kill her for her secret, and gamble for the cards. He wins on the first two but turns up the Queen of Spades as the last one, the fatal card which means his own death. The opera is laid in old Petersburg, and there are some extraordinary sets of scenes in the parks and along the Neva. These were painted by Dimitrovitch, a talented artist of before the war, who died of drink and an oversupply of Georgian mistresses.

He was one of two contemporary scenic designers, both addicted to the same vices, both equally talented. The other did the sets for *Romeo and Juliet* and for *Cinderella.* There seems to be no one to take their places today for the new ballets and operas have elaborate but vulgar decors. There's a pretentious Ukrainian opera just been produced at the Bolshoi, straight propaganda about life on a *kolkhoz.* The music is dreadful, and the libretto very bad indeed.

The most impassioned scene in the opera took place in a wheat field. The curtain went up to show the heroine laid out on the top of a haystack. "At last," we thought, "a little bit of sex," but as the hero drew near and glimpsed her lying in the sun, he plucked a paper from his bosom and burst into song—not at all a love song, but a detailed exposition of the new dam and the power plant to be built, the sluice gates, the gushing water, the mighty creative power of the Soviet people!

The music was so bad it didn't even remind you of anything you'd ever heard before, anywhere. It was simply noise, noise without melody or even real discord. The women's voices in Soviet opera are poor, the baritones and bassos usually quite good; but the acting is stiff, and the plump prima donnas and tenors make one think of our own early operatic performers before the days of streamlined glamor and the protein diet. The Bolshoi itself is always a grand sight, and the tiers of gold balconies, six of them, the crystal chandeliers, the crimson curtains, the width and depth of the stage, all very impressive. Think what it must have looked like with grand duchesses, in tiaras, leaning out of every box.

At the theater, in the lobbies, in the restaurants, the people are very quiet—silent, even. Time was, when the Russians liked nothing better than to meet together and talk, talk endlessly, talk about anything, everything, conclude very little, and next day start over again with the same arguments. Reading the nineteenth-century authors, there seems nothing but talk—talk and Chekovian soul-searching. Now, the people work so hard they've little time for their souls.

We wonder what really goes on in the minds of these people —what they look for and hope for from their rulers' promises. Someone who talked with one of the Embassy chauffeurs asked him what he visualized as Communism. "It may not come in our time," he answered, "but it will be a fine thing. Then no one will work more than two or three hours a day, and in the stores everything will be free. There will be no prices. There will be living space for all, and we will be happy." H. G. Wells never thought up a better Utopia, nor Southern California real-estate men a better promotion scheme. What a hoax it is! Millions upon millions of people fooled, their children fooled, their grandchildren fooled. The important thing is not to let ourselves be fooled.

Dad presented a note to Vishinsky, yesterday afternoon, answering the Soviet demand for a Foreign Ministers' Conference. Dad's visit lasted eight minutes. Vishinsky had a new interpreter, not a very good one, Dad said. Vishinsky himself looked tired and rather cross. The Foreign Ministry is not in the Kremlin, but in a large building not far from the Lubianka. The Lubianka is a vast block of building, handsome in a way. It looks what it is, the headquarters of the MVD, the Security Police, the very center of this Police State, and one of the most sinister prisons in the world.

Just the other day, we heard from the Italian Embassy of an Italian General lately released from seven years of prison within those walls, right here in Moscow. These officers had been taken in the war, and would have remained here for the rest of their lives if the Ambassador had not worked miracles in their behalf. One or two wives were also imprisoned. The women had been kept separate from the men, and they had not seen each other during the entire time. The men emerged very broken in health, none of them knowing anything of what had gone on in the world during the years of their incarceration. I dare say there are many such. These were the lucky ones.

Postmarked Moscow   *April 6, 1951*

SPRING IS HERE.
As Ed Freers exclaimed, "How wonderful, we can finally see the cement!" It's true there's no sign of budding leaf, no crocus in bloom, no daffodils or tulips. But now and again you do see people with flowers in their hands—*artificial* cotton hyacinths and stock—visible signs that winter is over.

Everywhere people have started windowwashing, and entry ways smell of fresh carbolic. Courtyards and side streets are seas of mud, planks' laid across from sidewalk to door. On the city outskirts, where big new apartment blocks have been built, it's even worse, no pretense having been made at draining or grading. I've never seen any landscaping attempts around the new buildings. They stand deep in winter snows; in spring and autumn mud; and in summer dust. Since the much publicized price reductions, shops have been crowded. There are queues for everything, even pickles, for the quantity of goods available is far less than the demand.

Getting in and out of the doors of the Mostorg is a feat in itself. One must hold tight to one's pocketbook and one's temper. This seems to be the time when the country people come to buy anything and everything. On all sides, one sees peasants in full lambskin coats, and old women in wadded jackets, fur hats, embroidered skull caps or shawls of flowered challis. These people wander about the city, gape at Lenin's tomb, stand on corners, chewing sunflower seeds, shuffle in and out of the museums and shops.

Now that the snow is off the ground, I'm going a little thought to our garden, even if we're not here to enjoy it ourselves. We've no more word of the poor old gardener. It's been two weeks since he disappeared, supposedly arrested after a drunken brawl in a café, where he was said to have hit a one-armed man. His wife went to the first prison to which he was taken. He'd been moved. She went to another, they had no record of him. Now she has engaged a lawyer, but neither of them has succeeded in getting any news. The gardener is sixty-five, not very strong, a pathetic man in spite of his drinking. His wife thinks she will never see him again, but she accepts the possibility with frightening resignation, and his disappearance seems to have made very little stir in the household.

Our meals are cooked, the kitchen windows are washed, and life goes on. Meanwhile, my seeds should be put into boxes and our cold frames repaired. We lost a yardman the week before the gardener was taken, so we are very short of help.

Postmarked Moscow　　　　　　　　　　*April 11, 1951*

I THOUGHT MOSCOW
and the Kremlin might defeat spring but, somehow, in some way, it's crept in, the air has grown balmy, and every house-

wife up and down the street has started windowwashing. It's going on at a great rate in Spaso; the three housemaids have their heads done up in towels and they are hard at work, splattering and smearing soap suds over the panes. They don't do a very thorough job—they leave streaks, and they don't wipe the corners, but the sun shines bright on the polished centers of the windows and lies in gay patches on the floor. Chantal Goffin has been at it, herself, and the panes of the Belgian Embassy are gloriously clean. I tell her only a Belgian or a Dutch woman would go to all that trouble.

Dad's Little Men have new hats—green-plush—and smart light-weight coats. They also have a new car, a Russian Zim. The young, black-eyed one has become quite friendly, smiling as I go out the gate. He is the one whom Dick calls Long Knife, because he carries a wicked blade that reaches almost from his armpit to his waist. I've gone so far as to send to Sears for blue-and-white-spotted dresses for the two women telephone operators, and for gay print aprons for the laundry women.

These ladies are still the bane of our existence, and we'd gladly turn them all out if the hotels would accept our laundry. A good many people do laundry in their bathrooms, but there are still sheets and flatwear to be taken care of. Some of the maids have become quite expert, so much has to be washed here that we would have cleaned at home. Except for a cleaning establishment run for the Bolshoi Theater clientele, there is none in Moscow; anything of our own that *must* be dry cleaned we send out to Finland or Sweden. Laundries are scarce enough, no wonder most Soviet citizens wear colored shirts.

It's true, however, that the race is not as dirty as one might imagine. The traditional weekly bath has a good deal to do with that, a weekly steam bath largely patronized by all classes. There are bathhouses set up in the villages, there always have been, and the men meet there as they would at a club. Several of our people have been to these establishments. Stu Warwick, our Assistant Air Attaché, is very anxious for Dad to go, because he wants to see what would happen to the Little Men. Where would they carry their weapons?

Lenin's tomb is open again. We saw the line forming yesterday. It was closed for more than a week. Perhaps they were washing the windows there, too.

I was wrong. The tomb is still closed. What I saw was merely a large out-of-town delegation, come to pay tribute. This is the longest it's been shut since we came, two years ago. Once it remained closed for a week, and there were stories about an ear being stuck back. Now it must be a more serious repair job, but they should have it finished by May Day.

This morning, over the radio, we heard that the President had relieved General MacArthur of his command. The word came on the ten o'clock BBC news broadcast. Having read the home and foreign papers, one knew it had to be. The British, especially, were very angry with him and I thought at once of the young woman in the shop on the Rue de Rivoli, last December, who said, *"Tout le même, Madame, est-ce que vous ne croyez pas que MacArthur est allé trop loin?"*

Now we must wait for the Soviet reaction. It won't come at once. As I have said, they always delay comment on any important event abroad until it can be discussed and revalued for propaganda purposes. Sometimes they never mention it at all for several days; or, if they do, they give it as a bare announcement.

Postmarked Moscow   *April 14, 1951*

STILL NO WORD IN
the Soviet press on the MacArthur removal. Even Radio Moscow has made no comments. Meanwhile, the town is filled with Chinese, businessmen's delegations, students, Government groups of all kinds. At the Tretchikov Gallery the halls have been newly decorated with pictures and statuary celebrating the Sino-Russian entente. How complicated it must be, here, when nations and men fall in or out of favor! So many records to be altered, so many pictures to be taken down and statuary

broken up. Ink eradicator must be a staple product of Soviet bureaucracy.

The Luxembourg Minister, one of Roger's friends, is going to send him a copy of the Soviet penal code and a most interesting little pamphlet embodying their instructions to their Foreign service officers. All these are unclassified, but difficult to obtain. Ed Freers tells me that the provisions in the penal code for punishment of escapees from the Soviet Union are particularly revealing. In the case of officers or soldiers, technically deserters, these may be shot on recognition, without trial or hearing.

Any members of their family or friends left at home who may have had knowledge of the escape are liable to ten years at hard labor—and, most terrifying of all, persons closely connected, even if they have no knowledge whatever of the "crime," are liable to five years' hard labor in the far north, being judged politically undesirable. The only distinction made is that escapees who are not members of the armed forces are allowed some kind of trial. So much for Soviet justice.

The gardener's wife has been unable to see her husband. He should have a hearing this month, but she gets no satisfaction when she goes to inquire at the prison. She doesn't even know that he is still there. We have applied for another gardener. Burobin is sending us a "yard woman," whom Bill Nagosky reports as a hefty creature, an ex-charlady who has a yearning for the great outdoors. She reports on Monday, and I am curious to see what this introduction of sex will do for the garden. Meanwhile, the man from the *Dacha* has come in to get our flat boxes and has taken them away to plant and put under glass. It's lettuce and nasturtiums I really count on, those are what grow best in Russia.

Where the Arakvi Restaurant manager found the roses that were on our table Wednesday night, I can't imagine. Tom Whitney and Harrison Salisbury, representing the AP and the *New York Times*, offered us a very grand dinner that evening. They rented the private room at the Arakvi, with a balcony that overlooks the main restaurant.

The Arakvi is a Georgian restaurant, and is considered the

most chic in the city. Its decoration reminds one of railroad station lavatories, gleaming white tile and bright, unshaded lights. The food is good, of its kind. We had caviar, which we were told to spread between layers of hot pastry like *mille feuilles,* and, with that, vodka and fresh green cucumbers and raw onions. I refused the onions but ate the cucumbers, quite a lot of them.

The orchestra came up from the restaurant below and played Georgian and Russian songs to us, all very sad and wailing as rendered on their strange instruments. As a great favor, they obliged with the White Russian anthem, and I wondered what the customers below must have thought. It was a very gay evening, and we were quite touched that the two men had treated us to such a lavish affair. Afterwards, next morning, I regretted that I'd eaten so many cucumbers. Dad quite meanly suggested it might have been the vodka.

Postmarked Moscow   *April 17, 1951*

ALL MOSCOW IS concentrating on the Great Ball, next Saturday—that is, all of our part of Moscow. MacArthur's homecoming pales beside the agitation created by our giving this costume party on the 21st. We have asked two hundred and twenty-five. They come at nine, are given a buffet supper, and then dance on into the night.

We ourselves intend to rent our costumes from the Bolshoi. I'm told they have rack after rack to choose from, and you can satisfy any fancy you may have and come as Peter the Great or the Black Swan if you wish. I incline towards a Czarina's mantle and a pearl headdress, as befitting an Ambassadress and the mistress of Spaso. Dick Service insists he wants to come as a swaddled baby, so restful he says, and he can be propped up against the wall and fed liquids.

To help out with supper, we should make a deal for the Afghan Ministers' five hundred hard-boiled eggs. The Egyptian Minister has four hundred and fifty, which are part of the same lot; the Danes, a hundred and eighty; the Swedes, another two hundred; and I think the Greeks and Turks were also in on the affair. It appears that the eggs were ordered from Denmark and were sent in through Russian customs.

The Russians have very strict regulations about the importation of foodstuffs; and, maintaining that the eggs might be diseased, they hard-boiled them all. Imagine receiving five hundred hard-boiled eggs! Along with the eggs, the Danes had ordered some onions and celery. The Russians peeled the onions and chopped the celery into small pieces, also for disease-control. But the eggs were the best of all, and that story entertained our dinner guests last night. We had a formal party of twenty-two in the state dining room, all a bit heavy until the Egyptian told us about the eggs.

I really think we might get some for next Saturday. We are going to have a time providing supper—hot dishes, cold meats and masses of salads without a lettuce leaf to go with them. Even cucumbers are five rubles apiece: a dollar and a quarter for a quite tiny one. I appreciate all those they gave us at the Arakvi; and, since stopping in at the florist's, I appreciate the roses we had on our table. I saw just six very faded ones, and they were priced at twenty-five rubles per, that's $6.50 per rose! Cut flowers, except for the garden variety to be found in summer, simply don't exist. We've a few lilac bushes along our side fence, but to trim the ballroom on Saturday night I fear we must resort to cedar boughs, a touch that is out of season for late April.

An enthusiastic committee of three is going to festoon crepe paper all around and suspend balloons. Dad has been making the punch, and a most delicious odor of rum and green tea hovers around the pantry. We've received the prizes we ordered from Finland, two first and two seconds, men's and women's, and now we must choose an anonymous committee of judges. The British, I believe, have organized groups and will make a dramatic entrance. We've saved as many flash bulbs as possible for Dad's Polaroid, and Dick will be stationed at the door, apparatus in hand. This camera of Dad's is most satisfactory. The pictures may not be fine, but it's great fun to get immediate results. The only trouble is that there's no negative, and the guests have to be prevented from slipping the prints into their pockets—once gone, no more can be made

Dad goes to the Foreign Office this afternoon to be received by Zorin in place of Vishinsky. The latter is still recuperating or still suffering, we're not sure which. Dad wants to tell Zorin of his trip to the Caucasus, and make sure that we are not shut into our hotel rooms over May Day but allowed to see whatever is going on in Tiflis at that time. Some of our people who were in Odessa last year were locked away for twelve hours.

Postmarked Moscow   *April 22, 1951*

IT WAS REALLY A good party. Dad had the orchestra play *Good Night, Ladies,* at four o'clock, otherwise the guests might have stayed on until the last drop of champagne and punch was gone. When the Brosios had been ceremoniously ushered out and there were only a few revellers left in odd corners, Dad marched into the ballroom, ordered up enough reserve bottles, marshalled the staff from pantry, telephone and kitchen, made them a speech of thanks for their hard work, and drank their health.

The men bowed; Frieda, the cook, wept; the older maids curtseyed; the younger tossed down their drink fast; and dear little Stepan, the pantryman, made a long and sentimental speech in response, saying that never before had there been so much happiness in Spaso, that they loved us both and were glad to do what they could. It was all very touching. We left three or four of our young men behind—Dick, Stuart Warwick, and a couple of the military—and through the doors, which we carefully closed, we could hear Stu playing, and much singing and Russian gaiety. It was Dick's birthday, and he started matters off by going straight down the line, kissing all the maids!

The costumes were very good. Everyone took great pains, and, thanks to the wardrobe of the Bolshoi Theater organization, those who had none of their own were able to hire almost anything they fancied. Dad was very fine in a bottle-green frock coat, lilac pants, his own checked vest, crossed with an immense gold chain, a ruffled shirt, stock, and beautiful red chop-whiskers. The British Ambassador was heard to remark, "Kirk looks very like an English squire. Come to think of it, perhaps one of his ancestors was one!" Surely the accolade!

I found a white-and-gold Russian court costume, quite new, made for some exposition, really very lovely. It fitted perfectly and I wore a glittering tiara, with ropes of pearls beneath my chin. The knowing told me that the number of ropes indicated age and status—virgin, married woman, widow, etc. It seemed wise not to inquire as to the exact significance of mine.

Dick and Jack Horner, who is staying here until he leaves next week for his post in Afghanistan, were Buryat princes, with splendid leather boots that turned up at the toes. Elaine Freers had a Latvian peasant costume, her boots were nice, too, knee length of soft red kid. Ed Freers had managed to find a stupendous outfit that made him look like the younger brother in the ballet of *Hunchback Horse*. There were a good number of Russian costumes, some of them excellent.

The Turkish Ambassador politely confided to me that he would have given mine the prize at once, but know I was *hors concours*. He and Wally, a billowing Grand Vizier, were the Prize Committee, assisted by Astrid Helgeby, the Norwegian Ambassadress. She looked very lovely herself in the dress of a boyar lady, but we felt that authentic and original costumes should receive the prizes.

It was a hard choice, but the woman's first prize went to Madame Hassan of the Pakistan Embassy who wore an Indian basket vender's costume, but a basket vender who had met with a rich rajah! Madame Hassan has the most marvelous jewels, and she had wrapped herself in them over saris she had looped into a full skirt. The texture and color were wonderful.

The second prize they gave to Mrs. James, the wife of our Air Attaché, who came as the "Lady Who's Known as Lou," a partner to her husband, the latter representing a dubious legendary ancestor, one of the James brothers.

The British Embassy staged a most impressive entrance. Thanks to the excellent classical education of their better public schools, they had evolved a Roman group, headed by their big military Attaché who was a stunning centurion. Behind him came gladiators, a vestal virgin, a sinister sybilline lady in black and vine leaves, with a stuffed raven on her shoulder, odd senators, and, last, the Emperor Claudius himself in flowing purple and a laurel crown. The Emperor had beautiful buskins to the knee, and his wife had curled his hair in authentic ringlets. He was most convincing, and well deserved the first prize. Men's second prize went to the Dutch Ambassador, who wore an Argentine Gaucho costume and flourished a lariat.

There were many others who might have been chosen. Captain Draim and his eldest daughter came, as Bo-Peep and the meekest of her sheep. Captain Draim, a large, quiet man, unexpectedly appeared as the sheep, in a full suit of white winter underwear and cotton batting wool. Charles McLane, one of our cultural Attachés, was such a good Dvornik in padded short coat and felt *valinkis* that we thought he had just wandered in off the street. A pretty young lady from the Persian Embassy felt so gay at supper that she went about with a tray or cakes on her head, offering them at each table. The Burmese Ambassador wore the most Burmese of his skirts and turbans, and took vast numbers of colored movies in all directions. We had quite a lot of cameramen, and Dick and Alec Sgourdeos, the Greek Chargé, did a rousing business.

We might have waited to hold the ball until Roger arrived —he should be here in June—but there's a time for everything; and the end of the season, with our colleagues' faces, conversation, evening clothes a bit tired and spotted, seemed the perfect moment. We enjoyed it ourselves. I think everyone else did. This morning the entire household is asleep.

The next project, and one we must take immediately in hand, is our trip to Tiflis. If Burobin and Intourist approve, we start out on Wednesday afternoon, a veritable safari. The Goffins are joining the party and there's Wally, the Freers, Stu Warwick, Dick, Jerry Barclay, a cheerful girl from the Canadian Embassy and ourselves, plus Dad's four bodyguards. We reach Tiflis Saturday morning, three nights and two days on the train. We are taking vast quantities of food and drink with us. One never knows whether restaurant cars will be provided, and, ever since Siberia, Dad and Dick are past masters of lavatory cooking, the basis of their meals being corned beef hash.

Postmarked Moscow   *May 7, 1951*

WE ARE SAFE BACK
in Moscow, and we spent a memorable ten days—six of them and six nights to match, in pre-Revolution Pullman wagon lits. It was quite an experience but great fun, and our party proved very congenial, even at the end. They all laughed at me as I dug out a pair of white cotton gloves to land in. I might deceive the friends who came to meet us, but my travelling companions knew just how dirty I was underneath. Air-conditioned travel will be a long time reaching the Soviet Union; and then, of course, they will claim to have discovered it.

We had a comparatively comfortable coach, going down, and felt quite fresh and elated at the start. They gave us an entire car to ourselves—they had to, as we were fourteen, all told, with the Goffins and the four Little Men. Each compartment was for two persons, and we had guards at each end. Our car was at the rear of the train, quarantined behind the diner. Stu Warwick claimed that we had six extra unofficial followers scattered elsewhere through the train, and he may have been right. He pointed three of them out to me, and they do have a look that is unmistakable.

I suppose they have to cover all possibilities. One of us might have been left at a station, or gone off on a separate trip, or stayed over a day. As it was, Dick and I took a stroll along the platform, one morning, having been told we had twenty minutes. The train left ten minutes early, and we had to swing aboard three cars up. I must say, walking through a Russian train is an education in itself. I was quite glad it happened. I was glad also that the forward-car door was open and that we didn't meet the fate of the poor young man who got off to go swimming in the Black Sea. Clutching his trousers in one hand and a large bouquet of wild flowers in the other, with the station master boosting him along, he made a dash for the train, almost got hold of the stair rail of our car, fell flat on the track, and there he was left behind, with his trousers down around his ankles.

Dick had toyed with the idea of a quick dip, himself, but gave it up after that horrid spectacle. Coming back, we really had an ancient and rattling example of the railroad wagon as known in 1903. I think the electricity had been installed only for us, as there were still shiny oil lamps in the compartments and corridors. It was a special type of car, half first-class—which means there are washrooms between every two compartments—and half second, without washrooms.

Louis Goffin said these cars were designed for people travelling with retinues of servants, the masters sleeping up front. The diner was pretty primitive and looked like a low class bar in a mining town. There was only one waitress, very dirty and very drunk, even in the morning. Fortunately, we took most of our food with us, and cooked our hash in the lavatory basin. One is certainly reduced to elementals when travelling in Russia. In fact, reading the 1903 Baedeker, with its recommendations on what to take along with one's baggage, I could see little difference. The list was quite applicable to 1951. What a country!

Tiflis and the Caucasus were worth the visit, however, and I'm very glad we went and delighted we chose May first to be away, as it poured rain for the parade here in Moscow, and the speech from the Tomb was reported as more insulting than usual to the Americans. The two happy and amusing incidents were that the Czech Ambassador's new blue felt hat ran streaks of blue dye down his face and neck; and that one of the British clerks got caught in the mob forming up for the people's demonstration and walked the whole way with them, passing in review before Stalin himself. He pretended to be deaf or dumb, whenever addressed, and somehow got by the militiamen whose files separate every five marchers. It was raining so hard that he almost looked like a Russian, although two of his countrymen in the stand spotted him as he went by and thought he had gone over to the enemy.

We didn't do too badly in the Tiflis parade. As I wrote, Dad had gone to the Foreign Office especially to inform them that we intended to spend May Day at Tiflis, and that he did not wish to find himself shut into the hotel, as had happened to some of our people in Odessa last November. May Day was on Monday, and, on the Sunday, Dad had Ed Freers tell "Salmon Shirt," the boss guard, that we had decided to spend the day picnicking in the country and would leave the hotel at a convenient time by a rear door, if he could arrange to have us do so.

The front door and all windows are sealed on such occasions, and we were told this would be done at eight-thirty in the morning and that we should be ready to leave at seven-thirty. "Certainly not a convenient time," said Dad, and he thereupon went into action and wrote off a stiff telegram to be sent in the clear to Hugh Cumming, left in charge in Moscow, protesting at the discourteous treatment, and asking that word of it be sent on to Washington.

The local authorities had intimated that we would be locked into the hotel, and not even allowed to raise the shades in our rooms if we remained after the appointed hour. Louis Goffin, the Belgian Ambassador, also sent off a telegram, slightly less militant but still firm. Chill silence of displeasure fell. There was considerable agitation observed on the part of our protectors. Dad and Louis remained quietly haughty, and thirty minutes later—that's fast work for Soviet bureaucracy—Ed was informed that special permission had been granted for us to leave at ten-thirty, by the main entrance, or, if we choose to remain, we could view the parade from our open windows, even now being unnailed. Triumph!

But there was better to come next morning, for, with the inevitable ten-minute delay in assembling a group of people and cars, we found ourselves bang in the middle of their parade, sandwiched between the biggest tanks. I hope never to be so near one of those engines of destruction again. . . . The militia maneuvered us with difficulty back onto the sidewalk, just in time to escape being crushed like beetles, then, when the tanks had passed, they waved us on to bring up the end of the procession.

Down the streets we rode between ranks of police and populace—why, I can't imagine. One would have thought they would have shunted us onto back alleys, but the Russian mind is unpredictable at all times. We must have looked like a delegation from the Politburo, to say the least. It was all we could do to keep from saluting the crowds, and it went on for blocks until we finally reached the turn-off and took the road out of town. It was especially comic, as, two nights before, Stuart and Dick and Jerry Barclay, who had gone out to watch the rehearsal for the parade, were picked up by militia, Dick and Jerry actually being escorted back to the hotel under guard. Then, on Monday, we found ourselves featured in the procession.

We had two pleasant days in the country, the first when we went to Mtesh, the old capital of Georgia, a quaint village on the river with a fine tenth-century church, set in a green meadow, surrounded by crenelated walls. We ate our lunch in Saint Nina's graveyard, which surrounds a smaller church of the same period, built over the remains of one dating from the fifth century.

It was a warm day, but cool under the trees. Dad took off his coat and got a stitch in his side, and Chantal Goffin took a chill, a visitation, we decided, from the outraged saint and the souls whose graves we had desecrated with sandwich boxes and bottles of red wine. It's true the Mother Superior of the convent next door had invited us into the grounds, brought stools and blankets for us to sit on, and called down blessings upon us when we left. Ed, our acting treasurer, pressed some money into her hand. She seemed grateful, but I fear Saint Nina held a grudge, as the two sufferers found out twenty-four hours later.

Our other picnic, the May Day one, we ate by the banks of a river after visiting Annanouri, once the fortress home of the Eristoff family, with two more old churches within the citadel walls, one very early. Annanouri is some forty kilometers up the Georgian highway, just where the road starts to climb out of the river valley. It's an isolated village, but we were cordially received by a nice old gentleman, a friend of our Russian Intourist guide. He was a clean old man, a bit purple in the nose, but he apologized, saying he knew he was a little drunk, but that it was a holiday and he hoped we would excuse him.

He showed us about the ruins and told us how wicked the Turks had been, hacking the carving and whitewashing the murals in the churches. He was as bitter about it as if it had happened yesterday, instead of hundreds of years ago. We climbed over the rocks, and the men took pictures from all angles—Dick taking great care to show those from the Polaroid to Salmon Shirt to quiet any fears that the Little Men might be taken with our group. None of us have ever attempted that, and it's a pity for I would so love a record of our two special familiars, Salmon Shirt and Long Knife.

Postmarked Moscow   *May 14, 1951*

THE PLANE COMES
in next Monday. I'm looking forward to our ten days spring outing. One piece of domestic good news is that the gardener has been let off with one year's imprisonment instead of five. He will probably be sent just outside Moscow, and his wife

can see him from time to time; but when his sentence has been served he can never live within the city limits again. This doesn't bother her too much, as her son will be in the same case when he returns from Siberia.

There are several categories of released prisoners, some being kept in the north, others allowed to live in specified towns or districts, and still others who can settle as close as a hundred and twenty-five kilometers from Moscow. The Soviet system is clever. He's given five years, but a kind, considerate Government reduces it to one! Now instead of being angry about her husband's arrest and imprisonment, his wife is grateful to the court for commuting his sentence.

Frieda had wanted to take food and medicine to her husband, but that was not allowed. Later, when he is in a permanent prison or work camp, she may do so. She could give him money the other day, and with that he could buy a few extra rations at the prison store. The regular food the men get is very poor, thin gruel in the morning, bread and soup at midday, and bread and water at night.

This business of visiting relatives in prison and hospital takes up a great deal of time in the life of most Soviet citizens. They go from one end of town to the other, shopping for little things and standing in queues, first to buy and later to wait for busses and street cars. Consumer goods are scarce, shopping facilities are scant in proportion to the population. It takes time just to live in the Soviet Union. While there is a theoretical eight-hour day, many trades and industries require their workers to spend twenty-four hours straight on a job, then allow them two days off. This is true of hospital nurses, taximen, and bus drivers—hardly occupations for tired men or women. The two free days either are spent on personal business, shopping and visiting, or very often the worker has an extra job during part of that time.

Moscow streets are always full of people at any hour, and this round-the-clock system seems to account for it. The housing conditions are so bad it's no wonder that people prefer to roam the streets rather htan stay home; that they are content to ride to and fro in busses; that they crowd into the parks even on wet, cold days. There's little recreation offered, simple recreation. It's all mixed with lectures and propaganda, and much of it costs money, so the average citizen goes out into the streets and shops just to amuse himself.

Postmarked Moscow   *May 20-21, 1951*

WE HAD OUR BIG Armed Forces reception here yesterday afternoon. The ballroom was hung with Navy signal flags, all the military attended in their best uniforms, and we lined up with the senior Attachés and their wives to receive the guests. With Dad's flag and the General's behind us, we looked like a recruiting poster.

The affair had been scheduled as a garden party, and the weather was just good enough to allow the guests to walk out onto the rear lawn—and come quickly back for a drink. It was bright, but chilly. The garden wasn't much to boast about. The grass is still brown from the solid freezing it got all winter, when we had a skating rink there with dire results. The vegetable garden is still under fertilizer, except for two patches, one of radishes and one of rhubarb. We now have one yard woman and one rather drunken youth working in the place of old Theodore. Neither one is very effective, and I fear we won't have much garden to look at this year—and less to eat. It's a pity, as right now there's very little to be bought in town.

Imagine, in this great city, supposedly "the greatest capital of the greatest country in the world," there wasn't a scrap of fresh fish in the markets last week and no canned or frozen vegetables. Meat and eggs are also scarce. Think of the poverty and monotony of the Russian diet. And still they live and multiply, millions and millions of them.

We had just five Russians at the reception yesterday, five

men, the highest-ranking being an Air Force Colonel. All came without their wives. They marched in together, shook hands with that rolling, crushing grip Russians have, left a horrid stink of sweet soap and cologne behind, passed on into the ballroom where each took one small drink, then out they marched again. The smell of them sticks, you have to scrub to get rid of it—and even then!

Some of the nicer members of the Diplomatic Corps are the Israelis. Two or three of their women are very pretty, and the men are intelligent. I talked with their Chargé the other night at dinner. He told me that there are about 45,000 Jews in Moscow. There was a synagogue, and he and his colleagues attended service there. They were never spoken to, however, by any members of the congregation, and not one individual had dared approach them privately or officially. There are even greater numbers of Jews in Odessa and Kiev. They live in misery, and many have been thrown out of their homes and jobs. On no account are they given exit visas or allowed to emigrate to Palestine, and their own Republic in the far north is a dreary and terrible place, little better than a prison colony.

Speaking of prison colonies, the Russians are building a big university center here in Moscow, or rather just outside on the Sparrow Hills, near the spot where Napoleon stood to look over the city. It is an extensive project, and will comprise many schools and research units. Every day, one sees the workers marshalled along the roads leading to this section. Most are forced labor and they march under guard, the rear being brought up by soldiers with police dogs. There are men and women in the groups, hundreds of them. Surely a terrible way to erect a temple of learning and a monument to men's free thoughts.

On the way to Tiflis, we passed several trainloads of prisoners; one, especially, was filled with women, crowded into cattle cars. We could see them looking out the small, barbed-wire-strung windows. It was broad daylight, anyone along the way or at the stations must have noticed them, and still the system persists and is accepted. Revolt won't come easily but revolt must be there, smoldering away underneath, even though overlaid with despair and the dull, dead necessity to live. What the end will be, we cannot guess.

Postmarked Moscow   *May 23, 1951*

OUR VACATION IS delayed. It's Wednesday now, our plane has been sitting in Tempelhof Aerdrome, in Berlin, since Saturday. The Russians assure us that they are "prodding" the Poles to give the over-flight permission. Yesterday the Poles asked for a flight plan—anything to delay and obstruct.

We've just lost another member of the staff, an officer who has been ill for some months. He was to have flown out with us, but went yesterday, with one of our young clerks who will care for him on the journey. It's another case where nerves have complicated whatever may be wrong with him. So few people at home can appreciate the peculiar difficulties of this place—or its peculiar needs. Lack of housing, and poor housing when we get it, head the list. Then there is the constant fight for repairs, and material to make them with, not to speak of men to do the work. This spring we have lost the greater part of our semiskilled Russian work force, lost them in such a way as to frighten any applicants for their jobs, and to discourage those left behind.

Then the servant problem.—If living were a little easier, one could "make do" alone, but for our young housewives the mechanics of shopping, and even cooking, are special. Marketing takes hours, and the gas pressure for cooking requires Russian submission to cope with. By and large, our personnel is very uncomplaining, but it's not an easy life. No wonder some break under the strain. Moscow tries men's nerves, as well as their souls.

THE POLES RELENTED.

The plane came in and we finally got away. Now we are back again after a smooth flight, the best we've ever had, straight across Poland over Warsaw, and Vilna, then on over the wastes of Russia, letting down the last hour so that we came in over the bumps, but I'd never give the Russian navigator the satisfaction of knowing I was airsick. Patriotic determination held me together.

We brought in masses of food, supplies enough we hope to last several months. On the way to the airport, Dick stopped to buy bananas, not just a dozen, but sixty-eight, an entire bunch, which he is distributing to our Embassy children. Even better than food supplies, we've a pretty lady visitor, Marian Achilles, from London. Her red hair and gay clothes will raise all the gentlemen's morale. A new face means a lot. It's great fun having her in Spaso for a fortnight's visit.

ALL THIS SUNSHINE,

and so little to do with it! It's not rained for nearly three weeks, the days and the nights are long and bright. Fortunately Dick gave me one of his black sleeping masks. I wake when the sun strikes down through the curtain, reach for the mask, clap it over my eyes, and go back to sleep. This can happen at any time from three-thirty on. Actually, there's a faint glow in the sky as the sun sets that shows it's only an hour or so before it will rise again.

Though the weather is warm and fine, there's a strong wind every day that blows all the dust of the steppes over the city. The law requires streets to be watered twice a day, just as it requires them to be cleared of snow in winter. There are carts going up and down the main avenues, but the side streets and the sidewalks must be done by the householders or the *dvorniks* of the buildings. At all hours, people are out with hoses, splattering about. I dare say it's a good idea, as otherwise the place would be too filthy. They've no green grass to water, except in the occasional parks, and those go without upkeep, except for a little sweeping of the paths.

Sweeping in Russia must be a discouraging business, for, as heaps of dust are gathered, the wind comes and blows them around again. The old women who do the work don't seem to mind. They sweep away mechanically, paid by the job rather than the result.

But it is exasperating to have this summer heat and be cooped up in the city without any chance to bathe, play golf, tennis, visit a friend over a country week end. The first year we were here, we tried to get permission to play tennis on some of the public courts.

There are no real public courts, but some do exist belonging to the Red Army, the big MVD organizations, various factories, and Government sporting clubs. The permission never came, and the Burobin authorities even refused to allow us to build our own court here, behind Spaso. We had no right to chop down fine old trees they said. The trees are no more than swamp maples, and last winter Averell Harriman told me he and Chip Bohlen used to take their exercise chopping at them during the war. Now the militia would rush in at the first sound of the axe.

But we did put on a good show on Wednesday afternoon. We have received a splendid power lawn mower from America, a kind of miniature farm tractor with attachments that allow it to plow, harrow, shovel snow. It's the pride of our engineer's life, and he came out to demonstrate it to us and to the Italian and Pakistan Ambassadors, both of whom had heard of its wonders. There's a kind of buggy seat that can be hitched on behind, and the sight of Wally Barbour running it up and down the lawn was superb. The Little Men goggled through the fence. People came from all over the square to look, and there were even MVD reinforcements called up. A report must even now be on file at headquarters.

We've also received a fine new truck at the Embassy, one of several that have been on order for over a year. It's a Diamond T, and is painted bright red. Wally was very much afraid, first that, the truck would never be licensed; and second, that we should have to change the color. Just to prove their contrariness, the Russians gave the license and said nothing about the color. Then, in order not to be too agreeable, they refused a driving license to our new master mechanic, an Army Sergeant of Engineers who has been at the game for twenty years.

To obtain a driving permit in the Soviet Union, they insist, at least for foreigners, that the applicant pass a mechanical test. They seem to consider this far more important than any knowledge of rules of the road and traffic regulations. Invariably, the questions are tricks designed to confuse and fail the applicant. This time, our Sergeant was thrown out when the examiner asked:

"When do you put acid in a battery?"

"You don't put acid in, you put distilled water," answered the Sergeant.

"Quite wrong, acid must be put in if there is a hole in the battery!"

The license was refused. One of our young Secretaries, the last one to apply, failed because he couldn't say what happened if a small bubble formed in a hydraulic gear shift. When you look at the stupid-faced *moujiks* that drive about the Moscow streets, it's hard to believe they know anything about that bubble. The final result of the Sergeant's test was a kindly lecture from the examiner, who advised him to return in three months' time after he had mastered some of the mysteries of internal combustion engines.

CURIOUS, AS I'VE
remarked before, how almost every nation chooses July for its
national holiday; it must be a very explosive month for revo-
tions. The Russians picked October, to be sure, but the French,
Belgians, Canadians, ourselves, all celebrate in July. This year,
every Allied Mission in Moscow has agreed to give an afternoon reception, instead of the big evening "do" of previous
years. So few Russians come to our parties, it's hardly worth-
while putting on a show to entertain them, and much more
fun to give private parties to our own friends. At the King's
Birthday the British had nineteen. It's quite likely that we
will have fewer. The Russians like to make a difference between us and the British—same idea as letting David Kelly
turn left in traffic, while Dad must drive round the block.

A few women came to their party, including Madame Sergeiv. Her husband used to be Ambassador in Brussels, and
both dined with us there. Some maintained that she had been
ordered to the post as Sergiev's wife, but as she is still with
him, the deal must have been permanent. She wears better
clothes than most, one of the few Soviet women I've seen in
a Western print dress.

It was Sergeiv about whom they used to tell the story in
Brussels. He sat next a rather naïve lady at the French Embassy.

"*Dites moi, Monsieur l'Ambassadeur,*" she said, "*ou sont
tous les Russes qui parlaient si bien le francais. J'en ai connu
tellement dans ma jeunesse.*"

"*Madame, ils sont tous morts,*" replied Sergeiv, and went on
with his soup.

Sergeiv was substituting at the British Embassy for Bogomolov, the Vice Minister in charge of the British area. It was
Bogomolov with whom I had my own passage-at-arms, last
year, when he remarked for my benefit, "*Oui, las generaux
Americans savaient parler touts les langues sauf l'anglais.*"

"*Au moins, Monsieur le Ministre,*" I answered, in as loud

a voice as I could muster, *"ils ont pu se faire comprendre."*

No pleasantries this year. The time for such is past, but I I still insist on these people shaking hands when we meet at receptions. I'd not give them the satisfaction of cutting me. We meet rarely enough, goodness knows, and top officials and their wives and families are never seen in ordinary public places. What do the women do with themselves? I never see any driving their own cars. Their housekeeping shouldn't take too long; and anyway, there always seems to be an old *baboushka* about to tend to such chores. Certainly they can't have too many rooms to clean and care for. Even the best of them live in close quarters, or so imagine.

The one spot in town that we know is used by them is a side street near the Lenin Library, where there is a block of old-fashioned, substantial apartment houses looking a little like some on Central Park West in New York. This short street is heavily patrolled and one sees big black cars go in and out at all times. One can walk through, but not unobserved. Then there's another large apatment building for what must be Government employees just across the Kremlin bridge. It was there, I was told, that Madame Kollantay the former woman diplomat lived, but the Swedish Ambassadress says that she is now in a sanitarium in the country; there are a number of these around Moscow. We thought we saw a whole new group of such buildings in a pine wood off the road to Zagorsk.

Motoring there last Thursday, I thought the Russian countryside had never looked more discouraging, at least the countryside in the immediate vicinity of Moscow. It was hot, dusty, dun-colored. The roads were crowded with trucks, and for miles the highway was under reconstruction by forced labor gangs—groups of men and women with MVD soldiers on guard with rifles at the barriers. What an unlovely country this is! We've been here just two years now. That's nearly long enough.

I think that just lately I've begun to be followed in the street. Perhaps I always was, but the other day I noticed a thin young man in gray suit and cap who popped up here and there, sometimes in front, sometimes behind me, as I walked along, from Mokhovaya. At the theater, when I've been without Dad, I've often seen one or more of our Little Men; and Stuart Warwick insisted, that time he took me into the subway, that his own men were joined by two or three others who must have belonged to me. It can't be a very profitable occupation for them. It doesn't really bother me, but it's an odd sensation.

Postmarked Moscow   *June 27, 1951*

AS WE STOOD ON the front terrace of the British Embassy, Tuesday evening, we looked across at the Kremlin where long lines of cars whirled out the gate. It was midnight, there were lights in the big palace, obviously a party had been given, and the guests were leaving, each important fellow with his guard-car behind. A "welcome home" dinner for Gromyko, we thought. He's just back from Paris, Vishinsky is still ailing in the country and he'd enjoy telling of his battles with the Western Ministers and Delegates. The Malik Cease-Fire Proposal has been out for several days. Dad waited until he was sure that Gromyko was back, and then asked for an interview, hoping to get clarification of Malik's suggestions. Yesterday, Wednesday, the 27th, Gromyko gave him the appointment for two-thirty.

Dad, Ed Freers, and Dick Service went down, Ed as interpreter and Russian expert, Dick as Far Eastern expert. Dad rather enjoys seeing Gromyko, first because he's a very bright man, a quick thinker, not given in private conversation to the prosy speeches so many of them make; and second, because the conversation can be in English on both sides. When official notes are exchanged, Gromyko reads his in Russian; he speaks in Russian when he must for the record; but the ordinary give-and-take of the interview is in English. I'd like to look on at one of these sessions. Ed and Dick tell me Dad does them with such style. He's a good Ambassador, a good diplomat, and I think even the Russians, or perhaps especially the Russians, respect him for it.

Dad asked Gromyko if he had enjoyed his weeks in Paris. They were long, said Gromyko, but Paris was indeed a beautiful city and yes, "French cooking is the best in the world." Quite an admission from the Deputy Foreign Minister of the U.S.S.R.!

Nothing to complain about as to the weather here these last weeks except that, as always, there's so little to do with it. The sun shines and shines, all day and nearly all night. Our garden is a collection of long green stems—that seems to be the way flowers grow in Russia. In the back, the lettuce and radishes are spreading all over the beds. The *dvorniks* took the best plot for cabbages, the one vegetable we can buy easily in Moscow, but after all it's a national dish, that and cucumbers. The poor old gardener is still languishing in jail. His wife hasn't seen him since his trial. She says the queues are too long at the prison door, but she seems cheerful enough and dreams of the good life they will have when both he and the son are released. As I've said, they will have to leave Moscow, and will never be permitted to live here again. That same system was true in Czarist times, I notice by the books I've read. Returned prisoners were allotted areas of residence, usually far from their former homes.

The ballet is closing now, for two months. We went to see *The Fountain* last night, and wish we might go to *Swan Lake* tomorrow. Instead, we dine at the Danes. Roger and Dick go to the Bolshoi in our places, the last performance of the season. Last night the theater was crowded with delegations of every kind, Indians, Chinese, and a few Americans, one in a violent pink-and-green sport shirt, wide open over a hairy chest. I notice he buttoned it for the second act intermission. *Nie Culturnie,* someone must have told him.

This week there are many parties, but they are earlier and quieter than last week's. The Italians' on Saturday was truly gay, that and the British bachelors' on Friday. I danced all evening and enjoyed quite a lot of cold champagne; the British had theirs in a great bowl, with strawberries floating in it. Their party was given at their *dacha*. They had strung lights along the porch, and, with warm breezes wafting in and out, it had a kind of "India in the Hills" atmosphere. The Italians' next night was a big "do," with rooms opened all over the ground floor, even space for the Afghans and the Pakistans to sit about along the edges. The Italians had a most wonderful spread—spaghetti, mountains of it, *risotto,* cold meats, and, on each side of the table, little suckling pigs.

So many of our colleagues are leaving; some have already left. The Goffins go to Teheran, where he will be Belgian Minister. We go tonight to say good-bye to the Jack Nicholls—he has been British Minister here; and to the Wynn-Popes—he was their military Attaché. The British party on Tuesday was for them. I like going to parties at their Embassy when the windows are open on that astonishing view, the river and the height of the Kremlin beyond. Their big drawing room is on the front and it's all very prewar, dancing about over a parquet floor—lights, music, women in pretty frocks—and the Kremlin just across the way. The British Embassy was another of the Morosoff houses, belonging to the richest of the Moscow merchant families. It's a rather terrible edifice, false Gothic throughout, even to the guest-room bath, which looks as though it had been designed for Sir Walter Scott's home at Abbotsford. At night, however, it becomes rather glamorous, the Kellys are hospitable folk, and they do it all in the traditional Embassy manner.

Postmarked Moscow   *July 6-7, 1951*

THE GLORIOUS

Fourth has come and gone. Our flag was hoisted at Mokhovaya, a good big one. It was a windy day and it waved bravely, streaming out over the heads of the passers-by. Here we put one over the front balcony, and inside the house we filled all the vases with red, white and blue flowers. One of our Embassy wives, Vaughan Pratt, and I went to market on Tuesday morning and bought all we could find. The Russians wanted to sell the flowers stalk by stalk, ruble by ruble. That's the way housewives buy cabbage and carrots, and their eyes grew round when we said, "Give us the whole bucketful." They knew we must be foreign capitalists. But this house is so huge, the ceilings so vast, if you decorate at all, it has to be done in a big way. My centerpiece, like the one Chantal Goffin did for me last year, measured three yards across. This time, we moved the big table from the state dining room into the ballroom, opened the doors onto the garden, opened all the windows, and put chairs around the edges and a couple of sofas for the tired Near Easterners to sit on. It looked very nice. We had a champagne bar, and there were iced cakes and sandwiches, along with two immense bowls of honest American ice cream, much appreciated by all the guests. Dad and I took station at six promptly. I wore a new blue Paris frock, and Dad looked very handsome in the best of his pin stripes with stiff white collar and dark tie. One of our Senior First Secretaries stood with us, alternating every quarter of an hour. The invitations read six to eight, and most of the guests came early and stayed until the very end; even the few Russians seemed to enjoy themselves.

We speculated as to who would turn up from the Foreign Office. Last year they sent a very scrubby lot, who stood in a corner, neither ate nor drank, and went away forty-five minutes later. This year, we had made our list shorter and checked it very carefully. Vishinsky is certainly ill; no one has seen him for months. Gromyko was invited, along with the other Deputy Foreign Ministers. None of them came—pressure of business, etc.

But we did draw a Senior Assistant Secretary, the man they call Secretary General of the Foreign Office. We had the head of the Consular Section, the Head of the Press Section, and two or three others, including the Chief of the American Division with his rather pretty wife, the first Russian lady, with the exception of Madame Gromyko, to accept an invitation to a party in Spaso. She and her husband are newly returned from the States. She wore an American-made frock, black-and-white print two-piece suit with a black velvet collar, a reasonable hat, and gloves. She spoke good English, replied pleasantly when addressed, and obviously had a very enjoyable afternoon. One of our Russian scholars heard her beg her husband not to hurry away. She said she liked the party.

Much to our astonishment, among the early arrivals were the Czech Ambassador and his wife, an elderly pair looking like a provincial couple just come from their golden wedding. Then who should turn up, toward the end of the party, but the Polish Ambassador, whom no one recognized when he first went down the line. Both these gestures must have been cleared and authorized, pre-Korean armistice manifestations, we suppose. This is the first time the satellites have been in Spaso since early last year.

Our young ladies and gentlemen did a fine job entertaining the special guests. The Czech confided to Vaughan Pratt that he'd come to the party hoping to find a good American cigar. Consternation. We rarely have cigars in the house, and none of the men living here smoke any. Vaughan rushed about, discovered that Dick had a box tucked away with some odd stores, and sent him off to find them. Meanwhile, Father Brassard, hearing the conversation, offered one from his own pocket, said he would be happy to have the Vatican supply a cigar to the Czech Ambassador. Unconscious of its origin, the gentleman smoked that one quite contentedly and put the three others Dick supplied in his own pocket to take home.

I had a pleasant conversation with the Secretary General of the Foreign Office. He was talking in French with Sohlman, the Swedish Ambassador. The Ambassador explained they had been colleagues at the United Nations last year. I asked how they liked the new building. Sohlman said the one thing he envied Lie was the flat on the top, a splendid place with its private tennis court.

"Are you putting a tennis court on the top of your new skyscraper on B Circle?" I asked the Secretary.

He almost winked, and said, "I hardly think the plans call for that."

Altogether, I found him very agreeable. What a stupid system that forbids our knowing these people, that cuts off any contact and divides us into hostile camps right here in Moscow. It's hard for anyone at home to visualize the situation. They can't believe that we see no one, that tiny incidents such as those on the Fourth of July are significant and exciting to us, that there is such drastic control the Secretary General is willing or not willing to pass a joke, the sentry at the gate is told when he may or may not salute, we are given theater tickets one week and none another, maids come and go—all depending on the headlines of the moment and the word that comes down from above. Nothing is too small for them to think of, no detail too obscure. On July Fourth, permission was given for polite speech, tomorrow that permission may be reversed. Tomorrow, on the other hand, we may be invited to dine off gold plate. One never knows.

The present attitude is mixed up with the Korean business, of course. Dad's name is prominent in the headlines these days, and his handling of the Gromyko interview was competent enough to merit their respect. Reading the American and European papers that have come in, I'm quite proud of him myself. He has a clear, direct approach which Gromyko understands. Both are strong men, both avoid innuendo and equivocation. It remains to be seen how much comes of the Cease Fire agreement. Our Far Eastern experts fear the Chinese will be slow to accept any admission of defeat, so that it may never be more than an inconclusive agreement.

Postmarked Moscow   *July 16, 1951*

NINETY-FIVE DEgrees. That's a lot of heat, especially in this dusty, ill-swept city. It's begun to smell bad. Odors drift in through the windows, odors from hundreds of old courtyards where dirt and refuse lie in the corners. The only breeze is hot, swept in off the steppes. On the stoops of the houses, in the doorways, people sit and stand, quite patiently, like dogs. One almost waits to see their sides heave and their tongues hang out.

This weather has beaten a seventy-five-year record. It's hotter in Moscow than anywhere else in the Soviet Union, hotter than Tiflis, hotter than Kharkov in the Ukraine. Moscow is hardly equipped for such heat. The Russians haven't gotten round to air conditioning—I've seen that only in Lenin's tomb! They've no fly screens at their windows, no fans. The problem of food conservation must be a big one, for an ice box is a rarity.

Come to think of it, I've never seen ice wagons going about the street; and we know with what curiosity and respect a frigidaire is looked on. There is ice, of course. They sell ice cream from small carts, and cold pink-syrup drinks from others. But ice for homes—I wonder what they would make of one of our vender machines—ten cents in the slot and out fall the ice cubes, another coin in the slot and out comes Coca-Cola.

Yesterday, Sunday, everyone got out of town, on trains or busses, or piled into open trucks. We went, ourselves, and picnicked in a wood on the road to the airport. Our Little Men were so pleased with us! Long Knife took off his jacket and shirt and went into a field to gather daisies. Where did he put his knife I wonder, slide it down his trouser leg? It was pleasant enough under the trees until the heat settled there too.

We came back to give a dinner party for Dick. He goes tomorrow to his new post in Brussels, and it will be strange at Spaso without him. This existence of ours is so full of comings and goings, one's heart pulls in and out like an accordion, and the music can be sweet or sour. Dad will miss him too. The pair of them sat up alone until four A. M., the other morning, talking, and then repeating what they'd talked about. Roger will miss him, for he's been a gay companion.

We think now to invite Bob Blake, a cheerful and bright young man, to take his place. We've room for him here and we shall all need some new interest and gay talk, so we'll be glad to have him join what's termed the "Spaso Collective."

He's an inveterate sightseer, so I expect him to take me tramping the town, once the weather cools off.

As a farewell to the staff, Dick is giving the Spaso servants a great party tonight. We are all out and Roger, now in charge of house management while Nagosky is on vacation, has arranged a big feed with an approximation of vodka, straight gin and whisky served up in water glasses. There will be twenty-five or more, counting the odd yard boy and the chauffeurs. The poor gardener, languishing in jail—how he would have enjoyed it. It will be held in the basement dining room, with the main course a great plate of beef stew, plus loaves of sweet sugared bread, all laced down with the liquor. There will be dancing—we're sending down a radio—and tomorrow everyone will look a little pale and tired.

Dick on his way home to bed, may stop off to drink a health with them. He takes the train tomorrow to Leningrad and Helsinki, flying from there to Brussels, where his family will join him.

Postmarked Moscow   *July 17, 1951*

OUR GOOD WALLY

left the other evening, after a terrific send-off. I'd like to be going away myself. We and the French and the British are some of the few Heads of Mission left in Moscow. The others are away vacationing, more trusting of events than we are. It's certainly holiday weather, hot again, very hot today. Last night, we dined with the Burmese Ambassador on the Moscow Hotel roof, ourselves, the Italians, and the French.

This sounds like a more glamorous affair than it really was —the Moscow roof overlooking the Kremlin, four Ambassadors dining together. The restaurant is set on a long terrace; in the middle there's space for an orchestra and dancing. It was crowded with people; men with shaven, polished heads, dirty white blouses open at the neck or sweat-stained blue jerseys;

soldiers in crumpled khaki; thick-necked women in sleazy prints, some still wearing their winter best, bottle-green crepe or wine-red, trimmed with bands of satin or velvet. Their hair lay frizzed in thick bunches or was braided around their heads. Most of the women wore watches—that's a sign of social standing in the Soviet Union—some had rings and brooches.

The Russians make an evening of it when they go to a restaurant. They get their money's worth, for they sit at table for hours, eat a little off one plate then another, drink a glass, drink another glass, still another. Often they drink until they literally cannot get up, and their heads go down on the table. I saw one man do that last night. He sat next to a party of three, the woman strung with silver chains, her face a kind of Oriental mask. She must have been Uzbeg or some such nationality. One man with her was correctly dressed in a gray suit, the other wore his blue shirt loose over white trousers. He was very talkative, gesticulating with his fork. At one point he grew so excited that to emphasize his point, he reached up and ran his fork through his hair!

The waiters wore loose white blouses and carried soiled napkins over their arms. They too, had shaved heads, a fortunate precaution, though I found a very long, very black hair in my salad.

Our table was covered with dishes of all sorts, little dabs of this and that, cold meat, raw cucumbers, whole tomatoes, caviar, slices of raw fish, mounds of toasted bread. Our host is a vegetarian, so he made out well enough, and we would have done better to make our dinner off what was before us. Later they brought in plates heaped with greasy, fried shoestring potatoes and a kind of chicken cutlet buried beneath a layer of hard fried fat. For dessert there were ice cream and compote of apricots. It's poor food, all of it, and hideously expensive. I shudder to think what the dinner must have cost the Burmese. We had some thin Georgian wine and warm soda water.

It grew very hot where we sat, in a kind of square alcove curtained off by what I think were string-bean plants growing out of boxes set on the floor. We finally moved our chairs out where we could catch a little breeze and watch the people. The moon came up over the Kremlin wall, just between the two largest red stars on the big towers. Madame Chataigneau, the French Ambassadress, speaks no English, the Burmese no French, Marie Noel Kelly rattled along in gallant diplomatic manner, Dad talked to Chataigneau and to David Kelly, who came late, having received a Quaker Peace Delegation at the Embassy. This is only the second delegation ever to come to the Embassy, the first being a brave group of students who showed their independence of spirit by calling on their Ambassador. Ordinarily, the delegations stay strictly away from us and it would be a rash man who would walk into Mokhovaya from the National Hotel's sidewalk outside is stiff with MVDs and militiamen.

At ten-thirty we'd had enough of the moon, the red stars, and Russian café society. The Little Men at their table near-by —there were eight last night, what with Dad's and Sir David's —had finished their beer so we rose, said good-night, and left the poor Ambassador to pay his very large bill.

Postmarked Moscow   *July 24-25-26, 1951*

THE HEAVENS OPENED, and the thermometer fell with a crash. The summer is probably over for this year. Actually, we've had our share of sunshine and heat so shouldn't complain. Dad is disappointed, as he had plans for going to the football game this afternoon, a terrific battle between the miners of the Dom Basin and the Red Army team. His Little Men grew discouraged last season, it was wet and cold and he never attended. Now they hope he will go again, for they prefer football matches to the theater or ballet, and come out in full force when the word is given, Salmon Shirt in the lead. Somewhere I read that football matches were first seen in Russia when the Vickers engineers came over from England to build the Moscow subway. The

Russans love the game, and no doubt they now claim to have invented it.

I'm not going to the football, Lady Kelly having invited me to come and dine with the Peace Delegation. These people insist they come as genuine peacelovers, not as Communist supporters. According to David Kelly, they've had the red carpet laid out for them wherever they've gone, and trips have been arranged in areas forbidden to us, sights shown them we never see—visits to farms, factories, hospitals, etc.—though, so far, they've met with no response to their request to see a prison and a corrective farm. They're not a group to be dazzled by the usual "vodka circuit" tour; they are men and women prominent in business and cultural activities, but they are Quakers, and they are convinced that war and armaments must disappear from the world. If the Soviets can persuade them that that is *their* program, it will be a real triumph.

Postmarked Moscow   *July 25, 1951*

I ENJOYED MYSELF very much at the Kelly's and was extremely interested in talking with the Quakers, all of whom seemed thoughtful, intelligent people. Their visits to nurseries and holiday camps impressed them with the care and concern shown for young children. Dad says the Russians in this are no different from animals, but it's quite true the children are affectionately cared for. It's true that they seem a happy lot until ten or twelve, when they turn very serious and solemn. A well-known doctor and child psychiatrist, Miss Creak, remarked that the women in charge were not young, many of them more than middle-aged. I've noticed that too. It seems to be part of the *baboushka* tradition. From babyhood the grandmother carries the swaddled child about the streets; then, when he is older, leads him along by the hand and watches over him as he plays in the parks.

This visit of the Quaker delegation is important because it's one of the first visits made by a non-Communist group, supposedly arriving with an open mind and a sincere effort to appraise the Soviet Peace Policy. I say an open mind, although their religion teaches them to abhor wars and preparations for war, so they are more ready to believe others who claim to profess the same. But it's also true these are hard-headed men and women of standing in their own country, so they should not be deceived by what seems to us a transparent and cynical approach.

In the Tretchikoff Gallery this morning I saw a number of them go in just ahead of me. I had told them to be sure to look at the room full of anti-American and anti-British caricatures and cartoons; but since my last visit, two months ago, the gallery had been completely changed about and the cartoons had all disappeared, only a few inoffensive ones left on a revolving file in a dark corner.

The Chinese pictures and sculptures had all gone, the big painting of the signing of the Sino-Soviet pact and the busts of Mao and Ho Chi Minh. Instead there were new paintings, huge ones covering yards of wall, of various Peace Congresses, of Stalin in his most benevolent moods, and an immense portrayal of Vishinsky addressing the UN; entitled the Voice of Peace. Down in one corner of the picture were the U. S. delegates, easily recognizable, behind them some haughty and sneering English and French, while on the other side, applauding Vishinsky's speech, were noble-browed Ukrainians and Czechs, their faces alight with hope and gratitude. Hung around all these pictures, almost framing them, were still lifes of flowers and mothers and children, Peace and Happiness for all, the great gifts of the Soviet Motherland.

I lost the Quaker party after we got into the gallery. I wonder what they made of it. The British Counselor in Charge of Internal Russian Affairs told me afterward he thought the whole business might well have been set up just for their visit. That seems fantastic, though by this time I should realize that nothing is too fantastic in this so strange land, that they go to any lengths and any expense to make their point, neither money nor labor being a consideration with them.

The Quakers have asked to see Stalin. It's even possible he may give them an interview, that he may take the occasion to make one of his historic pronunciamentos.

We wondered if Vishinsky would be at the Polish reception the other night. Apparently not, though we stayed such a short time, he might have come after we left. This was the first satellite function we have attended in a year. We went because the Pole came to our Fourth of July reception. I was rather glad to see the Russians, even if they looked more like dressed-up monkeys than ever. We would have stayed a little longer, but Blakeney, the Australian Chargé, came in with the shocking news of Admiral Forrest Sherman's sudden death in Naples.

Postmarked Moscow   *August 6, 1951*

ROGER AND BOB BLAKE
are just back from a trip to Vladimir, the ancient capital of the Princes of Moscovy. It's only a hundred and fifty kilometers away, one could easily drive there, but we are not allowed to take our cars out of what is called the Moscow *oblast*, the Moscow city limits.

Two of our girls went with them and they carried food and bedding—a wise precaution, as they weren't able to buy anything there, and both going and coming they could only get "hard car" tickets. Hard cars are what correspond to day coaches with us, and hard they are, with bare varnished wood shelves, three tiers one above another, the top shelves folding back against the wall.

Roger had asked for a taxi to meet them at the station, but none arrived and the party had to walk to the hotel, nearly a mile away. There the girls were given beds in a five-bed dormitory, the men in a similar building. That's the usual thing in Russia, private rooms being available only for special guests. From Vladimir, they tried to get over to Susdal, another ancient town, but found no one willing to drive them, nor could they engage a taxi to drive back to Moscow. They were told a delegation of Party Members had reserved all transportation over the week end.

I've not seen the girls, but the two boys looked very soiled and grubby and Chin has taken their clothes away to be dunked in a bucket of gasoline in the backyard. There are no drycleaning facilities available to us, and these things demanded instant treatment.

Bob said that the people looked miserably dressed and fed, that the town was wretched, and there were no signs of industry or construction anywhere. That may have been the reason no one followed them, for all of us have been thoroughly tailed lately, and no one stirs a foot in or about Moscow without a Little Man or Little Woman coming along.

Three shadowy figures appeared last Wednesday when I went with Roger and Bob to look at some old monasteries we had dug out of Baedeker. These monasteries were part of a ring of fortified places in a semicircle around the city of Moscow, protecting its vulnerable side. One or two I'd seen already, but Bob found three more, and they were most interesting, in spite of their sad state of decay and dilapidation.

Just next to the Donskoi Monastery we stopped to look at the main city crematorium, a big gray building with four chimneys, one on each corner, unpleasantly reminiscent of pictures of similar installations in the German concentration camps. It's true this building was set in a kind of garden cemetery, but it was neither neat nor pretty, and the whole place was pretty lugubrious. As we stood at the gate we saw a truck drive in, and Bob asked if I didn't want to walk closer to get a view of the proceedings as they unloaded at the door. "No thank you," I replied, and very wisely, for Bob described what he'd seen the week before:

"The body is laid on a stretcher and the mourning family sit around it in the open truck. If the person is to be cremated, it's rarely they've gone to the expense of a casket. In any case, the casket is always carried uncovered through the streets. Inside, the family follow the body to the receiving room and the doors of the crematorium proper. It costs just five rubles, a dollar and a quarter, to be cremated."

No wonder that's the preferred and encouraged form of disposal after death. Burial seems to be reserved for the pious and the elect, the most elegant cemetery still being the one behind the Nova Devitche convent, the second being that of the Donskoi. Stalin's second wife is buried in Nova Devitche.

These monasteries are all built more or less alike, a collection of churches and dwelling houses shut within strong walls, some surrounded with moats or deep dry ditches. All these monuments are falling into ruins, another few years and nothing will be left of them. It's too bad, for, the Kremlin excepted, Moscow has so little of historic interest, and politics aside, the Russian people should preserve these relics of former days. I sometimes wonder if the Russians ever had any idea of maintenance. Certainly the old chronicles and history books picture the country as desolate and disorderly, so it may not have changed as much as we think.

The cold weather keeps up. Friday night we went out to Tom Whitney's and Harrison Salisbury's *dacha*. Whitney is the AP correspondent, and Harrison is the *New York Times* man whose articles have aroused so much discussion. We didn't discuss controversial matters, and it was very pleasant sitting on their little lawn and dining on their front porch, even though we saw the next-door neighbor watching the proceedings through a pair of opera glasses and Dad's Little Men were posted at all four corners of the lot, their car drawn up in front. The *dacha* was little more than a shanty of unpainted wood with a sign over the door saying this was number hundred and seventy-eight, belonging to the Dacha Trust of Moscow. It was set in a quarter-acre lot, and across the way new log houses were being built for two Army officers.

Although primarily a *dacha* colony, Tom said, the community was now a suburban one, with many people living there all year round. The streets are wide strips of ordinary meadow, there's a mud track in from the main gate, and what happens after really heavy rains or snow I've no idea. Under the new system it's possible for individuals to buy or put up houses of their own, provided they get an allotment of land from the local Soviet. The houses are of wood, the traditional log cabin type. I saw none of dressed lumber. Some are small single cabins, others are double. They will all have electric light, but there is no running water available and everyone must use the village pump. Shower baths are taken under a barrel hung from a high tree. It's a primitive life.

Tonight we must go to a wedding reception at the Pakistan Embassy. There are seven daughters in the family and this one is the first to be married, a dark-eyed maiden wrapped in stange garments, silk-flounced skirt with a loose blouse over that, and then a *sari* on top. She and her mother and sisters are all draped alike, and all look alike. I can't think how the bridegroom will tell her from the others. The Pakistans are Mohammedans, so there will be no liquor, and toasts to the bride must be drunk in sweet pink lemonade. Not so at the wedding we are to hold here in Spaso on September 3, when Jane Breckenridge, the Minister Counsellor's pretty blonde secretary, marries Griff Edwards, one of our assistant naval Attachés. Dad has promised to give the bride away, and someone has produced a white organdy dress with veil. I always said a wedding here would be fun and am glad we can stage one before we leave.

ALWAYS, EVER SINCE my first arrival in Spaso, I've dreamed of holding a wedding in the Great Hall, of seeing Dad escort a bride down the Grand Stairway and up a red carpet to an altar arranged between the pillars at the far end of the room.

Now, after two and a half years, it's going to happen. Father Brassard, the American Catholic priest, is to perform the ceremony at six o'clock tomorrow afternoon, and Dad has shaken out his Admiral's uniform for the occasion. The whole Embassy is in a great state of excitement, has been for days, and now a directive has gone out inviting all the Chancery servants to watch the ceremony from the balcony, so Mokhovaya is also abuzz.

It seemed a simple enough idea, this holding a wedding, but it's not so easy. The bride and groom thought they could have a very quiet affair with a dozen or more of their closest friends invited, but they soon realized how bitterly disappointed all the rest of the Embassy would be, and there were numbers of people from other missions they would like to ask, so the list grew and was limited only by the space available. It's a hundred and fifty now, with four Ambassadors and five Chargé d'Affaires—quite an impressive group.

The gold chairs have been brought from the ballroom and set up in rows; the altar is waiting to be dressed; Lady Kelly is doing the flowers tomorrow morning; the floors have been cleaned and waxed by a corps of charwomen sent from Mokhovaya, who sloshed around for hours in their barefeet, washing and polishing; the red carpet has been laid down; and below in the kitchen the cooks are hard at work on the five-tiered wedding cake.

Jane's white organdy dress is donated by Vaughan Pratt, the wife of one of the First Secretaries, who wore it once and had put it away in its box, finding it too bridal for an ordinary dance frock. Jane says it will go back in the box and be sent to the Embassy file room to be handed the next bride, along with the veil which the Air Attaché's wife made out of a summer evening skirt belonging to the sister of the Australian Chargé d'Affaires. Lady Kelly, the British Ambassadress, loaned some Brussels lace; the prayer book was supplied by Jane's roommate and sent to Helsinki to be covered in white silk; the two crinoline petticoats were each loaned by other friends; shoes and stockings she fortunately had of her own.

Jackie Branaman, Dad's Secretary, will be maid of honor,

and we thought we were quite safe in ordering her a dress from Stockholm over two weeks ago. Couriers came and went, but the dress never appeared until yesterday when it turned up, a droopy model of cream net dotted with purple velvet bows. Consternation in Dad's outer office. Jackie telephoned me and I rushed down to Mokhovaya bearing my ice-blue satin skirt over one arm. We ripped the bows off, and put the skirt on over the top of the dress. With a cream net blouse it looked quite well, and someone produced a blue straw hat exactly the color of the skirt, so now the costume is complete, and very becoming.

Both Jane and Griff are Protestants, but the good Father Brassard has searched his records and his conscience and finds both permit him to perform the ceremony. To make everything quite legal, there will be a civil wedding in the morning at the Russian Registry Office, and Culver Gleysteen in his status of Consul, will witness the wedding here at Spaso. This is always done when Americans are married abroad, an impressive document being then given them to prove the marriage has actually taken place.

A sword had to be found for the bride to cut the cake with, so the Turkish naval Attaché obliged with a scimitar, and the four swords the ushers will use to make the arch as the couple leave the altar are rented for the purpose from the Bolshoi Theater costume reserve. Lanham Titchener, one of the British Embassy Counselors, is going to play the organ, a portable model lent by Father Brassard, and for days he has been practicing the Lohengrin and Mendelssohn wedding marches. His wife says he is more nervous than the bridegroom.

This morning our house manager and I have been to the market for flowers. Fortunately, this is the one time any amount can be had in Russia. Its just before the first frosts that flowers are really plentiful, and even then they are fairly dear in price, gladioli at 4 rubles apiece—a dollar in our money —and the best phlox, thirty cents a stalk. We fought our way through the crowds, bargained at each stall, and finally came away with big armfuls of lovely white flowers. These, combined with masses of sweet tobacco from our own garden, will be pretty, backed with greens which Bill has gone to cut in the woods.

Later—we are just back from the Registry Office, the bride and groom, maid of honor, best man, Jane's roommate, Roger, and I, plus Culver, our Acting American Consul. We toured about back streets for some minutes, finally coming to a big gray-plastered building where there was a notice on the door, saying this was the Marriage Registry Office.

I can't think there's much custom, or else the waiting room to which we were escorted is reserved for the special clients. In any case, it was all very quiet and orderly. We were given seats in a kind of corridor, furnished in the most approved Soviet manner, with two divans draped in Turkish rugs, an immense potted palm, a bust of Lenin flanked with red geraniums and, directly over him, a colored oil portrait of Stalin with his most benevolent smile. We sat for nearly half an hour. The Head Registrar had just stepped out. Finally, a severe-looking woman in a dusty dark-blue suit came through the door and disappeared into a room beyond.

"Please to come this way."

We trooped after the little blonde clerk, who motioned us along, and came into a room where there was a desk behind which the woman in the blue suit and two other younger women were seated. They indicated that we should all sit down, the bride and groom in armchairs opposite the three women. The two younger began to write, filling out forms and then more forms, copying data from their passports, their diplomatic cards, and their applications which had been made several days ago.

Both young women were near-sighted, both wrote with scratchy pens. It all took quite a long while. The only questions asked of the bride and groom were whether or not they had any children. After that they simply signed their names to two or three of the innumerable documents, and the marriage was over. The three women rose, read their names, their addresses and professions, repeated their statements that they had no children, shook hands with the happy couple. We all shook hands all around. The groom paid fifteen rubles, and was presented with a certificate stamped with a red seal. In the eyes of the Soviet authorities, they were now man and wife.

At Spaso we found Lady Kelly, Elaine and Winifred Cumming, hard at work. The men had stripped three trees at our *Dacha* and brought back a great truckload of greens. The busts of Benjamin Franklin and George Washington were removed from their places atop the columns in the dining room, the columns went between the big pillars at the end of the Great Hall. Lady Kelly filled gray tin trash cans with the oak and white flowers, and the cans, being fluted, looked part of the columns. Over the altar went a great piece of Bokhara embroidery, and, on top, my best Russian lace cloth. We banked it with candles, fat ones in holders Father Brassard brought from his chapel. The effect was superb. No florist could have done better, and when the chandelier shone down on all the red and gold and white, with the chancel banked in green, it was really beautiful.

Postmarked Moscow   *September 4, 1951*

OUR WEDDING WAS
really lovely. Dad and I are quite satisfied to have this our last Embassy occasion.

At four-thirty, the bride and maid of honor arrived to dress, attended by the Air Attaché's wife, who had charge of the veil and the bouquets, and the wife of the Assistant Air Attaché, who volunteered to take any last-minute stitches in the two dresses. Mrs. Titchener came up to take her place at the balcony rail, in order to signal her husband, the organist, when to start the music, and to give the word to Dad and the bride so they would know when to start down the stairs. Mrs. Titchener has done stage directing in England, so her advice was almost professional.

Our bride looked very pretty, and Dad was impressively

handsome in his Admiral's uniform. When we got the word that all the personalities had arrived and been seated, I went down, acting as the bride's mother, was escorted up the aisle by the head usher, and Lanham Titchener played the *Largo,* which was the signal for the groom and the best man to enter. After that, the wedding march. We all rose, and the bridal party appeared. Father Brassard conducted the ceremony very nicely, gave them his benediction, Lanham played the Mendelssohn march, and back down the aisle they went. It was all done with great style, and even the Russian Chief of Protocol, who attended, the lone outsider to be at the affair, was visibly impressed.

The reception was very gay, lots of champagne, the cake cut with the Turkish scimitar, pictures snapped on all sides—everyone enjoyed themselves. Belowstairs, the servants carried on with wine supplied for the occasion, and it was very jolly. The *dvornik* was found in the middle of the entrance driveway, toward midnight, and the yardwoman asleep in a back hall, but otherwise there were no casualties. And now I am quite satisfied—We've had our wedding at Spaso!

Postmarked Moscow   *October 4, 1951*

WHEN WE CAME
to Moscow two years and four months ago, time stretched far ahead. Now it's shrunk until we've just two days left. The trunks are packed, the cupboards emptied. The Russians stand about like vultures for anything we might discard. I've made my round of good-byes, I've called on the Swedish Ambassadress, on the Persian Ambassadress, on the Turkish Ambassadress, on the Dutch; we've lunched at the Pakistan Embassy, at the Indian Embassy and at the Norwegian Embassy, dined with the British and French Chargés d'affaires, and been to a beautiful evening party given for us by the Brosios, the Ital-

ians, real friends whom we hate leaving behind. I've been given presents and wept a few tears, for I'm very sorry to see the last of our own Embassy people—we've grown close to one another, almost interdependent—and the servants in the house go about with red eyes. Poor things, they've so little security.

But it's exciting, just the same, incredibly exciting that we should be leaving, actually leaving. I've had a last look at Red Square and the Kremlin by moonlight, a last walk down the crowded Arbat, followed by a dingy little man in a gray coat. I've crossed Spaso Square for the last time, watching the children playing like kittens in the sand, and looked across the roofs at the skyscraper, still askew and still unfinished.

Day after tomorrow we take off, at ten o'clock in the morning. The plane came in this afternoon, we've our Polish clearance, and our permits are in order. Two days more and we'll be arriving in Paris, with Moscow a dream behind us, a dream that's a conscious memory, a part of ourselves.

Russia one never forgets.

THE END